The Admirals' Advantage

The Admirals' Advantage
U.S. Navy Operational Intelligence in World War II and the Cold War

Lt. Comdr. Christopher A. Ford, USNR
with
Capt. David A. Rosenberg, USNR
and assistance from
Comdr. Randy C. Balano, USNR

Naval Institute Press
Annapolis, Maryland

Naval Institute Press
291 Wood Road
Annapolis, MD 21402

Library of Congress Cataloging-in-Publication Data
Ford, Christopher A., 1967–
    The admirals' advantage : U.S. Navy operational intelligence in
world war II and the Cold War / Christopher A. Ford with David A.
Rosenberg and assistance from Randy C. Balano.
        p.   cm.
    Includes bibliographical references and index.
    ISBN 1-59114-282-2 (alk. paper)
        1. United States. Navy—History—20th century. 2. Military
intelligence—United States—History—20th century. 3. Operational
art (Military science)—History—20th century. I. Rosenberg, David
Alan, 1948–   II. Balano, Randy Carol, 1959–   III. Title.
    VB231.U54F67   2005
    359.3'432'097309045—dc22

                                                    2004029615

Printed in the United States of America on acid-free paper ∞
12 11 10 09 08 07 06 05   9 8 7 6 5 4 3 2
First printing

*In memory of our Naval Intelligence shipmates
who gave their lives for
their country in the Pentagon on
September 11, 2001.*

Comdr. Dan Shanower, USN

Lt. Comdr. Vince Tolbert, USN

Lt. Jonas Panik, USN

Lt. Darin Pontell, USN

IT1 (SW) Julian Cooper, USNR

Ms. Angie Houtz

Mr. Brady Howell

Mr. Jerry Moran

He who commands the sea has command of
everything . . .

Themistocles

How can any man decide what he should do himself if he is ignorant of what the enemy is about?

Jomini

The art of war is simple enough. [First,] find out
where your enemy is.

Gen. Ulysses S. Grant

Nam et ipsa scientia potestas est. [Knowledge is
power.]

Sir Francis Bacon

Contents

Foreword

The Chinese strategist Sun Tzu, writing in the fourth century BCE, observed, "For to win one hundred victories in one hundred battles is not the acme of skill. To subdue the enemy without fighting is the acme of skill. . . . Thus, what is of supreme importance in war is to attack the enemy's strategy." The author was writing about land warfare at the time, but the observation aptly characterizes the success of the U.S. Navy's conduct of the long Cold War at sea—a prolonged confrontation that could have erupted into hundreds of land, sea, and air engagements while the fate of world civilization hung in the balance. American and Soviet government and military leaders closely tracked the size, capabilities, and deployment of the adversary's forces. Troops, platforms, weapon systems, strategy, and doctrine were carefully tabulated and analyzed, each side seeking to check its opponent's ability to gain an advantage.

The most dynamic aspect of this contest focused on submarine forces. Nuclear propulsion and nuclear weapons endowed these platforms with unprecedented stealth and firepower—the ability to wreak devastation on an opponent's home territory while submerged thousands of miles away at sea. Knowing the disposition of the enemy's nuclear-armed submarines was a primary intelligence imperative for both sides. The U.S. Navy developed the capability to consistently hold the submarine forces of the Soviet Union at risk. The Soviets' inability to check that advantage undoubtedly assured the success of the American national policy of deterrence.

In the pages that follow the reader will learn the critical role that U.S. Navy operational intelligence played in the Cold War. It was an evolutionary process that unfolded over four decades, built upon cutting-edge technology and old-fashioned brainpower. Perhaps most critical to its success was the ability of its practitioners not only to break out of the analytical box but also to break out of the confines of bureaucratic boxes, fusing intelligence from multiple sources into an effective weapon against a deadly adversary.

As the global war on terrorism presents us with new perils, the lessons learned from the development of U.S. Navy operational intelligence during the Cold War can provide relevant guidance for today's challenges. Twenty-first-century intelligence professionals seeking ways to confront and master new threats will find in this text a record of serious and protracted intelligence transformation that not only used our own resources to best effect but also kept up and even got ahead of the adversary. This process led from recognition of the threat to its comprehensive understanding based on hard information and finally to an analytical intuition that permitted accurate prediction of potential peacetime and wartime courses of action. The challenges we face today are different, but this book, prepared by a team of top Naval Reserve intelligence professionals, can offer insights and approaches that have continuing broad application.

Rear Adm. Richard B. Porterfield, USN
Director of Naval Intelligence

Preface

This study was prepared by members of the OPINTEL Lessons Learned Team of Naval Reserve Units Office of Naval Intelligence (ONI) 0766, 1666, and 0566 at the direction of six successive Directors of Naval Intelligence between 1994 and 2001.

Much of the data for this study was derived from the videotaped proceedings of the Operational Intelligence "Lessons Learned" Symposium held at the Navy and Marine Corps Intelligence Training Center in Dam Neck, Virginia, on September 12–13, 1998. The purpose of this classified symposium was to provide a forum for senior intelligence professionals to present their views, describe their experiences, and engage in conversations with one another about the evolution of naval operational intelligence since World War II. It also provided a forum for an exchange of ideas with contemporary practitioners of naval operational intelligence from the fleet and shore commands. This study captures the essence of those views.

Additional sources for this study include oral interviews and correspondence conducted with senior members of the intelligence community as part of an ongoing oral history project, as well as declassified portions of official Naval Intelligence institutional histories. The endnotes in this work document fully the sources used, and while most of the videotapes and interview records remain only in official, classified hands, that material is being preserved in the hope of its eventual declassification for research.

The information presented here is at the cutting edge of Cold War declassification. For that reason, it is skeletal in many places, providing provocative yet incomplete hints of icebergs of fascinating individual and organizational exploits hidden beneath the classification barrier. This story is being told now in this form because the general outline of the Cold War Navy operational intelligence experience can finally be publicly recounted in enough detail to make it comprehensible to interested readers. Perhaps more important, that story remains extremely relevant to intelligence professionals, seagoing operators, and other military and national security practitioners today. It is intended to help preserve and transmit this important history to current and future generations of naval intelligence practitioners and to make as much information as possible available to followers of good naval, military, and intelligence history and the general public.

Many people contributed to the completion of this study. First among them are the members of ONI 0766's OPINTEL "Lessons Learned" Team during 1996–99. Special thanks are due to Comdrs. James Tugman, Russell Milheim, Stephen Wendell Scalenghe, Marco Mizrahi, William Hunt, and John Volkoff, and Lt. Guy Noffsinger, all of whom conducted basic interviews, ran the symposium, or provided other support to this project. Thanks are also due to IS2 Timothy Francis, PhD, of ONI 0566, who provided editorial assistance. Special acknowledgment must be made of the support provided by Comdr. Randy Carol Balano, USNR, currently the Office of Naval Intelligence historian, who moderated a session at the 1998 symposium and went on to provide numerous acts of administrative, editorial, and security-related assistance, including leading the team that prepared the illustrations.

The OPINTEL "Lessons Learned" Team also wishes to give special thanks to the members of the OPINTEL "Lessons Learned" Senior Advisory Group: Adm. William O. Studeman, USN (Ret.); Vice Adm. Mike McConnell, USN (Ret.); Rear Adm. Donald M. ("Mac") Showers, USN (Ret.); Rear Adm. Sumner ("Shap") Shapiro, USN (Ret.); Rear Adm. Thomas A. Brooks, USN (Ret.); Capt. William Manthorpe, USN (Ret.); and Mr. Richard Haver, who have reviewed and commented on various portions and versions of the manuscript.

Profound thanks are also due to the Directors of Naval Intelligence from 1994 through 2003—Rear Adm. Ted Sheafer, Rear Adm. Michael Cramer, Vice Adm. Lowell ("Jake") Jacoby, Rear Adm. Perry M. Ratliff, Mr. Paul Lowell, and Rear Adm. Richard Porterfield—under whose sponsorship and encouragement this project originated and proceeded. Thanks are also due to the commanders of the Office of Naval Intelligence, Capt. Robert Simeral and Capt. Tom Bortmes, without whose patronage, facilities, and support this study could not have been completed. Finally, thanks to Capt. Ronald Blue, Capt. Michael Halbig, Capt. Michael Goss, and Capt. Thomas Breyer, commanding officers of Naval Reserve Unit Office of Naval Intelligence 0766; Capt. Stephen Nichols, commanding officer of Naval Reserve Unit Office of Naval Intelligence 1666; and Capt. Bruce Martin and Capt. Bradley Peterson, commanding officers of Naval Reserve Unit Office of Naval Intelligence 0566, who sustained the efforts of unit personnel to bring this project to its conclusion.

This study has been security-cleared by the Office of Naval Intelligence for public release. Any mistakes in fact or interpretation are the author's or project director's.

Christopher Ashley Ford
Lieutenant Commander, USNR
Principal Author

David Alan Rosenberg
Captain, USNR
OPINTEL "Lessons Learned" Project Director

Washington, D.C., and Arlington, Virginia
October 2004

Commonly Used Acronyms and Abbreviations

ACINT	acoustic intelligence
AI	Air Intelligence Officer (1350s)
AMHS	Automated Message Handling System
AOR	area of responsibility
ASAS	All-Source Analysis System
ASW	antisubmarine warfare
ATO	Air Tasking Order
ATP	Advanced Technology Panel
AUTODIN	Defense Department Automatic Digital Network
C^2	command and control
C^3	command, control, and communications
C^3CM	command, control, and communications countermeasures
C^3I	command, control, computers, and intelligence systems
C^4ISR	command, control, communications, computers, intelligence, surveillance, and reconnaissance
CAT	Crisis Action Team
CENTCOM	U.S. Central Command
CINCLANT/ CINCLANTFLT	Commander in Chief, Atlantic Command/ Commander in Chief, Atlantic Fleet
CINCLANTFLT	Commander in Chief, U.S. Atlantic Fleet
CINCPAC	Commander in Chief, U.S. Pacific Command
CINCPACFLT	Commander in Chief, U.S. Pacific Fleet
CINCUSNAVEUR	Commander in Chief, U.S. Naval Forces, Europe

CNA	Center for Naval Analyses
CNO	Chief of Naval Operations
CNO-IP	CNO Intelligence Plot
COMINT	communications intelligence
CSG	Cryptologic Support Group
CVBG	carrier battle group
DIA	Defense Intelligence Agency
DNI	Director of Naval Intelligence
ELINT	electronic intelligence
FIC	Fleet Intelligence Center
FICEURLANT	Fleet Intelligence Center Europe and Atlantic, Norfolk, Virginia
FICPAC	Fleet Intelligence Center Pacific, Pearl Harbor, Hawaii
FIST	Fleet Imagery Support Terminal
FITCLANT	Fleet Intelligence Training Center Atlantic
FITCPAC	Fleet Intelligence Training Center Pacific
FOFA	Follow-On Forces Attack
FOSIC	Fleet Ocean Surveillance Information Center
FOSICEUR	Fleet Ocean Surveillance Information Center Europe, London, England
FOSICLANT	Fleet Ocean Surveillance Information Center Atlantic, Norfolk, Virginia
FOSICPAC	Fleet Ocean Surveillance Information Center Pacific, Pearl Harbor, Hawaii
FOSIF	Fleet Ocean Surveillance Information Facility
FOSIF WESTPAC	Fleet Ocean Surveillance Information Facility Western Pacific, Kamiseya, Japan
GCCS	Global Command and Control System
GDIP	General Defense Intelligence Program
GIUK	Greenland-Iceland–United Kingdom
GRAB	Galactic Radiation and Background Electronic Intelligence Collection Satellite
HULTEC	hull-to-emitter correlation
HUMINT	human intelligence
I&W	indications and warnings
ICPOA	Intelligence Center, Pacific Ocean Area (World War II)
IMINT	imagery intelligence
INTELINK	intelligence Internet

IRBM	intermediate-range ballistic missile
IS	intelligence specialist
ISR	intelligence, surveillance, and reconnaissance
JAC Molesworth	Joint Analysis Center at Molesworth, England
JDISS	Joint Deployable Intelligence Support System
JFIC	Joint Forces Intelligence Command
JIC	Joint Intelligence Committee
JICPAC	Joint Intelligence Center Pacific
JICPOA	Joint Intelligence Center, Pacific Ocean Area (World War II)
JIRO	Joint Intelligence Research Office
JMCIS	Joint Maritime Command Information System
JOTS	Joint Operational Tactical System
LOCE	Linked Operations-Intelligence Centers Europe
NATO	North Atlantic Treaty Organization
NAVINTCOM	Naval Intelligence Command
NAVMARINTCEN	Naval Maritime Intelligence Center, Suitland, Maryland
NAVOPINTCEN	Navy Operational Intelligence Center, Suitland, Maryland
NAVSECGRU	Naval Security Group
NAVSTIC	Naval Scientific and Technical Intelligence Center, Suitland, Maryland
NEC	naval enlisted classification
NEO	noncombatant evacuation operation
NFOIO	Navy Field Operational Intelligence Office, at National Security Agency, Fort Meade, and Suitland, Maryland (1957–82)
NIE	National Intelligence Estimate
NIPS	Naval Intelligence Processing System
NIPSSA	Naval Intelligence Processing System Support Activity, Suitland, Maryland
NISC	Naval Intelligence Support Center, Suitland, Maryland
NMIC	National Maritime Intelligence Center, Suitland, Maryland
NMJIC	National Military Joint Intelligence Center, the Pentagon
NOAA	National Oceanic and Atmospheric Administration

NOIC	Navy Operational Intelligence Center, Suitland, Maryland
NOSIC	Navy Ocean Surveillance Information Center, Suitland, Maryland
NPIC	Naval Photographic Interpretation Center, Suitland, Maryland
NRIP	Naval Reserve Intelligence Program
NRL	Naval Research Laboratory
NSA	National Security Agency
NSG	Naval Security Group
NSOC	National SIGINT Operations Center
NTIC	Naval Technical Intelligence Center, Suitland, Maryland
OBU	OSIS Baseline Upgrade
OIC	Operational Intelligence Center
ONI	Office of Naval Intelligence
OOA	out-of-area operations
OP-009J	Soviet Doctrine Division, Office of the Director of Naval Intelligence (1980s)
OP-094	Chief of Naval Operations Directorate for Command, Control, and Communications (1970s and 1980s)
OP-603	Chief of Naval Operations Strategic Concepts Branch (1970s and 1980s)
OP-95	Chief of Naval Operations Directorate of Naval Warfare (1970s and 1980s)
OPINTEL	operational intelligence
OPNAV	Office of the Chief of Naval Operations
OSIS	Ocean Surveillance Information System
OTH/T	over-the-horizon targeting
PHOTINT	photographic intelligence
PRC	People's Republic of China
PT	photographic intelligenceman
RDSS	Rapidly Deployable Surveillance System
RIU	Radio Intelligence Unit
ROW	rest-of-world
SABER	Surface Analysis Branch for Evaluation and Reporting Division, Office of Naval Intelligence
SAG	Submarine Analysis Group

SAM	surface-to-air missile
SAP	special access program
SCI	sensitive compartmented information
SDI	Strategic Defense Initiative
SECNAV	Secretary of the Navy
SIGINT	signals intelligence
SIOP	Single Integrated Operational Plan
SLBM	submarine-launched ballistic missile
SLOCs	sea lines of communication
SNA	Soviet Naval Aviation
SOSUS	Sound Surveillance System
SPEAR	Strike Projection Evaluation and Antiair Research Division, Office of Naval Intelligence
SSBN	nuclear-powered ballistic missile submarine
SSG	Strategic Studies Group, Naval War College
SSN	nuclear-powered attack submarine
SSO	Special Security Officer
SURTASS	Surveillance Towed Array Sensor System
SWORD	Submarine Warfare Operations Research Division, Office of Naval Intelligence
TAD	temporary active duty
ULTRA	World War II code word for extremely sensitive communications intelligence
USSR	Union of Soviet Socialist Republics
VTC	video teleconferencing
WWMCCS	Worldwide Military Command and Control System
YN-2505	designation for yeoman Intelligence Clerk

The Admirals' Advantage

1

OPINTEL and Its Origins

For centuries, with perhaps the sole exception of siege warfare, naval and military commanders have always had one set of questions foremost in their minds in the days and hours before battle is joined: "Where is the enemy, in what strength and disposition is he present, and what is he doing *right now?*" In this fundamental question, without some answer to which a commander cannot be expected to function intelligently in formulating or executing his immediate war plans, lies the genesis of a vital part of the profession of intelligence: the provision of "operational intelligence" to the warfighter.

Operational intelligence, or "OPINTEL" in U.S. Navy parlance, is difficult to define with precision. One former U.S. Director of Naval Intelligence (DNI), however, defines it as "the art of providing near-real-time information concerning the location, activity, and likely intentions of potential adversaries."[1] Simply put, it is "that intelligence information needed . . . for planning and conducting operations" in the most immediate sense.[2] Its emphasis upon timely warfighter support should be distinguished from "other varieties [of intelligence]: the analysis of strategy, doctrine, leadership, or equipment."[3] According to an official Navy statement of concept in 1948, OPINTEL is intelligence that is "directly concerned with the operating forces" and "intended for use by the operating forces in the near or immediate future and . . . shaped for this use by every echelon of command."[4]

On land, this sort of intelligence was traditionally provided in a haphazard and rudimentary form by cavalry scouts and all manner of human spies. In naval affairs, however—where opposing vessels could routinely operate out of sight not only of one another but also of land itself—picket ships could provide only the most immediate warning of impending engagement.[5] Since its foundation in 1882 upon the issuance of General Order Number 292, the Office of Naval Intelligence (ONI) has been charged with collecting and recording "such naval information as may be useful to the [Navy] Department."[6] Naval officers have also long understood the need to join the surveillance of foreign warships with the tracking of those merchant vessels upon which such ships might prey.[7] Yet it was not until 1903, with the arrival of the radio aboard naval vessels, that real OPINTEL was able to overcome the tyranny of visual distance in the dissemination of intelligence to forces operating at sea.[8] Thus, as one historian of U.S. Naval Intelligence has observed, operational intelligence is "a relatively new intelligence concept that came into its own subsequent to the development of radio."[9]

By World War I, radio interception was already providing time-urgent intelligence to British naval commanders, just in time to play a pivotal role against the new naval threat presented by German submarines.[10] Of necessity, these innovations sparked what was in effect a new discipline: providing "intelligence . . . to produce results in the immediate future" by means of a highly efficient intelligence organization devoted full-time to "locating and identifying U-boats, plotting their movements, and providing analysis of them."[11] This text is the story of the OPINTEL revolution and of how it played out during the climactic years of the twentieth century in which vast political and military power blocs—the Axis and the Allies during World War II, and then the North Atlantic Treaty Organization (NATO) and the Warsaw Pact during the succeeding half century of the Cold War—contended with one another for control of the planet.

OPINTEL in World War II

World War II was the crucible in which modern OPINTEL first began to take shape. Numerous historical accounts—now available due to the gradual declassification of records shrouded in history for many years after the war—attest to the vital role that intelligence played in making possible the Allies' overwhelming victory in 1945. For example, Gen. Thomas Handy reportedly believed that Allied intelligence triumphs shortened the war in Europe by at least a year, and Gen. Dwight Eisenhower estimated that it saved thousands of British and American lives.[12] Similarly, Adm. Chester Nimitz, commander in chief (CINC) of Allied forces in the Pacific theater, believed that the good intelligence he received was worth as much as an entire additional fleet.[13] Indeed, it has been clear for some time that "no history of naval warfare in World War II can now be regarded as complete without mention of the information which was available to the Allied admirals."[14]

But World War II was more than just a triumphant success story for the intelligence profession. Fundamentally, the war also set the tone—and laid the conceptual and organizational foundations—for postwar intelligence practice. The quantity and quality of the intelligence available to Allied commanders during the war created an entirely "new dimension in war," one that required "a new dimension in thinking on the part of our commanders."[15] Allied leaders came to use intelligence as "an actual planning factor" and learned to employ it along with "systematic efforts to exploit the techniques available."[16] As they did so, the organizational methods and analytical tools they used to exploit intelligence information laid the foundation for the succeeding fifty years of intelligence practice.[17] This was no less true for operational intelligence in naval warfare than it was in other intelligence arenas, for naval intelligence "mushroomed during the war, to become a recognized leader in intelligence collection and processing."[18]

All-Source "Fusion": The Power of Analysis "as a Sensor"

The strength of operational intelligence in modern practice lies in the methodology known as "all-source fusion": the systematic effort to collect information from multiple sources and piece it together in such a way as to see broader patterns. This concept of "the interdependence of all sources of intelligence"[19]—that is, the basic insight that the value of intelligence can be far more than the sum of its fragmentary parts—did not originate in World War II.[20] Nevertheless, that war saw the development of high-level all-source fusion in an *operational intelligence* context for the first time. In fact, a key to Allied intelligence successes during the war was precisely the ability of analysts to draw upon a broad range of information sources. As the U.S. Pacific Fleet's official intelligence history put it in October 1945, "All of the products of intelligence must be available to all branches and all specialists. Collation is the heart and soul of intelligence."[21]

All acquired intelligence information exists, and must be understood, in its particular context. Sometimes the value added by multisource analysis by experts who are knowledgeable not only in collection techniques but in the underlying subject matter can lie simply in explaining a single piece of information in that context. For example, British Prime Minister Winston Churchill may have been misled by raw high-grade communications intelligence ("ULTRA")[22] into pressing for untimely offensives against Erwin Rommel's *Afrika Korps.* Reading intercepted messages without an analyst's background knowledge or any corroborative information, Churchill failed to understand that Rommel's reports of his perilous situation were as much an effort to coax reinforcements from Berlin as they were accurate descriptions of the *Korps'* morale and order of battle.[23] On other hand, multisource analysis adds value by making intelligible aggregates out of individual fragments that are meaningless when viewed in isolation.[24] A good example is the legendary analyst with the wartime U.S. Office of Strategic Services who could reportedly tell the number of Japanese troops at an encampment by analyzing aerial photographs of their latrine.[25] According to one British veteran of wartime naval OPINTEL, while "no single source [may give], on its own, a complete picture . . . in combination and with intelligent deductions by officers with deep background experience of [enemy] procedures, they [can] reveal the enemy's plans clearly enough."[26]

Intelligence may be a matter of "trying to assemble a jigsaw puzzle,"[27] but one can often discern the picture even when many pieces remain missing. Intelligence "fusion" is the only methodology that can provide these pieces. During World War II, intelligence professionals became adept at "combining inputs from all the many sources available"—from radio intelligence to photo reconnaissance to prisoner interrogations—and then rapidly providing the result to operational commanders.[28] When practiced at a high level, all-source operational intelligence becomes an art form. Ultimately, it becomes the aspiration of good operational intelligence officers, nourished by their "all-source" perspective upon the enemy's activities, to begin to think like him—not only reporting his position and activities but also anticipating his next move. This, for example, is what Admiral Nimitz demanded of Edwin Layton, his fleet intelligence officer after Pearl Harbor:

> I want you to be the Admiral Nagumo of my staff, I want
> your every thought, every instinct as you believe Admiral

Nagumo might have them. You are to see the war, their operations, their aims, from the Japanese viewpoint and keep me
advised what you are thinking about, what you are doing,
and what purpose, what strategy, motivates your operations.
If you can do this, you will give me the kind of information
needed to win this war.[29]

Proper intelligence fusion, however, requires more than simply
piercing the veil of the enemy's operational secrecy and "getting into
his head." Good operational intelligence also requires penetrating
one's customer—that is, in Navy vernacular, it requires understanding
"Blue" forces as well as "Red." Without a solid grounding in one's own
operational practices and current operational disposition, it will be
impossible to fully understand either the enemy's activity—which,
after all, is presumably at least partly a reaction to one's *own* deployments—or the immediate needs of one's own commanders.[30] For this
reason, OPINTEL practitioners have always recognized that their work
"cannot be complete until it includes an interpretation of any pertinent
input from its own forces' operations staff."[31]

Finally, good operational intelligence requires timely dissemination, since "information can be acquired and evaluated until hell
freezes over, but it does not become *intelligence* until delivered to the
commanders who can make proper use of it."[32] This is why the development of real operational intelligence in naval warfare had to await
the arrival of radio communications aboard combat vessels. And even
then its first real flowering did not occur until World War II, by which
point the advent of long-range radio links and transoceanic cable communications made it possible for centralized analysis centers to rapidly
"feed" intelligence to operational commanders hundreds or even thousands of miles away.

With adequate near-real-time dissemination, all-source fusion can
turn operational intelligence into an enormously powerful tool. Spectacular successes in particular collection techniques—for example, the triumphs of Allied code breaking represented by the "cracking" of German
and Japanese codes—certainly contributed enormously to the outcome
of World War II. It is often forgotten, however, that real progress in using
such intelligence came through humbler means: the analytical tool of
multiple-source fusion and the development of dissemination systems
capable of providing analytical products to the warfighter.[33] This was the

contribution of OPINTEL's "Founding Fathers" during World War II. By bringing such sources and methodologies together for the first time, they were able to use intelligence analysis itself, in effect, as a new type of "sensor"[34]—a means with which to see and understand far more about the enemy than ever before.

The British Model

Modern OPINTEL was invented in London shortly before the outbreak of World War II. In order to obtain useful intelligence on enemy fleet movements, the British Admiralty had for centuries sent agents into foreign ports, tracked warship sightings, and debriefed friendly merchant captains returning from abroad.[35] It was not until the late 1930s, however, that the emerging technology and organization of "fused" operational intelligence came together in a systematic fashion.

As Alan Bath has recounted, the British "grew to realize that no single type of information could, without integration of data from many other sources, provide a sufficiently authoritative picture of what to expect from their enemies."[36] By 1939 it was understood that some kind of "central assessment machinery" would be required and that Britain required "integrated intelligence inputs" to meet anticipated wartime needs.[37] Initially, the British military services took advantage of the Joint Intelligence Committee (JIC), which had been created three years earlier by the chiefs of staff, to provide all-source intelligence to the national leadership: the prime minister, his war cabinet, and the chiefs of staff.[38]

Within the British Admiralty, this understanding of the need for—and potentialities of—all-source fusion had earlier led to the creation of a dedicated operational intelligence architecture, the Operational Intelligence Center (OIC). The OIC was the creation of Adm. Sir William James, RN (Royal Navy), the deputy chief of the British naval staff. He had headed the British Admiralty's cryptographic bureau, known as "Room 40," during World War I, and understood the occasional difficulties that office had faced when forced to depend for analysis and dissemination of information upon operational staffs who were not familiar with the intelligence function. The problems experienced by Room 40—candidly assessed during the interwar period in at least two admiralty studies—helped ensure that the OIC would be permitted to become a real *intelligence center* rather than simply a cryptographic bureau.[39]

Thus, mindful of the successes that British forces had enjoyed during World War I by combining the skills of cryptographers with inputs from a network of radiogoniometry (direction-finding) stations—as well as being aware of the need to ensure better coordination between intelligence analysts and operational staffs—James encouraged the British Director of Naval Intelligence (DNI) to replicate and improve upon this process in peacetime by creating "a proper intelligence section" capable of "put[ting] two and two together." As a result, in June 1937 the British Naval Intelligence Directorate (NID) was told to establish an "all-source intelligence center," the OIC. Headed by a former Royal Navy paymaster named Norman ("Ned") Denning, this center initially focused upon following the movement of Italian submarines and German forces supporting the Nationalist cause during the Spanish civil war.[40] Though small and at first focused only upon Spanish issues, Denning's new OIC was in its own way revolutionary, for its area of operations it became "the co-ordinating centre for *all* information from whatever sources with full responsibility for analysis and evaluation."[41]

Crucially, the fledgling OIC was in an ideal position to expand to meet the admiralty's wartime needs vis-à-vis German U-boats. After starting with no more than a "skeleton crew," the OIC had acquired a staff of fifty by October 1938—nearly a year before the outbreak of hostilities—and soon moved into a new, underground "war room" built for it in the basement of the admiralty building in London.[42] The move clearly identified the office as the distant progenitor of the U.S. Navy's own Ocean Surveillance Information System (OSIS) of half a century later. A second British OIC was established in Singapore in 1938 to provide tailored theater-level intelligence to His Majesty's Far East fleet. In 1939—thirty-three years before the U.S. Navy would establish an analogous facility at Rota, Spain, for identical reasons—a "scaled-down version" of the admiralty OIC was also set up in Malta, providing more tailored information to the Royal Navy's Mediterranean commander than could the national-level watchfloor in London.[43] Under the stewardship of Rear Adm. John Godfrey, RN—who became the British DNI in 1939 and believed it "the most important duty of naval intelligence in wartime to be providing information on enemy warships"[44]—the admiralty's OICs were quickly prepared for global war.

After the outbreak of war in Europe in 1939, the OIC performed splendidly and before long emerged as "arguably the single most effective intelligence organization of the Second World War."[45] Under the leadership of Comdr. Rodger Winn—a remarkable London attorney who had studied at both Harvard and Yale before being directly commissioned into the Royal Naval Reserve[46]—the OIC's tracking room became "the primary intelligence weapon against U-boats, providing Royal Navy operational commanders with up-to-the-minute information on the strength and locations of German wolf packs."[47] With the tracking room operating in close coordination with the crucial comprehensive master plot of surface activity maintained throughout the war by Denning,[48] the OIC was essential to the admiralty's conduct of the Battle of the Atlantic.

American Practice

The Atlantic Theater

The hallmark of integrated OPINTEL systems is that their effectiveness increases with the number of effective "nodes" and with the number and variety of intelligence inputs brought into the fusion process. For the Royal Navy—locked as it was in a maritime battle for survival against the depredations of Germany's submersible commerce raiders in the early stages of World War II—this dynamic produced great incentives to join intelligence forces with the U.S. Navy. Indeed, British DNI Godfrey already wished to work more closely with existing U.S. communications intelligence (COMINT) and direction-finding networks. This desire to coordinate more with the United States increased markedly in the spring of 1941, when the U-boats' operational areas expanded to the waters west of Iceland, bringing them into the new U.S. maritime security zone.[49]

   Fortunately for both of the soon-to-be wartime allies, the effectiveness of Commander Winn's OIC was not lost on naval planners on the other side of the Atlantic. Over time the Americans also came "to appreciate the responsiveness of the British naval intelligence system to the needs of the forces it supported."[50] One key player in this process was Rear Adm. Alan Kirk, who became the U.S. DNI in March 1941 after returning from a posting as U.S. Naval Attaché in London. Kirk had become familiar with the admiralty's highly effective OIC from his time in Britain and was "impressed by the effective meshing of the British Navy's intelligence and war planning organizations in the Combined

Operations Intelligence Center."[51] Kirk's penultimate predecessor as DNI, Rear Adm. Walter Anderson, had already recommended to President Roosevelt that the United States follow the British practice and set up a joint-service defense planning body.[52] While interservice rivalries and some admirals' suspicions of the British did not make such mimicry easy, the U.S. armed forces nonetheless established a loose combined-service intelligence planning structure in early 1942.[53]

More importantly for present purposes, in January 1941 the U.S. Navy also established a dedicated OPINTEL "'war room' capable of supplying complete combat or operational intelligence," designated OP-38W within the office of Chief of Naval Operations (CNO) Adm. Harold Stark.[54] Unfortunately, though created "in straightforward imitation of the British," this plot room had been placed "under an admiral who didn't understand [intelligence] fusion or really want the job."[55] In December 1941, therefore, the OPINTEL function shifted to the staff of the newly appointed U.S. Fleet Commander in Chief (COMINCH[56]), Adm. Ernest J. King, under the designation F-35 (later F-32), the Operational Information Section of the Operations Division of COMINCH headquarters.[57] By May 1943—when another wartime reorganization of the Navy Department put Admiral King in charge of the entire Atlantic naval theater of operations—King's apparatus had finally fully duplicated the intimate relationship between the British OPINTEL staff (OIC) and the Atlantic operational commander (the First Sea Lord).[58]

The early American wartime reorganizations of the Atlantic command structure were particularly important in that they brought operational command of American forces and the new intelligence center under the same roof. One of the reasons that the British Admiralty had proven so receptive to Admiral James's call for the establishment of the OIC in 1937 was that the admiralty—unlike the War Office or the Air Ministry—enjoyed operational control of combat forces. This centralization of operational control created a corresponding "demand" for centralized intelligence analysis.[59] By contrast, the U.S. Navy Department, which lacked this kind of operational command, was initially less receptive to such ideas. The wartime reorganization of the COMINCH staff, therefore, removed an institutional obstacle to national-level operational intelligence on the British model.[60]

F-35 initially consisted of no more than a "rudimentary plotting room for U-boat movements."[61] Operational intelligence also soon came to reside almost exclusively in the hands of the operational planning staff rather than the Office of Naval Intelligence. The U.S. Navy observed a strict distinction between "intelligence required for current naval operations [i.e., OPINTEL], which was to be provided directly from the operational headquarters to the forces involved, and intelligence for planning, which was to be provided via the joint/combined staff" system.[62] This arrangement may well have contributed to the legendary rivalry between ONI and OP-20-G, the Communications Security Section of the Office of the CNO, that by 1943 left OP-20-G with a "virtual lock on naval operational intelligence," while ONI functioned merely as "a producer of basic and static intelligence such as ship and aircraft characteristics or geographic area studies."[63] Throughout the war, OPINTEL would remain an intelligence function run out of the fleet operational staffs: even the Navy's highly successful radio intelligence (e.g., COMINT) operations were shifted from under the aegis of ONI's Far East Section (OP-16-FE) to the COMINCH staff in July 1943.[64]

To be sure, ONI set up an "Operational Intelligence Section" (OP-16-FO) in April 1943, with the mission of ensuring that information was properly processed and made available to operational commanders. However, this office was disbanded after only a few months. Another ONI effort in early 1942 resulted in the establishment of an Intelligence Center (C-1) within the office's C-Branch (OP-16-C) for the purpose of evaluating and disseminating "current information from all sources." This office was redesignated the Foreign Plot Section (OP-16-FP) in March 1943. Unfortunately for ONI, the Plot Section provided information only to the Secretary of the Navy's morning briefings. It did not, as a matter of policy, "handle or plot [either] any material concerning the strength or disposition of Allied forces" or high-grade cryptologic intelligence. ONI would therefore have little role in OPINTEL until after the end of the war, when COMINCH was dissolved.[65]

Nevertheless, though this function clearly fell under War Plans rather than ONI, the U.S. Navy was now emphatically in the OPINTEL business. F-35, the main U.S. Navy tracking room, was headed by Comdr. George Dyer. King's COMINCH staff had a further Atlantic Section tracking room, F-11, under Lt. George Laird, that focused upon U-boat activity. After Rodger Winn's visit to the United States in 1942, Lt. Comdr. Kenneth Knowles became head of F-11. Knowles had himself visited London to study Winn's methods, and in late 1942 he began teaching the British approach to his F-11 staff. In December 1942 F-11 was redesignated F-21. Within it, there was later established an even more restrictive component, the F-211 "Secret Room," to handle raw cryptographic information. Knowles's F-21 quickly emerged as an able counterpart to Winn's effort at the admiralty OIC. By late 1943, in fact, the Americans had acquired the dominant role in producing cryptographic intelligence on the U-boat war, thanks to the acquisition by OP-20-G cryptologists of new high-speed "bombe" computers (from the original Polish word *bomby,* used by the Poles in 1938 to describe the first mechanical devices to decrypt German Enigma codes).[66]

Although the U.S. plot did not maintain a twenty-four-hour watchfloor as the British did, both tracking rooms learned to fuse all-source information, such as high-grade cryptologic products (e.g., ULTRA decrypts), direction-finding plots, COMINT traffic analysis, and sighting reports.[67] The resulting comprehensive track of Allied and neutral combatants, merchant shipping, and German warships and submarines proved indispensable to wartime efforts to protect Atlantic merchant convoys against U-boats and commerce raiders, and would ultimately help Allied forces destroy Adm. Karl Dönitz's U-boat fleet.[68] Modern OPINTEL had arrived.

In the footsteps of the British OIC's approach to distributing OPINTEL fusion nodes among regional commands, when the U.S. Navy set up separate Atlantic theater "Sea Frontier" subordinate commands, scrambled telephone links were established between the COMINCH OPINTEL staff and the new Sea Frontier tracking rooms.[69] The U.S. Navy's efforts to build its OPINTEL architecture into an integrated theater-wide network still lagged behind the efficient and experienced British OIC, but the Americans made great strides—and cooperation with the admiralty tracking room was "superb."[70] From May 1942 through the end of the war, the British and American submarine plots employed a uniform U-boat designator scheme and exchanged daily U-boat estimates.[71]

In addition to establishing this formal architecture of OPINTEL collection, fusion, and dissemination, the Americans also took important steps toward institutionalizing OPINTEL as a permanent feature of the U.S. naval system. In December 1942 the Navy established an advanced OPINTEL training program; by the end of the war this school had produced some thirteen hundred naval officers who were specifically trained in operational intelligence.[72] By providing specialized formal instruction in the arcana of the OPINTEL art in addition to the formidable on-the-job training provided in its new Atlantic- and Pacific-theater intelligence cells, naval intelligence not only helped meet fleet operators' wartime needs but also began to lay the groundwork for future OPINTEL successes. The cadres of skilled OPINTEL specialists produced by such programs would prove invaluable some years after the war when the Navy set about reconstituting its OPINTEL architecture in the face of an emerging naval threat from the Soviet Union.

The Pacific Theater

This successful adoption by the U.S. Navy of the admiralty's OPINTEL concept was not limited to the Battle of the Atlantic. As early as March 1942, suggestions had been floated that this approach be adopted in the Pacific as well, and in May 1942 Admiral Nimitz endorsed the establishment of an Intelligence Center, Pacific Ocean Area (ICPOA) based at Pearl Harbor, Hawaii. Capt. Arthur McCollum was instrumental in this process. He had headed ONI's Far Eastern section in 1941 and was among the many U.S. naval officers who had been impressed by the British OIC. With lobbying from McCollum and others, Admiral King approved the ICPOA concept on June 12, 1942.[73] Established within two weeks of King's decision and operational within two months, ICPOA thus "applied [the OPINTEL system] equally in the Pacific war."[74]

In the autumn of 1943, when Admiral Nimitz became Commander in Chief, Pacific (CINCPAC), the young ICPOA became JICPOA, the Joint Intelligence Center, Pacific Ocean Area. This "Joint" center had modest beginnings, developing simply because Nimitz's naval staff lacked adequate maps to support land operations in the Pacific theater's developing "island-hopping" campaign. According to a memorandum prepared in October 1945 by the U.S. Pacific Fleet's assistant chief of staff for intelligence, the new organization's map and chart facilities "were not designed to meet all theater needs."[75] More specifically, as one participant recounted,

> Admiral Nimitz realized that we lacked one major element: maps. Hydrographic maps by the Navy are great for sea areas, but they are not very good ashore—not very good for land ops ashore even on a small island. So Admiral Nimitz

found at Fort Shafter an Army topographic battalion that was unemployed. So he took that Army battalion together with its [commanding officer], Colonel Joseph J. Twitty, and formed and integrated them into ICPOA—and put a "J" in front of the name. And we had the world's first [Joint] Intelligence Center . . . [because] we needed something that the Army could provide that the Navy didn't have.[76]

JICPOA, however, quickly became a large and truly all-service intelligence staff—containing nearly two thousand people by war's end—that seated Navy intelligence professionals alongside their counterparts from the Army, Marine Corps, and Coast Guard.[77]

Containing major sections dealing with radio intelligence, air intelligence, and photo interpretation, JICPOA was principally concerned with strategic intelligence estimates for major Pacific operations, and to this end it drew together "information from every source of intelligence from radio intercepts to prisoner of war interrogations."[78] It also included a dedicated OPINTEL cell with its own situation plot, displaying "all known or suspected locations of enemy forces,"[79] and thus marked the United States' first experience with a genuinely "purple" (i.e., joint-service) operational intelligence architecture. One participant credits JICPOA with having been "one of the most effective intelligence organizations in military history."[80]

Like its admiralty and COMINCH counterparts, the JICPOA organization provided a valuable template for intelligence organization, and its structure soon provided "a pattern for ensuing advanced centers elsewhere in the Pacific"[81] at places such as Dutch Harbor, Pago Pago, Auckland, Brisbane, and eventually Guam.[82] A separate Australian system of national-level and regional joint-service Combined Operational Intelligence Centers (COICs) had also been set up beginning in August 1940. The national-level COIC in Melbourne was co-opted by Gen. Douglas MacArthur's staff in April 1942, thus bringing the Australian network into the rest of the Allied system.[83] In a dynamic that would repeat itself in the Cold War environment of the 1970s and 1980s, operational intelligence during World War II was increasingly devolved as "frontline units, advanced intelligence centers, [became] true focal points for fusion of all-source intelligence data."[84]

OPINTEL's Contribution

While it might not quite have been true, as Churchill once put it, that "the defeat of the U-boats carries with it the sovereignty of all the oceans of the world,"[85] the OPINTEL methodology that helped accomplish this defeat played a vital role in the successful conclusion of World War II in both the Atlantic and Pacific naval theaters. As noted above, it is commonplace to credit the Allied cryptologic successes of ULTRA and "MAGIC" (its Japanese analogue) with greatly advancing the war effort—from the Battle of the Atlantic[86] to the Battle of Midway[87] and beyond. According to one study cited by naval historian John Winton, in fact, "without Special Intelligence the war would have been much longer, and more costly, and indeed might never have been won."[88] After the British began sharing ULTRA COMINT with the U.S. Navy's OP-20-G in June 1941 through the British embassy in Washington, D.C., therefore, one might suppose that the intelligence war was all but won.[89]

Serious students of intelligence tradecraft, however, will recognize this as an incomplete picture. The phenomenal successes of Allied code breakers *did* contribute immensely to the outcome of the war, but these breakthroughs alone were not enough. To begin with, ULTRA information included data that were more than just code breaking: it was the code name applied to all of the high-grade fused intelligence produced by tracking rooms such as F-21 and the admiralty OIC, and it included information acquired by other means, such as direction-finding and radar contacts.[90] More importantly, ULTRA information was only as good as the system that managed, analyzed, and distributed it. ULTRA and MAGIC would have meant much less if Allied intelligence staffs had not learned to use such material in the production of finished, all-source intelligence supplied as tailored near-real-time operational support to warfighting commanders by an efficient system of subtheater-level intelligence-fusion nodes.[91]

Functioning within this sophisticated OPINTEL system, intelligence officers were thus able to provide remarkably effective answers to the age-old commander's query, "Where is the enemy, and what is he doing *right now?*" All-source intelligence support—heavily based upon ULTRA decrypts—supplied to operational commanders through the OIC architecture, for example, was vital to British operations against German tankers and supply ships that supported the battleship *Bismarck.*[92] Even where decrypts did not directly reveal planned operations, this combination of code breaking and sophisticated all-source analysis by experts in German operational methods provided excellent general intelligence support. As Winton recounts, the OIC became expert at "interpreting the tell-tale signs and hints the Enigma decrypts provided that something was afoot." Surface ship operations in the North Sea, for example, could be deduced by the "increased number of Luftwaffe reconnaissance flights, movements of fighter squadrons from Germany to Norway, sailing signals and route orders of escorts and minesweepers, the transfer of operational control over ships from one flag or regional authority to another, unusual instructions to U-boats to report on British air and sea patrols and radar surveillance, or an increase in traffic in the 'Officer only' key."[93] Though temporary breaks in ULTRA coverage—resulting, for example, from the introduction of a fourth wheel to the Enigma machine's multiple-rotor electromechanical encryption system—were obviously formidable problems for the OIC, their accumulated expertise developed so that under such circumstances they could still often produce useful educated guesses.[94]

Most of all, however, all-source intelligence was used in the evasive routing of merchant convoys from June 1941 until the end of the war, thereby enabling Britain to survive the U-boat blockade. Such effective intelligence support also enabled Allied forces to take active measures against the U-boats. By the spring of 1944, OPINTEL-driven attacks helped force the Germans to completely revise their tactics, requiring their submarines to remain underwater by day and to attack only at night. Even apart from their escalating losses, this change alone represented a major defeat and helped ensure that they would no longer be able to threaten Britain with isolation or impede the transatlantic logistics support required for the liberation of France.[95]

ULTRA alone did not ensure victory. Rather, it was a triumph of intelligence organization and coordination, the hallmarks of sophisticated operational intelligence: "There is no question that the synergetic efforts of the American, British, and Canadian naval intelligence organizations were key to Allied intelligence success in the Battle of the Atlantic, providing more and better information on U-boat operations than any one of them could have done alone."[96]

In the "battle of wits" that was the Atlantic war,[97] "sound organization and good intelligence" carried the day.[98] Efficient OPINTEL, Allied commanders discovered, could work wonders. As one British participant recalled, "by the end of [each morning's briefing] there was little or nothing we did not know about what the U-boats were up to in the Atlantic at the time."[99] According to another participant, Winn's tracking room helped give the Allies "a comprehensive and accurate picture of the whole operational U-boat fleet including the dispositions and movements of those boats actually at sea in the North Sea and the Atlantic."[100] The experts at the admiralty's submarine tracking room were able to produce daily charts detailing the location of every German U-boat: "We were generally current in our reading of U-boat signals and sometimes knew more about the true situation at sea than did the [U-boat high command]."[101] As time went by, tracking room experts even got to know the personalities and idiosyncrasies of many individual commanders, giving them an "uncanny" or "eerie" ability to understand German activities and predict their moves.[102] Nor was this expertise entirely tactical: OIC analysts "rubbed minds daily against those of the [U-boat high command] and his staff,"[103] enabling them to assess German strategy and doctrine as well.

The importance of good OPINTEL organization—as opposed to merely good intelligence sources—can also be seen through negative inference by comparing Anglo-American with German practice. The German *B-Dienst* code-breaking service, for example, did manage to break the Royal Navy's main code and the code used for Anglo-American-Canadian communications in the Atlantic (Naval Ciphers Nos. 2 and 3, respectively). Despite the insights these cryptologic successes gave into virtually all Allied naval operations, however, the German naval staff never developed a successful operational intelligence system and was unable to effectively plot and assess the ever-changing situation at sea.[104] In a dramatic illustration of the importance of ensuring timely intelligence production, only a small proportion of British signals broken by *B-Dienst* were readable in time for operational use.[105] The Battle of the Atlantic, therefore, was won not just by Allied OPINTEL successes but also by high-level OPINTEL failure by the Germans.

As in so many other ways, methodologies pioneered by the Allies during World War II laid the foundation for naval warfare during the next half century. As the Germans' new Type XXI *schnorkel* boats became operational later in the war, OPINTEL formed the core of a strikingly modern Allied antisubmarine warfare (ASW) effort. By integrating data from COMINT, direction-finding hits, sighting reports, ASW "barrier" patrols, and even hydrophonic listening devices, they coordinated the hunt for these elusive targets in a three-dimensional maritime environment.[106] In the years to come, Navy operational intelligence would play a similar role against the submarines of the Soviet navy.

The impact of the OPINTEL methodology was no less dramatic in the Pacific theater. As John Prados has chronicled, "Intelligence remains the missing piece in the puzzle of explaining [the outcome of] the Pacific war." As in the Atlantic, however, these Pacific successes were not those of high-grade cryptology alone, though this clearly played a pivotal role. Rather, the real story of the Allied intelligence victory lies in "the day-to-day accumulation of a fund of knowledge concerning the adversary" built up through the integration of information from many sources.[107] Good intelligence sources, combined with highly effective intelligence methods—for fusion analysis, tailored operational support, and rapid dissemination—made Allied admirals far better informed and knowledgeable than their Japanese counterparts. By allowing Allied commanders to be, in John Adams's words, "possessed of all this knowledge, well digested and ready at command," operational intelligence helped make possible the destruction of the Japanese empire.[108]

Some Recurring Operational Intelligence Themes

As noted above, OPINTEL practice during World War II laid the foundation for operational intelligence in the postwar world, in which allied Western nations would again come to face a powerful continental dictatorship with an expanding naval capability. It is useful, therefore, to identify some recurring themes of OPINTEL practice that emerged during the 1939–45 war and that would help shape operational intelligence during the Cold War.

Collection, Dissemination, and the Aspiration to "Real Time"

First, as discussed earlier, good operational intelligence requires good communications systems and prompt dissemination, for sound analysis cannot influence a battle unless it is made known in time to the commander who needs it. World War II made abundantly clear that the most successful commanders "'tended to be those whose radio-interception services were able to bring them the promptest and most accurate information about the intentions of their opponents,' and the same applied at sea."[109] Particularly in naval warfare, where many battles took place in which ships never actually came within sight of one another, providing prompt and accurate information about the location of the enemy was the heart and soul of OPINTEL. "Intelligence is a perishable commodity. Battles are won and lost and campaigns are decided often on the basis of which side is most proficient in the use of intelligence—that is, the acquisition, evaluation, and dissemination of military information in time for commanders to act upon it. No matter how accurate the information, it is militarily useless unless it is made available soon enough for command decisions."[110] As a rule, "dissemination tends to be intelligence's Achilles heel,"[111] because "the best intelligence in the world is wasted if it is not passed in time to those who can use it."[112] Such pressures are particularly demanding for operational intelligence.

In World War II, modern technology—in the form of scrambled telephone communications, high-frequency radio nets, and transoceanic cables—was first enlisted to the cause of OPINTEL collection and dissemination. Through such means, all-source information could be rapidly collected and, once analyzed, sent to operational commanders faster than ever before. Organizationally, the establishment of subtheater-level regional fusion centers, each dedicated to providing OPINTEL and other intelligence support for a particular local commander in chief, greatly accelerated the speed of this intelligence cycle. It was always a struggle, of course. According to an assessment prepared in October 1945 by the U.S. Pacific Fleet's assistant chief of staff for intelligence, for example, "one of our most difficult problems was dissemination."[113] Ultimately, however, Allied intelligence staffs were indeed able to "distribute this information to the forces that needed it—in time for them to use it."[114]

These principles—a push to utilize the most advanced available communications technology and organizational devolution—became enduring themes of operational intelligence practice into the twenty-first century. They were part of the core ethic of what would later be called the "OSIS culture" of "when in doubt, push it out . . . to the operating forces as rapidly as possible."[115] When the collection and dissemination components of the OPINTEL process are compressed as much as possible, the resulting "battlespace picture" given the operational commander can be tremendously advantageous.[116] The commander who has the OPINTEL advantage can make well-informed decisions faster than his adversary, a well-understood strategy for victory in maneuver warfare.[117] At sea, where *all* warfare is maneuver warfare, this advantage can be particularly decisive.

Role of Technology

In addition to the importance of technology for rapid collection and dissemination—and the resulting incentive continually to seek "higher-tech" solutions to such problems—technology plays a crucial role in making possible rapid and meaningful operational intelligence analysis.[118] This was clearly shown during and after World War II, as the information flows entailed by modern all-source intelligence fusion made it increasingly difficult for analysts to keep up with events. The needs of time-sensitive OPINTEL analysis, therefore, emerged as "the major factor making automation necessary."[119]

The drive for automation in U.S. military intelligence, in fact, began even before World War II. In the 1930s, for example, intelligence officers pioneered techniques of applying (then) state-of-the-art business machines to code breaking in order to increase the speed and accuracy of their attempts to crack foreign encryption systems. Such rudimentary automated systems as letter-frequency counters, card sorters, and keypunch machines aided considerably in speeding the cryptologist's job.[120] At the suggestion of Thomas Dyer and Joseph Wenger of the OP-20-G intelligence section, the Navy's Bureau of Ships was able to rent crucial IBM keypunch equipment and hire two full-time operators to help run it, for an initial investment of only five thousand dollars. Rear Adm. Edwin Layton attributes the advance of U.S. machine-based cryptology ahead of British efforts in the 1930s to this decision alone.[121] Too much should not be made of this, however, as the National Security Agency's (NSA's) history of U.S. cryptology notes the equipment's arrival was delayed for a year, and the naval intelligence officer who received it was forced to spend precious time personally training two clerks in its operation.[122] In addition, apart from code breaking, operational intelligence as a whole was still done by hand at war's end in 1945. Nevertheless, these first steps had shown the way forward, and Navy OPINTEL would thereafter be at the forefront of applied automated data processing (ADP) and database management in the years ahead.

Pushing OPINTEL to the Front

As suggested previously, a crucial innovation of wartime operational intelligence, pioneered by the British and enthusiastically followed by the Americans, was its increasing devolution toward "the front"—that is, the establishment of dedicated OPINTEL functions with local warfighters at increasingly junior levels of command. It was fundamental to Admiral Nimitz in the Pacific, for example, that he maintain his own fleet intelligence section and that its staff concentrate specifically upon the most immediate issues (e.g., Japanese message traffic) affecting the Pacific Command. His intelligence staffs believed that analysts in Washington, "being so distant from operational headquarters" and removed from "the uncoiling snake of Japanese military power," would give insufficient attention to operational intelligence. Local analysts, in contrast, could provide the information Nimitz needed to know in the fight against Japan: "what the Japanese *were doing,* could do, and would probably do."[123] The proliferation of subtheater-level fusion centers (e.g., Advanced Intelligence Centers) in the Pacific suggests that other operational commanders felt the same way. Their needs could best be understood and met not by Nimitz's command-level staff at Pearl Harbor but by their own dedicated all-source fusion centers.

This idea is fundamental to the nature of operational intelligence for at least two reasons. Most obvious, of course, is that a dedicated OPINTEL cell at a subregional command can spend all of its time addressing the intelligence needs of that command and need not rely upon more broadly focused or only part-time support from higher-echelon intelligence staffs. As has been suggested earlier, however, the effectiveness of OPINTEL support also corresponds directly to the ability of intelligence analysts to understand their "Blue" customer as well as the enemy. Almost by definition, a dedicated command-level staff will understand the situation and requirements of that command better—and will provide information more effectively—than a higher-level structure with a wider scope of responsibility. Operators and intelligence professionals, in other words, can gain enormously from the kind of intimate understanding and trust built up by a shared working environment and operations-level perspective.

The gradual devolution of OPINTEL during the course of World War II reflects this dynamic. Ultimately, the first fledgling steps were even taken toward building up a meaningful operational intelligence function aboard individual ships. In early 1942, for example, Vice Adm. William Halsey embarked a Radio Intelligence Unit (RIU) aboard his task force flagship, the aircraft carrier USS *Enterprise* (CV-6), in early 1942—the first RIU to be so employed, but not the last.[124] Not all commanders were ready for such a step or willing to use such new capabilities properly at this highly devolved level of intelligence support. In particular, such arrangements required an unprecedented degree of intelligence/operator mutual understanding and trust. As Layton recalls, for example, RIU embarkations often placed young lieutenants in the awkward position of instructing an admiral on the enemy's real intentions.[125] Fortunately, such floating collocation also helped foster mutual confidence in ways that life in a shore command could not match: both lieutenant and admiral, after all, would literally "sink or swim" together according to the quality of their working relationship.

Though it still remained difficult to make the concept work consistently at the level of individual unit commands, the U.S. Navy built up a highly evolved network of interrelated OPINTEL cells at all major levels of command—partially overlapping and supporting one another in service of the warfighter's needs. Even at the afloat level, the Navy made great strides in this regard during the course of the war. As Rear Adm. Donald ("Mac") Showers recalls from his own days with Admiral Nimitz's intelligence staff:

> In the beginning of the war, we had very few Intel officers on ships. They were mainly staffs ashore. It was only after we started offensive operations that we placed radio intercept teams on the ships with the flags. These teams became able to listen to tactical communications in the vicinity of an engagement or in battle, and provide early warning information to the commanders. And commanders, to a man, became appreciative of this capability. It was very useful to them and highly valued having an Intelligence officer on board who could provide them with this information. Little by little, that system grew.[126]

By war's end, "fusion began right at the top, with the President's Map Room, and extended down, ultimately, to every major warship, where fusion took the form of the combat information center."[127] Such moves toward "afloat OPINTEL" were an important beginning for what the Navy would turn into a potent and robust methodology later in the century.

Informal versus Formal Communications

Part of the genius of this interconnected network of mutually supporting intelligence fusion centers was that it allowed analysts to engage in informal "back-channel" consultations with one another. Carried out via modern near-real-time communications links, such as Teletype printers and scrambled telephones, this bypassed the more restricting (and accountable) formal dissemination of center "products." The U.S. and British submarine tracking rooms devoted to prosecuting the U-boat enemy, for example, exchanged informal analytical comments and questions in addition to the official daily analytical summaries they dispatched to the fleet. This transformed the special direct signal link between the two centers into the vehicle for "a completely free and unfettered exchange of ideas and information."[128] "To encourage the most frank and unconstrained exchanges of ideas, these [informal] messages were treated as personal notes and no regular dissemination of their contents was made outside the two tracking rooms, although on occasion the commander in chief, U.S. Fleet [Admiral King] and the first sea lord used this 'back-channel' to exchange views on submarine matters."[129]

As a means through which analyst and operational commander alike could hone their understanding by interaction with their counterparts in other commands, therefore, the highly integrated OPINTEL network provided an important service. This would continue to be the case when the U.S. Navy revived the OPINTEL concept during the Cold War—with such ad hoc interconnectivity ultimately becoming the animating principle of the "intelligence Internet," INTELINK, in the 1990s. Indeed, it was to be a recurring theme of postwar intelligence organization that the time, security, and bandwidth pressures of modern OPINTEL organization helped lead naval intelligence to create communications systems sometimes more effective than those used for operational command and control. As Adm. David Jeremiah would later recount, "In many ways, the communications systems in the early days were better in the Intel world than they were in the unrestricted line organizations. That's always been an important part of the integration of intelligence and the operational community."[130]

Sanitization Issues

Because by its nature, all-source intelligence fusion can involve the integration of information from extremely sensitive sources as well as more pedestrian ones, the OPINTEL process often presents problems of "sanitization." It presents dilemmas, in other words, of whether, how, and to what degree intelligence staffs can provide sensitive-source information to operational commanders—many of whom may not themselves be permitted to know that such a source even exists. During World War II, these problems particularly came to the fore with regard to high-grade cryptologic intelligence from ULTRA and MAGIC decryption.

In the U-boat war, the British initially resisted sharing ULTRA-derived information with U.S. intelligence, fearing that the Americans would inevitably "leak" it. Alternatively, they feared that U.S. commanders would leap into action precipitously on the basis of ULTRA information, thereby compromising the closely guarded cryptologic effort at Bletchley Park by reacting too effectively to the announcement of German plans.[131] The British preferred to use special intelligence somewhat passively, employing it principally to help convoys avoid U-boat attack. The Americans were inclined, however, to use the information more aggressively—as a means of helping to more quickly force an Allied victory by seeking out and sinking submarines with "hunter-killer" groups.[132]

It was often unhelpful, however, to "sanitize" such information by disguising it as simple agent reports, since this encouraged uninitiated intelligence consumers to treat highly reliable ULTRA information with the same skepticism that tends to greet most uncorroborated single-source human intelligence (HUMINT).[133] Despite reservations by the First Sea Lord, Adm. Sir Dudley Pound, by June 1943 the British had acceded to American proposals to use ULTRA information as the basis for aggressive prosecution of German U-boats—for example, the so-called *Milch Cow* refueling submarines that sustained U-boat "wolf pack" operations at sea.[134]

At some point, the British discovered, operational security had to take second place to operational success—or at least the imperative of preventing catastrophic operational failure. R. V. Jones, who headed the British scientific intelligence office during the war, recounts an example of how British concerns for cryptologic secrecy could—if accorded too much weight—lead to grave problems. According to Jones, ULTRA decrypts allowed the British to read the entire German plan for the invasion of Crete three weeks in advance. Despite this extraordinary information, they were unable to prevent or defeat the invasion, "partly because our Commander, Lord Freyberg, could make only the most limited use of the foreknowledge for fear of giving the Enigma secret away."[135] Analogous restrictions upon information in the U-boat war, it came to be seen, could lead to Britain's defeat.

Bowing thus to necessity, the admiralty established a special secure radio Teletype circuit for ULTRA material between the U.S. and British submarine tracking rooms.[136] For dissemination of ULTRA to other commands as the war progressed, the British set up a system of Special Liaison Units (SLUs) tasked with receiving and carefully managing the distribution of ULTRA information to the most senior operational officers.[137] The intelligence arms maintained a list of "ULTRA-indoctrinated" officers to whom—and, in theory, *only* to whom—information could be revealed in detail. These officers were expected never to put themselves in any position in which they might be captured.[138] In U.S. practice, special "ULTRA officers" (aka "Special Security Officers," or SSOs) performed this function,[139] and any change in operational patterns at the COMINCH level on the basis of high-grade cryptologic information (i.e., ULTRA) had to be specially approved.[140] Operations undertaken on the basis of ULTRA information had to have a plausible "cover story."[141]

As the British had foreseen, however, the aggressive use of ULTRA information on the offensive was a gamble. According to F-21 chief Knowles, the U.S. Navy was willing to take "calculated risks" in this regard—even though they sometimes "skated on some pretty thin ice" with regard to operational security.[142] Over the course of the war, U.S. Navy "hunter-killer" groups of escort carriers and destroyers tracked down and sank fifty-four U-boats. The Germans, in yet another analysis failure, concluded that the continuing success of these groups meant there must have been some two hundred "hunter-killer" groups deployed in the Atlantic. The real number, however, was only six. Fortunately, the lack of German OPINTEL paid off for the Allies.[143]

In the Pacific theater, high-level Japanese decrypts were apparently initially so tightly held that valuable information sometimes failed to reach those who needed to know it. In Layton's account, for example, MAGIC in early 1941 was "hedged with a fetish of secrecy so overwhelming that its value as intelligence began to erode."[144] In his eyes, some of the blame for the Navy's disastrous surprise at Pearl Harbor in December of that year must be laid at the feet of Washington's decision to cut off Adm. Husband E. Kimmel, then-commander of the Pacific Fleet, from decrypts of Japanese diplomatic messages ("Purple").[145]

Such barriers began to erode in the face of wartime exigencies. In 1942 U.S. Navy COMINCH Admiral King issued a directive governing the control of COMINT that permitted sensitive information to be passed to commanders subordinate to the Atlantic and Pacific commanders in chief, though only in the form of operational directives. Meanwhile, King declared, "Every effort must be made to avoid indicating any correlation between the source of intelligence and the outcome of operations."[146] The rules were soon loosened further, so that radio intelligence products could be provided to commanders in pithily summarized "gist" form—"without making direct reference to the sources of the information"—as ostensible radio direction-finding "hits," or simply without attribution.[147] (For the most part, however, the Americans handled sanitization on an ad hoc basis.)[148] Despite continuing difficulties, however, the combination of sanitization, the use of "special crypto systems" for secure dissemination, and limited distribution enabled U.S. intelligence staffs to get information "directly to commanders who needed it and could act on it."[149]

This sort of tension between security and access—not simply by operators but by the broader intelligence analytical community involved in fusion efforts—would become characteristics of OPINTEL in the second half of the twentieth century. The challenge is to use sensitive intelligence information enough to ensure operational success, but not so much that it (a) is inadvertently (or deliberately) compromised by one's own forces or (b) is used so obviously or frequently that the enemy suspects one's recurring advantage is due to more than good fortune. Winton describes this latter problem by analogy: "When one player consistently knows which cards his opponent holds, how much and how often dare he go on winning before his opponent begins to suspect and changes the cards or the game?"[150]

As former DNI, NSA Director, and CIA Deputy Director William Studeman has put it, the metaphorical "stovepipes" of controlled access to highly sensitive intelligence sources have both "strong attributes and strong tyrannies simultaneously." Finding the right balance between restriction and distribution is a key challenge of operational intelligence professionals, who "must manage dissemination to [the] lowest classification levels; sanitization is an important and sophisticated process."[151]

During World War II, the Allies walked the tightrope between restriction and dissemination by combining the relative strengths of their two approaches to the sanitization issue: "The Americans' sometimes-reckless zeal to produce the most helpful product was tempered by well-founded British concern about protecting the source of the information. As [Capt.] Kenneth Knowles put it, 'Perhaps it is fair to say that the British were more clever in [ULTRA's] use, and we, more daring.' Combining these talents produced a vastly superior product than could have been achieved individually."[152] Managing the tension between security and access would remain a recurring theme of postwar operational intelligence.

The Importance of People

The years of World War II were for many naval intelligence professionals "exciting years, requiring great initiative from . . . intelligence officers," who found themselves expected to adapt to changing circumstances and organize a full-scale intelligence war effort with no clear plan of action from headquarters.[153] Wartime intelligence structures were not carefully planned ahead of time but were rather "created out of necessity."[154] As discussed earlier, the Navy did provide a well-attended OPINTEL training curriculum. Individual intelligence organizations such as JICPOA also provided in-house training in a variety of different subjects.[155] For the most part, however, wartime structures and practices evolved on an ad hoc basis, in response to the needs of operational commanders as they were understood at the time.

This evolutionary, vaguely Darwinian model of adaptation without an OPINTEL "master plan" would become a recurring theme of operational intelligence during the second half of the century. As one former DNI recalled, OPINTEL "evolved over the years because of our changing requirements and our changing sources of intelligence. It's not something you can plan. It evolves."[156] As the Pacific Fleet's assistant chief of staff for intelligence recounted at the end of the war, the young joint intelligence center "grew empirically and without prior plans, [so that] the only guidance was the need dictated by the progress of the war."[157]

To be sure, it was not that there were *no* models for how to organize a successful OPINTEL system: the admiralty's OIC provided the U.S. Navy with a working template, just as the practices of World War II would provide a conceptual and organizational model for postwar operational intelligence. But it is the nature of OPINTEL—grounded as it is in an ethos of highly tailored support for the operational commander—that no rigid master plan is ever possible. Since no campaign precisely mirrors the last, OPINTEL is destined always to be a creature in the middle of adapting to a changing environment.

The U.S. Pacific Fleet's assistant chief of staff for intelligence, Brig. Gen. Joseph Twitty, described this challenge in October 1945.

> The history of JICPOA is a history of continued changes. It has been a continuing struggle to adapt the organization to constant changes both in the needs of the operation forces and in the sources of intelligence available. . . . An efficient intelligence organization had to stay in step with the changes. Before the war ended, JICPOA was on the verge of a reorganization to adjust itself to the intelligence needs of operational forces invading Japan in coordination with intelligence produced by [the commander in chief of U.S. Air Forces in the Pacific].
>
> The beginning of another war, in another theater under different conditions, would probably find that an organization patterned after JICPOA, manned by similar personnel, would provide only the makings of an intelligence center that would require immediate adjustments before constructive work could be commenced.[158]

As with other operational intelligence centers, for JICPOA all that was foreseen—indeed, all that one *could* have foreseen—was that it would "grow . . . as a flexible mechanism adapted to changing needs with the progress of the war."[159]

Success in such endeavors places a premium upon attracting, motivating, and retaining high-quality personnel—the "human capital" with which flexible, innovative organizations purchase success in dynamic environments. As Brigadier General Twitty summarized in 1945, "The careful selection of personnel for ICPOA and JICPOA assured a high quality of intelligence product. The research done in the various sections was painstaking and as complete as necessary for operational purposes. There was so much of this work to be done that we organized against deadline production dates rather than for 'apple-polishing' perfection."[160] As this terse summary suggests, one key to OPINTEL's success appears to have been to select and retain quality intelligence professionals. The Navy required—and got—people of sufficient caliber to be able to handle the demands of providing enough information in time for it to be useful during a continual process of "on-the-job" training.

As the admiralty had done with its choice of Rodger Winn to head the OIC in London, for example, the U.S. Navy during World War II successfully identified and nurtured intelligence professionals who were able to accept these challenges and thrive. According to the Pacific Fleet's intelligence history,

> Starting with a small nucleus of officers groping their way in a relatively unknown field, this center grew with the war until it could supply all types of the most detailed information on every phase of Japanese military, Naval, industrial, agricultural, political, and social development. Men drawn from all walks of civilian life—lawyers, forest rangers, architects, newspapermen, geologists, engineers, scholars, and teachers—became qualified linguists and experts in the short space of two and three years. Working with professional military men, they supplied the information concerning the enemy forces to Pacific Ocean area commands.[161]

Such personnel successes would become the continuing challenge of postwar OPINTEL, and of naval intelligence today.

All in all, operational intelligence during World War II pioneered methods of globe-spanning information sharing and coordination and did so in remarkably successful ways. As is usually the case with historical scholarship, simply retelling such a tale may create the impression that the outcome was preordained, or that it seemed simple or straightforward to its participants. Nothing, one suspects, could be further from the truth. The very nature of "on-the-job" adaptation and innovation that characterized the evolution of OPINTEL during the war meant that participants could have very little, if any, idea where their journey was taking them. To them, the progress recounted herein must have seemed a decidedly contingent and unpredictable path. As the Pacific Fleet's intelligence history put it, in such ad hoc development, "there were mistakes, overlapping efforts, [and] blind alleys, that at times impaired efficiency."[162]

Nevertheless, viewed from our vantage point of more than half a century later, it is possible to judge their experiments a success. Perhaps more importantly, it is possible to discern patterns in their journey—or, in the words of Brigadier General Twitty, "certain principles that are believed to be immutable"[163]—that would emerge as enduring themes of operational intelligence to the present day.

2

The Postwar Years

Demobilization and Rebirth

Thinking about World War III

The Navy's sense of relaxation after the defeat of Germany and Japan in World War II did not last long. Eastern Europe fell seemingly irretrievably under Soviet control, Moscow acquired nuclear weapons, and a new era of global alliance rivalry began. This was not "hot" war, and for a time, at least, "the fact that we were identifying the Soviet Union as our [intelligence] target was a very, very sensitive subject."[1] The world soon settled into a tense "cold" war, however, in which always being more or less on the edge of global conflict became a way of life. Not surprisingly, the constant prospect of war had a profound influence upon Western military institutions, including the U.S. Navy. Indeed, "a third world war was the unifying strategic concept underlying much of late twentieth-century military planning, programming, procurement, and operations."[2] Just as global war had given birth to modern OPINTEL and given that art its distinctive shape, so the continued imminence of another such war—sure to be greater and more terrible even than the last—elicited its rebirth and evolutionary development.

Until the mid-1950s, Western military planners imagined that war with the Union of Soviet Socialist Republics (USSR) would take the form of what has been described as a "multiphase protracted conflict." It would begin with a massive Soviet attack in Central Europe reminiscent of the final phases of World War II, followed by a "small" atomic air offensive by the West, and then a bloody reinvasion of Europe. With the "nuclear revolution" of the 1950s until the first years of the 1960s, this conception changed to one in which massive nuclear exchanges would be followed by a series of smaller nuclear exchanges. This new scenario imagined there to be little role for traditional military mobilization, conventional combat having been replaced by a cataclysmic nuclear brawl in which the Americans ultimately expected to attack more than one thousand targets with over three thousand weapons—at the cost of perhaps 285 million immediate casualties.[3]

It was not entirely clear what role the U.S. Navy might play in such scenarios, except to provide a carrier-borne complement to Strategic Air Command bombers assigned to attack specified "targets of naval interest." In the late 1950s, however, the Navy's distinct sense of *at sea* missions began to return with the development of modern submarine fleets. As in so many arenas of modern military technology, in 1959 the United States led the way by fielding the first attack submarine capable of operating with—or, crucially, against—a modern battle fleet: the USS *Skipjack* (SSN-585). The submarine's hull was teardrop shaped and thus optimized for submerged speed, while its nuclear power plant permitted essentially infinite submerged range. Moreover, *Skipjack* took to sea within two years of the deployment of nuclear-armed cruise missiles in converted diesel-electric missile submarines. With a range of five hundred miles, these *Regulus* cruise missiles gave the submarine force the capability of immense power projection ashore.[4]

These twin innovations began to carve out a strategic role for the Navy in a world dominated by nuclear weapons. From the perspective of naval operational intelligence, however, these innovations were more significant for what they meant could be expected from the Soviet navy. Sure enough, a new competitive arena had opened up, and by 1957 the Soviets had developed the Zulu-class diesel submarine capable of carrying SS-1b SCUD-A short-range ballistic missiles. From 1961 onward, diesel-powered *Golf*-class and nuclear-powered *HOTEL I*–class Soviet ballistic missile submarines became operational. Their medium-range SS-N-4 SARK and SS-N-5 SERB medium-range ballistic missiles made it possible for the Soviet navy, if it could get close enough, to threaten the United States itself. By 1963 the USSR had deployed some thirty-two submarines carrying ninety-five ballistic missiles of various types.[5] The advent of nuclear power in the Soviet naval order of battle also allowed Russian submarines to operate more effectively against modern battle groups at sea—that is, to potentially threaten U.S. carrier battle groups.

For U.S. naval planners, these developments raised the specter of a new U-boat war of unprecedented ferocity: a struggle for control of the seas against nuclear-armed "wolf packs" capable of threatening merchantmen, surface combatants, and coastal U.S. population centers alike. The Navy's mission in the Cold War world—in which the principal adversary posed much more of a land and aerial threat than a naval one—had initially been unclear.[6] By the late 1950s, however, the Soviets were able to threaten the vital sea lines of communication (SLOCs) to America's European allies within the North Atlantic Treaty Organization (NATO).[7] These developments had profound implications for Navy OPINTEL, for against such a new U-boat threat, what could be more appropriate than a revival of the highly successful operational intelligence system of World War II?[8]

OPINTEL's Rebirth

Organizational Changes

In the immediate postwar years, however, this resurgent submarine threat was still in the future, and the Navy found itself a shadow of its wartime strength, with neither the need nor the opportunity to reconstitute the far-flung OPINTEL apparatus that had proven so successful in 1941–45. This is not to say that the Navy had forgotten OPINTEL, for it had not. After Japan's surrender and the subsequent dissolution of the COMINCH architecture, the Office of Naval Intelligence finally acquired the dominant role in Navy operational intelligence. The DNI had established an Operational Intelligence Branch (OP-16-O) in February 1945, and after the war's end this was redesignated as ONI's Operational Branch (OP-23Y).[9] The branch was given the mission of disseminating intelligence to the Operations Division of the CNO's staff (OPNAV) and to the commanders of operating forces. The former COMINCH Combat Intelligence Section was also pulled within ONI, becoming OP-23Y2, thus ending the turf battles between the Plans Division and ONI over the control of the OPINTEL function and placing it for the first time under Naval Intelligence.[10] By 1950 OP-23Y had been redesignated OP-322Y.[11]

Navy operational intelligence continued to maintain close links with the U.S. cryptographic community. Very early on, this took the form of placing cryptologists and naval intelligence analysts in the same workspaces, as "we created a group of people to sit with the analysts in the Naval Security Station on Nebraska Avenue" in Washington, D.C.[12] In 1946 ONI's Operational Intelligence Branch (OP-322Y) set up an entire cryptologically focused Special Intelligence Branch at Arlington Hall known as Y1, from its designation OP-322Y1. (Y2 was the Fleet Intelligence Unit at the new Pentagon building, while Y3 was ONI's Current Intelligence Section.)[13] With the establishment of the National Security Agency, the Navy's Y1 was relocated to the new NSA complex at Fort Meade, Maryland, and renamed the Navy Field Operational Intelligence Office (NFOIO) on August 26, 1957.[14]

As suggested by its convenient colocation with NSA, the mission of the new NFOIO revolved around signals intelligence (SIGINT). Specifically, NFOIO was tasked with exploiting "all sources of special intelligence for the purpose of producing operational intelligence for timely dissemination to commanders of operating forces."[15] While NFOIO could thus not be said to have engaged in true all-source fusion, it nonetheless provided valuable SIGINT inputs to more broadly focused OPINTEL efforts. It also kept the Navy closely tied to valuable national-level sources of information, a lesson the Navy had learned well in the era of MAGIC and ULTRA.[16]

As part of the same Navy reorganization in 1957, ONI's Current Intelligence Section (Y3) was redesignated OP-922B4 and assigned to maintain a twenty-four-hour watchfloor in the Pentagon to support the OPNAV duty officer and give daily briefings to the Chief of Naval Operations and other senior Navy leaders.[17] The direct ancestor of today's CNO Intelligence Plot (CNO-IP) in the Navy Command Center, OP-922B4 represented an important national-level OPINTEL node—one of the few locations at which all-source operational intelligence was still performed during the 1950s.[18] The other location was in Tokyo, Japan, where, in September 1950, the commander of U.S. naval forces in the Far East—worried about the possibility of outside Communist intervention in the Korean War—established a Far East Plot to monitor Communist Chinese and Soviet shipping from the Taiwan Straits to the coast of Siberia.[19]

"The People Factor"—Intelligence Professionals

It has long been understood that "large-scale military science is a matter of winning at keeping good people" in one's employ.[20] This has certainly always been the case for naval intelligence, which, in the words of one former DNI, "utterly depends upon the expertise, dedication, close working synergy and continued professional growth of all our people, civilian and military."[21] This was certainly not a lesson ignored by Navy operational intelligence during World War II, when the Navy excelled at attracting and retaining highly effective professionals capable of the innovation and flexibility required in wartime OPINTEL support.

After 1945, however, the large-scale wartime OPINTEL apparatus was largely dismantled, leaving in its place only a skeleton crew of national-level OPINTEL practitioners in OP-23Y and its alphabet soup of successor organizations. Significantly, however, to keep this functional OPINTEL core alive—and to provide a nucleus of experience around which all the functions of the postwar ONI could be rebuilt—the Navy turned in the early postwar years to veterans of the wartime OPINTEL system, especially Naval Reservists.[22]

To accomplish this, in March 1946 Navy Secy. James V. Forrestal authorized naval intelligence to begin training officers of the regular Navy and the Naval Reserve in navy intelligence.[23] In 1947 the Navy created a new category of restricted line officers with a new 163X designator (Special Duty Intelligence) "to provide career opportunities for World War II Naval Reserve intelligence personnel with significant expertise."[24] Though reservists thus led the way, the active-duty Navy was not long in catching up: a new category of generalist intelligence professionals, officers with the 1630 designator, was made available to unrestricted line officers in 1948.[25] Intelligence officers were thereafter divided into 1630s and 1350s, the latter being a specialist air intelligence officer, or "AI."

The 1630 and 1350 communities were very different. As one observer somewhat uncharitably explained, the "AI" was a "rag-tag," "brown-shod aviation ground-pounder" who served as "a supporting character in the Naval Aviation community." He did such things as taking pilot debriefs, managing threat training, and holding down "a variety of collateral duty assignments in the squadron to free the aircrew for other critical duties." The 1630, by contrast, was "a cerebral type who served as a sort of counselor to the line Commander, or as a Naval Attaché."[26] The two communities would remain sharply divided for some years.

Nor were the personnel changes of the 1950s limited to the officer corps. World War II had also shown the value of having specialized enlisted personnel assist with the arcane tasks of photo interpretation, photogrammetry, and cartography.[27] Peacetime funding constraints limited ONI's ability to recruit and train such persons in the immediate postwar years, but in 1958 the Navy established the specialist enlisted rating of photographic intelligenceman (PT). This was followed in 1959 by the creation of a Naval Enlisted Classification (NEC) code for yeomen who were qualified to provide support to offices handling sensitive intelligence material (intelligence clerk, or YN-2505).[28]

The numbers of such intelligence professionals remained small into the 1960s. In 1955, in fact, the Navy's entire 1630 population numbered only 50.[29] Even as late as 1959 the Navy had in its officer corps only 104 regular intelligence specialists—and these were mostly 1350s, who filled operational billets at sea with carrier air wings—supplemented by 125 reservists on active duty.[30] It would not be until 1963, with the selection of Rear Adm. Rufus Taylor to be the Director of Naval Intelligence, that a 1630-designated officer became DNI.[31] Nevertheless, these personnel changes make clear that the Navy had taken critical steps to create and maintain the core of professional expertise necessary to sustain naval intelligence during the Cold War.

Early Stirrings of a Technological Revolution

Automated Data Processing

Though these efforts would not bear much fruit until the 1960s, naval intelligence started down two roads that in the years ahead would make possible enormous strides in the development of modern operational intelligence. The first of these was the beginning of ONI's efforts to develop usable automated intelligence databases. In 1959 ONI began work on developing a general-purpose automated data storage and retrieval system.[32] Originally intended as a way to speed the analysis of voluminous data on global merchant ship activity, this effort had profound implications for information management as a whole. By streamlining some of the crucial tasks complicating the life of OPINTEL analysts, it enabled them to provide more "real-time" support to operational commanders. The conceptual descendant of the early IBM keypunch machines rented by Navy cryptologists in the 1930s, this database system, which would mature into the SEAWATCH system some years later, was a flexible and expandable scheme that marked OPINTEL's first small steps into the computer age.

SOSUS

The second technological development that began during the 1950s was the commencement of work on the Sound Surveillance System (SOSUS). This network of hydrophone (underwater microphone) arrays was designed to be deployed on the ocean floor to listen for nearby ships or submarines and feed their data via underwater cables back to shore-based processing and analysis centers. Harvard professor Ted Hunt initially proposed the idea of exploiting deep ocean sound channels for the detection of submarines with underwater hydrophones. Antisubmarine warfare had used passive hydrophones in an effort to detect submarines since World War I,[33] but passive acoustic detection did not come of age until the discovery by Maurice Ewing and J. Lamar Worzel that a "deep sound channel" existed in deepwater portions of the oceans that trapped and focused low-frequency sound, allowing it to propagate over long distances.[34] With project KAYO in 1949, the U.S. Navy began looking for ways to use passive acoustic arrays to detect the low-frequency sounds radiated by enemy submarines, and by 1950 the so-called Hartwell Report had discussed the possibility of using both submarine-mounted and fixed seabed surveillance arrays of passive acoustic sensors to detect snorkeling submarines at long range.[35] This idea became the foundation for an elaborate global hydrophone network.

Initial development of SOSUS began under the code name CAESAR, and the first hydrophone arrays were under test as early as 1948.[36] In 1952 a chartered British ship installed an initial forty-element hydrophone array off Eleuthera Island in the Bahamas for the U.S. Navy, and by 1954 the first processing center commissioned in Ramey, Puerto Rico.[37] By November 1955 six SOSUS stations had become operational, and the Navy had established a Sound Surveillance Evaluation Center to deal with the increasing volume of information they produced.[38] This growing surveillance system was not an intelligence asset per se, for it belonged to OP-95, the OPNAV mission sponsor for anti-submarine warfare, and was thus a technical adjunct to the operational Navy.[39] SOSUS was an enormous boon to naval intelligence, however, because the vessel-location data it provided could be, and were, a unique and valuable component of all-source fusion analysis. Indeed, early in its existence SOSUS was so highly classified that in some respects *only* intelligence professionals could make full use of it![40]

Precisely why SOSUS proved to be so vital to naval intelligence may be seen from an examination of the peculiar geographic constraints in which the Soviet navy found itself. If Soviet forces wished to sortie against NATO's SLOCs in the Atlantic, for example, their best route would be to travel around Norway's North Cape and travel southward down through the Greenland-Iceland–United Kingdom (GIUK) gap.[41] In the Pacific, vessels leaving the Soviets' ice-free ports were somewhat less restricted, but they would still have to deal with surveillance and opposition naval forces based in Japan and the Aleutian Island chain.[42] This placed a great handicap upon Soviet naval deployments, as their strategists realized: "For an exit to the ocean, our Navy was forced to cross enormous water expanses and force its way through choke points and straits either controlled by NATO navies or constantly under observation by their allies."[43] Though possessed of the longest coastline in the world, this tyranny of climate and geography meant that with regard to ice-free access to the open ocean, the Soviet Union was "actually all but landlocked."[44]

This was the genius of SOSUS—and the secret to the enormous impact it would eventually have upon Navy operational intelligence. If underwater listening devices could be placed in the key choke points (e.g., the GIUK gap) through which Soviet forces would have to pass in the event of war, the naval all-source OPINTEL picture could be revolutionized by the acquisition of this new and unique source of acoustic intelligence (ACINT). Moreover, in the emerging era of nuclear power, such ACINT might be the only way to locate enemy submarine commanders when they did not wish to be found. SOSUS became especially important because of its potential to "provide Navy commanders with timely and accurate information on all hostile or potentially hostile submarines, including missile-carrying ones, in large ocean areas."[45] SOSUS did not become a particularly extensive system until at least the 1960s, but it had huge potential. In that era of preparations for what would be, in effect, a new war against nuclear-powered and

-armed U-boats, SOSUS became the "most important submarine detection and tracking system."[46]

Allied Intelligence Coordination

One of the earliest lessons naval intelligence gained from World War II
was the importance of intelligence coordination with one's allies, as
exemplified by the superb cooperative effort mounted by British and
American OPINTEL watchfloors during the Battle of the Atlantic. This
lesson was not forgotten, and during the Cold War the United States
built up close intelligence relationships with its allies in the global
struggle against communism.

Perhaps the closest of these relationships, not surprisingly, was
with the United Kingdom; though now it was the United States, with
its truly global perspective and unmatched financial and military
resources, that played the role of senior partner. In 1948 Rear Adm.
Thomas Inglis, the American DNI, signed an agreement with his British
counterpart, Rear Adm. E. W. Longley-Cook, to establish an active
OPINTEL liaison relationship between the U.S. commander in chief in
the Eastern Atlantic and Mediterranean and the British Admiralty's
Naval Intelligence Division (NID). This special naval channel supplemented other avenues of intelligence sharing—for example, naval
attaché relationships or high-level intelligence sharing between the
Defense Department and Britain's Ministry of Defense (MoD)—and was
devoted specifically to operational intelligence issues.[47] A broader
Anglo-American intelligence sharing agreement was later reached in
1951.[48]

Operational Experience for the Intelligencers

As discussed in chapter 1, the embarkation of Radio Intelligence Units
aboard USS *Enterprise* had marked the advent of "afloat OPINTEL."
Such approaches remained largely embryonic, however, until some
years into the Cold War, and intelligence officers had little opportunity
to gain firsthand experience of naval operations. Referring to the newly
created 1630 intelligence officer designation, for example, DNI Rufus
Taylor is reported to have declared that "we don't send junior 1630s to
sea."[49] The other intelligence officer category, Air Intelligence Officers
(1350s), *did* go to sea. They remained heavily focused upon intelli-

gence issues relating to carrier strike operations and played little, if any, OPINTEL role for the fleet. Given the importance of operational "Blue force" understanding to the provision of good operational intelligence—a subject also addressed previously—this was unfortunate.

The situation began to change in the early 1960s, however, when junior 1630s *did* begin to go to sea—beginning with then-Lt. William Manthorpe.[50] This development was a watershed. One of the postwar strengths of the U.S. Navy was its heavy emphasis upon forward-deployed operations and "the profound importance of *operational experience.* A strong operational orientation during the Second World War and into the 1950s led the U.S. Navy to emphasize deploying its forces at sea, and developing strategic plans based on current capabilities and actual operational experience."[51]

When, in the late 1950s and early 1960s, the Navy's intelligence professionals began to deploy at sea as well, they obtained the chance to partake in this experience—and thus to significantly enrich the quality of the OPINTEL support they could provide to operational commanders. The full benefits that were ultimately obtained from this dynamic still lay some years in the future, but here as well, the Navy was laying the groundwork for future OPINTEL successes. Many of the 1630s who began to go to sea would in the future provide the core of the Navy's senior OPINTEL leadership. At the same time, many of the operational counterparts with whom they began to develop long-term relationships of trust and mutual understanding would go on to become the senior leadership of the naval service itself.

3

The 1960s

Laying the Foundation for OSIS

Soviet Naval Threats and "Flexible Response"

After a decade during which U.S. military planners expected that war with the Soviet Union would simply be a series of massive nuclear exchanges, NATO began attempting to develop and maintain a capacity for "flexible response" to all possible levels of Soviet provocation. As one scholar of the period has noted, this was a tacit admission of nuclear stalemate.[1] Almost by definition, a flexible response entailed a more significant mission for the U.S. Navy, since it might be called upon to engage the Soviet fleet in all manner of shifting, escalatory scenarios. During this period, however, NATO still envisioned the Navy's basic role as a defensive one. Its job was to create barrier forces in the North Atlantic to prevent Soviet combatants (principally submarines) from reaching and disrupting the sea lines of communication linking America and Western Europe. These lines were more important than ever, now that war planners expected to have to fight "flexibly" for an indefinite duration on the Central Front. Allied naval forces were therefore expected to absorb an "initial [Warsaw] Pact attack" at sea, contain it, and then reassert control over key ocean areas such as the Mediterranean.[2]

Continuing a trend that had begun with the first emergence of a growing Soviet submarine threat in the late 1950s, this new strategic thinking helped make naval operational intelligence more important than ever. Just as U.S. submarine developments—specifically, the deployment of the Polaris submarine-launched ballistic missile (SLBM) in 1960—began to give American naval forces a greatly increased strategic nuclear role, Moscow's submarine fleet was rapidly becoming a potent threat to the United States and to U.S. naval forces.[3]

Throughout the 1960s and into the 1970s, the Soviet navy emphasized the deployment of submarines armed with nuclear missiles of various capability, and promoted the large-scale development of Soviet naval aviation (SNA) assets capable of threatening U.S. carrier battle groups in the North Atlantic.[4] As one Russian naval historian put it, the Soviet fleet came to place particular emphasis upon "destroying [U.S.] carriers before they approached the deck-based aviation launch points" in order to prevent nuclear air strikes against the Soviet homeland. The Soviet fleet also emphasized "combating [U.S. and other NATO ballistic missile] submarines before they launched ballistic missiles."[5] Although it was exceedingly difficult to threaten Western ballistic-missile submarines (SSBNs), the prized carriers seemed increasingly vulnerable. The 1960s saw the deployment of numerous *Echo I*– and *Juliet*-class submarines armed with variants of the SS-N-3 *Shaddock* cruise missile designed for antisurface warfare (ASW)—that is, missiles designed to be carrier killers. An even more advanced missile, the SS-N-7 *Siren,* took to sea in the *Charlie I*–class submarine in 1967.[6]

From an OPINTEL perspective, these developments meant that tracking the new "Red" U-boats had never been more important. The difficulty of finding submerged submarines at sea, moreover, meant that if the U.S. Navy was to accomplish its mission, it would have to develop more sophisticated means of all-source intelligence fusion than ever before. As one veteran of the Navy's OPINTEL system put it, "Submarines are hard to find. They are impossible to find if the analytical approach is confined to a single discipline."[7] When Moscow's submarine fleet began to engage in out-of-area (OOA) operations, the Navy had little choice but to reconstitute a robust and responsive OPINTEL system in response.[8] The growth of Soviet naval aviation, armed increasingly with long-range cruise missiles, themselves designed to threaten U.S. carrier battle groups, also added to OPINTEL's importance.[9] In these urgent needs lay the seeds of the worldwide Ocean Surveillance Information System (OSIS) that the U.S. Navy gradually constructed and made operational by the early 1970s. "With the growth of the Soviet Navy," one participant recalls, inevitably came OSIS: "*We had to have it!*"[10]

Soviet Naval Developments: The OPINTEL Threat

Year	Soviet Advances
1959	First deployment of nuclear-powered attack submarine (SSN), *November*-class
1960	First deployment of *Echo I*–class nuclear-powered cruise missile submarine (SSGN), carrying SS-N-3 missiles and designed to target U.S. aircraft carriers
1962	First deployment of *Echo II* SSGN
1964	Soviets begin maintaining continuous presence in Mediterranean
1967	First deployment of a nuclear-powered ballistic-missile submarine (SSBN), *Yankee*-class, armed with SS-N-6 missiles with ranges of 1,300 nautical miles
1968	First *Yankee* SSBN patrol in the Atlantic
1969	First deployment of *Charlie*-class SSGN
late 1960s	Soviets begin operations in Indian Ocean, Caribbean, and off Africa's western coast
1971	First *Yankee* SSBN patrol off the U.S. Pacific Coast
1972	First deployment of *Delta I*–class SSBN, larger than the U.S. Navy's own *Lafayette*-class SSBNs, and armed with SS-N-8 missiles. The *Delta* was the first SSBN able to threaten the continental United States without leaving Soviet-controlled waters.
	First development of a titanium-hulled submarine, the *Alpha* SSN, with phenomenal deep-diving capabilities
	First deployment of *Kiev*-class vertical/short take-off and landing (VSTOL) aircraft carrier
1980–85	First deployments of *Typhoon*-class SSBN, *Oscar*-class SSGNs, *Mike*-class SSN, *Sierra*-class SSN, *Kilo*-class SS, *Akula*-class SSN, and *Delta IV*–class SSBN
1985	First deployment of the nuclear-powered *Kirov*-class heavy cruiser

Navy OPINTEL Matures

The Proliferation of "INTs"

The 1960s saw the proliferation of specialized intelligence inputs to the all-source fusion process from communities devoted to the production of increasingly specialized "INTs" such as COMINT (communications intelligence, a subcategory of SIGINT, or signals intelligence) and PHOTINT (photographic intelligence, later known as IMINT, or imagery intelligence). While human intelligence (HUMINT)—the traditional reporting of "agents," "assets," and other human sources[11]—played only a minor role in naval intelligence during this period,[12] the Navy soon came to exploit a wide variety of other types of information. Indeed, by the mid-1960s, a veritable revolution was under way in the number and variety of specialized "INTs" available for all-source OPINTEL fusion.

As noted in chapter 2, the Navy was already receiving invaluable information via the Navy Field Operational Intelligence Office (NFOIO) at Fort Meade from the national-level SIGINT community headed by the new National Security Agency (NSA). Beginning in 1965, however, joint NSA and Navy operations began in which specialized intelligence ships—the *Belmont* (AGTR-4), *Georgetown* (AG-165), *Jamestown* (AG-166), *Oxford* (AG-159), *Private Jose Valdez* (TAG-169), and ill-fated *Liberty* (AGTR-5)—collected SIGINT to satisfy national requirements and collect data for electromagnetic propagation studies. These efforts soon expanded to include the conversion of small cargo ships for this purpose (among them the equally ill-fated *Pueblo* [AGER-2], which was seized by the North Korean navy in January 1968).[13]

The Sound Surveillance System of underwater listening devices—optimized for the tracking of Soviet submarines—has also been discussed previously. From small beginnings in the 1950s, however, the SOSUS network grew throughout the 1960s into a sprawling undersea intelligence network all of its own, feeding increasingly valuable information to the Navy's antisubmarine warfare and intelligence communities. ONI's first dedicated analytical facility for processing acoustic intelligence became operational in June 1962 as part of the Naval Scientific and Technical Intelligence Center (NAVSTIC).

An increasingly specialized PHOTINT community, moreover, was also springing up within the Navy to help meet the needs of intelligence analysts and operational commanders. The Naval Photographic Interpretation Center (NPIC) began to carve out an important OPINTEL role for itself during the Cuban Missile Crisis of 1963.[14] NPIC rapidly analyzed photographs of Soviet and Cuban activity on the island as the world teetered on the brink of conflict over Soviet Premier Nikita Khrushchev's decision to deploy intermediate-range ballistic missiles there. Assigned the mission in 1961 of preparing "strategic and operational reports and studies based upon analyses of sensor images derived from subsurface,

surface, air, and space reconnaissance systems,"[15] NPIC received plaudits for its "immediate analysis and timely distribution of intelligence photography" during the Cuban crisis.[16]

From a time-sensitive OPINTEL perspective, useful photographic intelligence was still limited, at this point, to imagery taken from reconnaissance or other aircraft. As NPIC's 1961 mission statement indicates, however, the era of "overhead" (i.e., satellite) reconnaissance was just beginning—the Central Intelligence Agency's first CORONA photo reconnaissance satellite having been launched in August 1960—and the timeliness of such products would in time improve dramatically. Moreover, by the late 1960s naval aircraft were being equipped with new and more flexible aerial sensors, supplementing traditional aerial photography with side-looking radar imagery and pictures from infrared imaging equipment such as that first fitted onto RA-5C Vigilante aircraft in February 1968.

Another aspect of the revolution in satellite reconnaissance was the advent of signals intelligence collection from space. In June 1960 the Naval Research Laboratory (NRL) launched the first so-called Galactic Radiation and Background (GRAB) satellite. Ostensibly a research probe, as its name indicated, GRAB was really America's first spy satellite—an orbital receiver for electronic intelligence (ELINT) such as the emissions given off by the operation of Soviet radar sets.[17] Initially, radar ELINT focused upon land-based Soviet radar sets, whose location was vital to know in planning for nuclear war operations. In the years ahead, however, "overhead" ELINT would become a vital part of Navy OPINTEL.

All in all, the volume of information "inputs" to the emerging Ocean Surveillance Information System was growing exponentially. In 1967 the Navy's all-source fusion OPINTEL effort began receiving regular inputs from a SOSUS-derived "submarine contact file," as well as weather information from the Fleet Weather Central circuit, and merchant ship location data from the Movement Report Control Center.[18] The sophisticated operational concept of the admiralty's OIC had now been fully revived and was being played out with the benefit of everything that modern technology could offer.

The Ocean Surveillance Concept

Together, such new specialized "INT" communities—all providing information that could be incorporated through all-source analysis into "fused" OPINTEL products—helped make it possible for naval intelligence to begin building a true worldwide ocean surveillance *system*. By the late 1960s the overarching concept of "ocean surveillance information" had become a clear focus of U.S. intelligence planning. This concept was defined as "information that is derived from the systematic observation of sea areas by all available and practicable means primarily for the purpose of locating, identifying, and determining the movements of ships, submarines, and other vehicles, friendly and enemy, proceeding on, under, or above the surface of the world's seas and oceans."[19] Simply put, "ocean surveillance information" was OPINTEL painted on a global canvas and incorporating a wider variety of sensors and analytical inputs than ever before imaginable.

The parallel developments of new dynamics in U.S. war planning, the Soviet threat, and the development of specialized national-level intelligence subcommunities set the stage for the efforts of naval intelligence in the 1970s to bring all of the intelligence pieces together into a smoothly functioning, integrated whole. A staff study approved by the Director of Naval Intelligence in 1964 endorsed the development of a comprehensive information processing system for ocean surveillance information. This study had far-reaching implications, for according to Capt. Wyman Packard—the dean of ONI historians—it would become the conceptual core of OSIS.[20]

That such a project was conceivable, let alone possible, is testimony to the strength of the OPINTEL concept pioneered in London and developed to such a high art—within the parameters of existing technology—by the British and Americans during World War II. Ultimately, "operational intelligence" was as much a process or approach as a specific type of information provided to operational commanders. The OPINTEL approach, "proven to be the most successful method of examining a hostile submarine force," could "easily be applied to any aspect of military analysis."[21] As "a process, an ethic, a set of organizations, technologies and complex architectures," the OPINTEL concept had the potential to be "universally applicable to the intelligence enterprise."[22] In Navy practice, it would prove to be enormously resilient and adaptable, both in the establishment of an "ocean surveillance information" system and thereafter.

OPINTEL and Automation

All of this information, however, had somehow to be processed if meaningful operational intelligence was to be extracted from the flood of data now available. Accordingly, the process of applying state-of-the art data processing equipment to the production of operational intelligence was accelerated dramatically in the 1960s. In 1964 the NPIC was renamed the Naval Reconnaissance and Technical Support Center, and transferred from the director of the Navy Field Support Activity (formerly the Commander, Fleet Activities Command) directly to the supervision of the Director of Naval Intelligence. A new Data Processing Department was established within the new center, devoted to "support [for] the Navy's rapidly expanding Integrated Operational Intelligence System."[23] Thereafter, one of the center's principal tasks was to "provide miniaturized and automated intelligence data bases and intelligence production support to the operating forces of the Navy."[24]

A new operational requirement was promulgated within the Office of Naval Intelligence in 1964. The requirement was driven by the increasingly urgent need for "an afloat capability to collect various items of tactical information and to process, analyze, and correlate the information for near real-time use by the operating forces." The resulting development was the Naval Intelligence Processing System (NIPS), designed to provide automated intelligence database systems for ordinary ships of the line, which would then be connected through communications links to more centrally located Fleet Intelligence Centers (FICs).[25] The concept grew out of the success of the Integrated Operational Intelligence System (IOIS), already field-deployed in the *Saratoga* (CV-60) during 1962. The IOIS processed multisensor (e.g., infrared imaging) information from RA-5C Vigilante reconnaissance aircraft to produce an intelligence product aboard the aircraft carrier.[26]

The NIPS concept improved the carriers' afloat processing capabilities and was also expected to facilitate distribution of "digital and photo miniaturized intelligence to shipboard tactical [intelligence systems] . . . and to Fleet Intelligence Centers for in-house and fleet command support."[27] NIPS was even expected to make "afloat OPINTEL" feasible on smaller ships as well, a process that began in 1968.[28] These efforts to "devolve" operational intelligence production were an important part of the sophisticated OSIS system taking shape as data flow increased.

To improve the capabilities of shore-based OPINTEL facilities, a high-speed data link was established in 1966 between the ONI automated data processing center at Arlington Hall and the CNO's Intelligence Plot (CNO-IP) at the Pentagon. The ADP center had itself been created in 1964, in part to improve computer-driven intelligence processing following the procurement of new IBM mainframes for the Fleet Intelligence Centers at Norfolk and Pearl Harbor.[29] In 1968 a similar high-speed link was created between Arlington Hall and the NFOIO at Fort Meade, to assist in the transmittal of SIGINT from national-level sources managed by the NSA.[30] In 1969 further high-speed circuits were set up between NFOIO, the Pacific Fleet, and the commander of U.S. Naval Forces in Europe (CINCUSNAVEUR). Whereas OPINTEL analysts had previously done their work with graph paper, acetate overlays, and colored pencils, their art now became increasingly automated.[31]

Despite efforts to improve afloat information processing, the growth of this emerging Navy OPINTEL information-sharing network was driven in part by the *limitations* of shipboard intelligence staffing. As one former DNI recalls, the exploding information burdens of intelligence analysis during the 1960s—driven by the emergence of automated processing at shore-based centers—helped create powerful incentives to develop efficient near-real-time information exchange with ships at sea.

> One of the reasons we became so proficient at OPINTEL as early as we did—and other [U.S. military] services did not—was because of the physical nature of our flagships. . . . The fact is, most of our numbered flagships back in the 1960s could accommodate an Intel staff of about five people. As new sources of information became available—overhead [imagery], SIGINT, acoustic information, or whatever—it quickly became apparent that five people on board ship with limited communications ability cannot keep up with the picture. So we had to devise a system that can take all of this data, put it together, boil it down to critical information required by the Fleet, and then send that out in a single thread to this heavy cruiser.[32]

Under pressure to make things work despite these limitations, the Navy led the way in developing a robust, worldwide information-sharing network built around distributed data processing at national and regional intelligence "nodes," and fleet-specific broadcasts of condensed intelligence information for additional shipboard tailoring. Beginning to harness the power of an emerging computer age, therefore, naval intelligence was well on the way toward building a "bold new system, based upon unprecedented connectivity" between analytical nodes.[33]

Intelligence Personnel: Thriving upon Change

Like many "revolutionary" changes in the history of warfare, OSIS became possible not through the sudden discovery of some new technology or process but through the gradual refinement and improved application of existing techniques. This was accomplished by an innovative and flexible organization that recognized the need for change even if not always being sure of its ultimate destination.[34] As it had during World War II, therefore, a sophisticated Navy operational intelligence system developed ad hoc, without a "master plan."[35] When combined with an acute sense of the need for operational intelligence in the face of a growing Soviet threat and an appreciation of the potentialities of emerging collection, processing, and dissemination technologies, merely possessing the concept of OPINTEL developed by the admiralty OIC in the late 1930s was enough.

In such a technologically volatile time, with the equipment and analytical techniques of OPINTEL changing at such a dizzying pace, it was more important than ever that naval intelligence attract and retain personnel capable of the innovation and flexibility that this environment demanded.[36] The people who made OSIS possible, therefore, were the Navy's new cadres of intelligence professionals—high-quality officers and enlisted men whom it trusted to make decisions and to whom was given the responsibility of meeting the fleet's needs in this new era. As one OPINTEL veteran put it, Navy OPINTEL had a "TQL" (total quality leadership) philosophy long before that management technique was in vogue.[37]

The Operational Focus and "Know Thy Customer"

An important step in creating an officer corps capable of such feats occurred with the consolidation of intelligence officer designations. Intelligence officers, who were previously divided into 1350 (air intelligence officer) and 1630 (intelligence generalist) designations, were merged in 1968 to create a new, unified career path of 1630s.[38] At the time of union there was some danger that the 1350s would swamp the far less numerous 1630 officers: according to Adm. William O. Studeman, there were at that point "nearly 700 AIs and only 200 1630s, so the 1350 community dominated."[39] Despite such fears, however, the merger went well, enabling the new aggregate community to combine the operational focus of the 1350s with the analytical focus of the 1630s. This merger was of great importance to Navy operational intelligence, for it permitted *all* intelligence officers to do tours of sea duty in strike warfare billets with aircraft carriers and amphibious groups—on the "front line," as it were, with the Navy's operational commanders.[40]

Unique Operating Environment

This importance of having intelligence professionals at sea with the fleet is hard to overstate. As we have seen, good operational intelligence production benefits enormously from an understanding not just of "Red" forces but of "Blue"—that is, of one's own operational needs, perspective, and culture. This provides the key to understanding the peculiar strength of operational intelligence in the U.S. Navy in the middle and late years of the Cold War. The nature of activity in the naval environment—three-dimensional, of relative uniformity, and lacking all but the most rudimentary "frontiers"—provided a radically different experience from that of other U.S. services. This afforded a unique perspective that gave the Navy some advantages in developing a sophisticated modern OPINTEL system.[41]

Army and Air Force units during the Cold War expected to operate "against" the adversary's actual forces only in the event of war and for the most part had no operational contact with their likely opponent. Based in garrisons, they generally maneuvered against "opponents" infrequently, and only in simulated form: in exercises other U.S. or NATO units played out scenarios where they acted as "Red" forces. By contrast—a point repeatedly and emphatically made by senior active-duty and retired Navy officers during the preparation of this study[42]—the Navy continually operated "inside and among our opponent['s forces],"[43] maneuvering against real Soviet units on a daily basis in an everyday life of "war without the shooting" on, above, and below the sea's surface.[44] In other words, far from merely eyeing each other across a frontier or demilitarized zone, the Soviet and U.S. navies flew and sailed around and under—and occasionally into—each other as a matter of course.[45] During the Cold War, "the ships and maritime aircraft of East and West tracked each other unceasingly, using and producing above-water and underwater operational observations in the process."[46] As one former DNI recounted, "This gave us a wonderful opportunity to learn and develop and become experts in operational intelligence."[47]

Operator/Intelligence Integration

In addition to the opportunities for OPINTEL development provided by its operational environment, the Navy enjoyed some organizational advantages over the other services. In no other service, after all, did the warfighter and his intelligence staff literally *inhabit* their weapons platform.[48] The Army and Air Force during the Cold War tended to organize their intelligence structures into separate battalions, brigades, squadrons, or wings—generally existing and operating somewhat separately from operational commanders. By contrast, naval intelligence officers and staffs tended to be much more closely "integrated into operational units."[49]

Especially after naval intelligence officers began routinely serving at sea, this unique learning environment gave them a peculiar advantage in the OPINTEL art. "We are *in* the wing, squadron, or assigned to the ship. And when we are [junior officers], we are part of ship's company, we are part of the squadron. We bunk and live with and interoperate with our operational brothers—and that's a huge advantage."[50] As one former DNI has written, the Navy became good at OPINTEL "because its operators and intelligence professionals share the same floating environment and operate in it, side by side, day in and day out."[51] By virtue of their job of studying "evidences of the enemy in action," intelligence officers have always had "a certain 'front-line' mentality" that separates them from other public servants.[52] In the Navy, however, the uniqueness of this perspective—and the OPINTEL strengths that flowed from it—were taken to unprecedented heights. "What really defined OPINTEL," one veteran of this period remembers, "was being out at sea. This gave the Navy a strength that no other service had."[53]

In addition to providing an unequaled education in both Soviet activity and the needs of U.S. operational commanders,[54] this operational experience also better equipped naval intelligence professionals to persuasively deliver useful intelligence to the warfighter. As noted in chapter 1, the embarkation of the first Radio Intelligence Units

aboard carriers in World War II placed intelligence officers in the position of tutoring senior naval commanders on the nature and extent of
enemy operations. Such awkwardness was, to some degree, inherent in
the nature of "afloat OPINTEL." After 1630s went to sea in the U.S.
Navy in the 1960s, however, intelligence officers were better equipped
to hold their own, because their commanders knew that they were
receiving information from someone who really understood their operational world.[55] Serving aboard ship with the operators, noted Vice
Adm. Thomas Wilson, "You learn their culture; they learn *your* culture. You're friends together in a living situation as well as a working
situation. It's hard to replace that interaction, hard to duplicate in any
other way. . . . It's almost [that] you are [yourself] an operator first and
foremost."[56] After all, as one OPINTEL veteran put it, operators and
intelligence professionals afloat simply "can't avoid each other—a
ship's a small little world."[57]

Operator/Intelligence Relationships

The "immersion" in operational culture created by this system of "integrated proximity" would prove to be a great advantage for Navy OPIN-
TEL.[58] As former DNI Sumner ("Shap") Shapiro recalls, these twin
factors of serving aboard ships constantly deployed "eyeball-to-
eyeball" with the Soviets "gave us a wonderful opportunity to work
cheek-and-jowl [with operators], to live with them, to get them to
depend upon us Intelligence officers to provide them with the information they needed to do their job. So we have evolved as a result, and
established remarkable working relationships with the operators."[59] The
strength of these relationships with the operational community,
according to former Director of the (Intelligence) Community Management Staff and Deputy DNI Richard Haver, were "one of the differences, frankly, between Naval Intelligence officers and, frankly,
intelligence officers raised elsewhere."[60]

　　This had profound implications for the efficacy of the "service
industry" of intelligence production—especially in a time-urgent operational intelligence context.[61] Michael Herman has suggested a market
metaphor for the intelligence cycle, seeing it less as a rigid process of
responsiveness to formal user requirements than a semi-entrepreneurial
one. Operational consumers of intelligence are the intelligence officer's
"clients," and it is his job not only to provide a better service but also to

study the "market" carefully and to "sell" his clients what they need *in a form that they will "buy" and continue to desire in the future.*[62] Crucially, therefore, just as a client would be reluctant to purchase surgical services from an unknown or inexperienced doctor, so an operational commander will be reluctant to listen to an intelligence officer he does not trust. Naval historian Jon Sumida offers the story of a June 1937 exercise by HMS *Hood,* in which the British battleship's fire control team hit nothing because they ignored accurate aerial target-spotting reports given them by an air-spotting officer whom they neither knew nor fully trusted.[63] Such a result during operations against the Soviet navy, of course, would have been catastrophic.

To be both useful and used, therefore, intelligence must be relevant to the needs of the operator at the moment of delivery, conveyed in a form intelligible to that operator, and communicated by someone who enjoys the operator's trust and respect. Even the most "accurate and elegant intelligence possible" would have been "quite useless had it not also been able to be related to naval operations, both current and projected." Its successful provision, therefore, requires "regular and frequent communication between operations and intelligence staffs together with at least a modicum of mutual respect—in short, a meeting of minds."[64] Provided that the relationship between intelligence professional and operational commander does not become *too* close— thus imperiling "that independence of thought which is an essential prerequisite to objective assessment" so that "intelligence starts to see what operations would like it to see, not what they ought to see"[65]— such a "meeting of minds" between operations and intelligence is essential to good OPINTEL.

Ultimately, the value of even the best intelligence depends upon its consumers: "It is only useful if they take it seriously. Close relationships play a major part in determining intelligence's credibility and educating [consumers] on how to use it properly."[66] Information that is not believed is worthless, making operator trust a priceless commodity for the good intelligence officer.[67] This insight—well understood by naval intelligence professionals, who have long conceived of their work as providing an "on-demand *service* to consumers, vice *products*"[68]—underlines the important bonds of mutual understanding and trust built at sea in the late 1960s between Navy intelligence officers and their operational commanders.[69]

"Know Thy Collector" Too

The good analyst needs to be close not only to his customers—the operational commanders he supplies with OPINTEL services—but also to the collectors who provide the all-source fusion process with its various inputs.[70] "The all-source analyst must be close to his collectors, both to steer their collection and single-source analysis and to discuss interpretations with them. Part of his job is to know the pitfalls of the various sources, and when their collectors are carried away by professional enthusiasm for them."[71]

This had been clear to the analysts of the admiralty's wartime OIC—who developed a productive relationship with code breakers at Bletchley Park[72]—and it proved true for the postwar U.S. Navy as well. In part, this was why the close working relationship developed between Navy OPINTEL and the national-level SIGINT community at NSA was so useful. A generation after MAGIC and ULTRA, naval intelligence still relied heavily upon COMINT. This relationship with cryptology was so valuable to Navy OPINTEL that positions at NFOIO were considered a choice assignment for "hot-running" young intelligence officers, and an NFOIO "old boy network" ensured that the cream of ONI's crop was sent there on a regular basis.[73]

The importance of this relationship may be seen in the complicated nature of the intelligence tasking process in the Navy during this period. Line officers did not directly task intelligence collection. Rather, OPINTEL personnel translated operator information needs into various formal standing and ad hoc requirements—and then had to persuade operational commanders to endorse their requests.[74] This system placed a great premium upon operator/intelligence mutual understanding and trust, and upon the OPINTEL professional's keen understanding of the potential and limitations of collection.

OPINTEL's relationship with national-level SIGINT became more important still after 1965, the year that the Navy first became involved in operations on a large scale in Indochina during the Vietnam conflict.[75] The operational intelligence needs of Vietnam helped drive NSA and the national SIGINT community into "tactical" support for the first time. Efforts were made at all levels to provide U.S. forces in Vietnam with information about the location and disposition of infiltrating Viet Cong guerrillas, Soviet arms supplies, North Vietnamese military units, surface-to-air missile (SAM) site locations and status, and other vital targets.[76] The war thus helped force SIGINT, in one participant's words, out from behind the "Green Door" of the ship's cryptologic spaces by creating incentives to push such information quickly to U.S. forces for operational use.[77]

The exigencies of wartime operational support also encouraged NSA and other U.S. SIGINT staffs to improve their own variety of all-source fusion, by forcing them to use "bits and pieces [of information] in [an] operational environment—not [just] code-breaking."[78] Their successes in these endeavors showed the value of SIGINT in tactical operations, and laid the groundwork for the great strides of the 1970s in integrating a wider variety of SIGINT inputs into the OPINTEL picture.

4

OSIS Comes of Age

FOSIFs, FOSICs, and Fusion in the Electronic Age

Increasing Soviet Threats

With regard to the threat perceived by the U.S. Navy from the Soviet navy, the early 1970s continued the trend of increasing alarm that had been building strength in the late 1960s. For the most part, the U.S. Navy continued to envision a defensive role for itself in the event of conflict with the USSR, "focused on countering the Soviet submarine threat to allied Sea Lines of Communications (SLOCs), and on the newly formed Soviet Naval Aviation (SNA)."[1] The Soviets, however, not only continued developing their submarine and naval aviation capabilities, but under the leadership of Adm. Sergei Gorshkov also began to develop an increasingly powerful conventional surface fleet capable of projecting power outside of Soviet home waters. This effort to create a more "balanced fleet" caused even more alarm in the Navy Department:[2] "The specter of a powerful Soviet Navy leaving home waters, overwhelming U.S. and Allied defensive chokepoints and barriers, and proceeding into the open oceans to disrupt the SLOCs grew to near-crisis proportions from the late-1960s through the mid-1970s."[3] By 1974, moreover, the Soviet navy had acquired its first submarine-launched ballistic missile with a truly intercontinental range (the SS-N-8), thus making it possible for Soviet submarines to threaten U.S. population centers without having to transit such choke points and antisubmarine warfare barriers.[4] All in all, the prospect of having to fight a campaign against such forces made it more important than ever that Navy OPINTEL develop into a fine art.

OPINTEL Returns to the Fleet

From the end of World War II until the late 1960s, Navy OPINTEL had largely been a national-level enterprise, performed principally by watchfloors in the Pentagon and specialized analysts in offices such as NFOIO. By the end of the 1960s, however, automated data processing (ADP) systems made possible a meaningful OPINTEL capability aboard individual naval vessels themselves—or at least initially aboard aircraft carriers and fleet command ships. The various Fleet Intelligence Centers also acquired state-of-the-art computer processing capabilities. This process of devolution continued rapidly in the early 1970s with the formal establishment of a worldwide Ocean Surveillance Information System combining national-level analytical nodes with fleet-focused regional OPINTEL fusion centers and ever-expanding "afloat OPINTEL" capabilities. By the early 1970s, therefore, OPINTEL had truly returned to the fleet.[5]

Success usually has many fathers, and OSIS is most safely described as a concept arrived at by many different people at about the same time through a process of convergent evolution driven by fleet operators' urgent need for such a capability.[6] Of the various specific genealogies claimed for OSIS, however, two stand out. As noted in chapter 3, a staff study approved by the Director of Naval Intelligence in 1964 endorsed the development of a comprehensive information processing system for ocean surveillance information. According to Capt. Wyman Packard, these conclusions led directly to the creation of OSIS.[7] Vice Adm. David Richardson dates the origin of OSIS differently, tracing it to a luncheon in Washington, D.C., in August 1968 at which he asked for the establishment of a Mediterranean Surveillance Net. As commander of the U.S. Sixth Fleet in the Mediterranean (COMSIXTHFLT), he wanted more support for his operations in the face of increasing Soviet activity there.[8] Whatever its specific parentage, however, OSIS emerged in the early 1970s as the highest expression of the Navy's OPINTEL art.

FOSIF Rota

Tailored Fleet-Support OPINTEL

In 1970 the Fleet Ocean Surveillance Information Facility (FOSIF) at Rota, Spain, began operations as a specialist OPINTEL cell devoted to supporting Sixth Fleet operations in the Mediterranean. Particularly concerned by the Soviets' growing presence in the Mediterranean—as shown dramatically by large-scale Soviet exercises such as "OKEAN-70" in the spring of 1970—FOSIF Rota evaluated Soviet operations "in context of SIXTHFLT operations" and "littoral political and military activity." The locations and activity of Soviet units, Sixth Fleet and allied naval forces, and merchant marine activity were put together as all-source, "fused" operational intelligence for use by the fleet in day-to-day activity.[9] Crucially, Rota's immediate loyalty was to COM-SIXTHFLT, not ONI or any other institution in Washington, allowing it to focus intensely upon meeting the fleet's needs.[10] Rota thus became "the prototype of a global system to provide direct support to operating forces" on a regional basis.[11]

The Rota facility focused upon systematized collection, processing, and dissemination with an eye to indications and warnings (I&W) intelligence; exploitation of Soviet command, control, and communications (C^3) activity; more efficient surveillance; and the appropriate sanitization of the resulting product for fleet operators. Rota provided a daily report at 0500 Greenwich Mean Time—or 0500 "Zulu" hours in military parlance—that was designed to reach Sixth Fleet aircraft carriers in time for each morning's briefing. Special "FLASH"-precedence advisories were also issued, as circumstances demanded, on high-interest or rapidly developing events such as Soviet air activity.[12]

Innovations in the Cryptologic Relationship

FOSIF Rota contributed much to naval intelligence by pioneering fleet-support operations within the "node-driven" decentralized approach OSIS took to operational intelligence. Among its greatest successes in this regard is its role in reshaping the relationship between the cryptologic community and Navy OPINTEL. As we have seen, a close relationship between the OPINTEL and SIGINT communities had been important from the very earliest days of OPINTEL at the British Admiralty, the COMINCH tracking room, and ICPOA. Its importance continued into the Cold War with the establishment of the Navy Field Operational Intelligence Office in the National Security Agency complex at Fort Meade, Maryland. As OPINTEL devolved back toward the fleet, however—and as the demands of the Vietnam War forced NSA increasingly into the production of "tactical" intelligence—this relationship came under some strain, for it was difficult for a national-level architecture to meet such diverse demands efficiently or systematically.

At FOSIF Rota, Navy intelligence officers placed a high premium upon Soviet C^3 exploitation—developing a highly effective approach that subsequently "became a recognized methodology within OSIS."[13] To help acquire the SIGINT information vital to this endeavor, the new facility enjoyed a secure communications circuit to the National SIGINT Operations Center (NSOC) at NSA, and in-house analytical support at Rota from the Naval Security Group (NSG or NAVSECGRU)— the Navy-wide cryptologic activity that operated under NSA's aegis.[14] Though FOSIF Rota enjoyed "excellent" relations with NSA at the "analyst level" in Spain, Rota "bombarded" NSA with requests for Mediterranean-related SIGINT, souring relations with NSA headquarters.[15] The local NAVSECGRU function at Rota also looked at the new OPINTEL facility with some suspicion, initially viewing it "as [a] competitor, or worse."[16]

These problems were solved, however, by the creation of a new SIGINT support staff, the Cryptologic Support Group (CSG)—under Officer in Charge Comdr. James McFarland—to take over FOSIF Rota's interface with the SIGINT community. The CSG, although still technically under the supervisory aegis of NSA's SIGINT command architecture, soon shared workspaces with the FOSIF analytical staff and "worked together and played together" well.[17] In practice, the CSG and FOSIF contingents became essentially indistinguishable, functioning so smoothly as a team that the cryptologists became de facto FOSIF Rota personnel—owing "allegiance to nobody but the SIXTHFLT."[18] Similar innovations also occurred under Officer in Charge Thomas Brooks at the FOSIC in Norfolk, Virginia, that served Commander in Chief, U.S. Atlantic Fleet (CINCLANTFLT)—where CSG personnel and even career NSA analysts joined naval intelligence officers and provided access to NSA "technical data" (raw information) "right there on the [watch]floor."[19]

Needless to say, the effective co-option of the CSG cadres annoyed senior NSA leadership. As one NSA civilian expressed it in a trip report filed after visiting FOSIF Rota,

> It is impossible to discern the players without a program and there is no distinction between the FOSIF and the CSG. In fact there is not any physical distinction because they all share the same space! Worse yet, the CSG is reviewing and

has access to *raw* SIGINT thus duplicating the analysis of the [NSG] field station, as well as NSA. Even worse, it is reporting first on many Med-related [Mediterranean] events without any oversight from SIGINT authorities. The CSG officer in charge knows the system and is only concerned with supporting the fleet in whatever manner he can with or without a proper charter. We have created an unchecked monster in Rota.[20]

From an OPINTEL perspective, however, this "unchecked monster" maniacally devoted to fleet support was precisely what was needed to ensure that the Sixth Fleet received superb SIGINT-related operational intelligence. These innovations provided a model of smooth coordination that was soon adopted throughout the OSIS system.[21]

Especially with regard to Soviet submarine and C^3 analysis,[22] the FOSIF/CSG team "worked miracles" in supplying OPINTEL to the fleet.[23] Their combined efforts broke NSA's national-level monopoly on Soviet C^3 exploitation and provided operational intelligence of enormous sophistication. Indeed, Vice Adm. Daniel Murphy Sr., then serving as COMSIXTHFLT, described FOSIF Rota's Soviet C^3 report as the most important single intelligence report he received during the Arab-Israeli war of October 1973. This was especially critical since the Soviet navy had dispatched more than one hundred naval vessels to the Mediterranean during the conflict, placing OPINTEL at an unprecedented premium.[24] Rota's C^3 reporting also helped identify Soviet operational practices and command linkages for potential attack or other "countermeasures" in time of war, thus providing valuable feedback into Navy targeting and strategic planning.[25] Ultimately, NSA itself recognized the value of FOSIF Rota's intelligence, subsequently incorporating this Soviet C^3 report as a regular NSA reporting vehicle.[26]

Other OSIS Nodes

NOSIC

The national-level node of the decentralized OSIS system developed out of the Ocean Surveillance Branch of NFOIO, which was detached and moved to a temporary Butler Hut building at Suitland, Maryland, in July 1970. (NOSIC was literally, as well as symbolically, wedged into the structure of the naval intelligence establishment: a crane unceremoniously lowered its Butler Hut into the courtyard at one of the ONI buildings in Suitland.)[27] There, it became the Ocean Surveillance Information Division (OSID) of an entirely new Navy Ocean Surveillance Information Center (NOSIC),[28] a national-level OPINTEL cell that incorporated many of the OPINTEL-related fusion lessons and experience then being pioneered by FOSIF Rota.[29] The first operational watch was established at NOSIC in January 1971.[30]

NFOIO continued to provide SIGINT-related "operational intelligence support to the major fleet commands on an all-source twenty-four-hour-per-day basis, as well as to SECNAV [the Secretary of the Navy], CNO [the Chief of Naval Operations] and other appropriate commands and agencies."[31] The new NOSIC, however, was a modern incarnation of the British Admiralty's Operational Intelligence Center of World War II—a specialized submarine tracking room that quickly became "the authoritative expert" on all Soviet submarine issues.[32] Some of the intelligence support NOSIC provided concerned generalized support to the fleet on such matters, including a new and much-acclaimed all-source weekly report begun in January 1972 on Soviet out-of-area submarine operations.[33] Other NOSIC products were more specialized. In December 1975, for example, NOSIC began producing a detailed all-source daily message on "Soviet Submarine Operations and U.S. ASW [antisubmarine warfare] Sensor Encounters."[34] More exotic still was the work of the Fleet Support Section within NOSIC's staff of Soviet submarine experts, which had the job of providing "specifically tailored support on a world-wide basis to fleet units engaged in sensitive operations."[35] In a less dramatic vein—but no less important to fleet operations—NOSIC also became the OSIS system's principal repository of merchant shipping OPINTEL.[36]

Additional Fleet Nodes

Following the model of FOSIF Rota in the Mediterranean, OSIS quickly sprouted a network of fleet-support OPINTEL nodes around the world. The OSIS system was "hierarchic in design but operated in a dispersed manner,"[37] with high levels of reciprocal information flow between the fleet nodes and the national "hub" of NOSIC at Suitland. OSIS became operational on "a worldwide system basis" in 1972 with the establishment of another FOSIF at Kamiseya, Japan (also known as FOSIF WESTPAC), to support the commander of fleet operations in the

Western Pacific. Similar facilities, designated Fleet Ocean Surveillance Information Centers (FOSICs), were set up in London, Pearl Harbor, and Norfolk, Virginia, to support U.S. naval forces in Europe, the Pacific Fleet commander and eastern Pacific operations, and the Atlantic Fleet, respectively.[38] (At Norfolk, the new FOSIC LANT [Atlantic] was located within the CINCLANT/CINCLANTFLT Command Center's all-source Current Intelligence Operations Center; at Pearl Harbor FOSIC PAC it was located next to CINCPACFLT's command center on the top floor of the Fleet Intelligence Center Pacific [FICPAC]; while in London, FOSIC EUR was colocated with CINCUS-NAVEUR's headquarters at Grosvenor Square.) The FOSICs combined their operational intelligence functions with more general staff support to the local commander, while the FOSIFs concentrated more upon "pure" fleet OPINTEL,[39] but together the FOSIFs, FOSICs, and NOSIC itself functioned as an integrated whole, the first truly global ocean surveillance system in history. By 1973 an informal program review found that "the operational OSIS was noted to be very successful and enjoying wide fleet acceptance and support."[40]

All-Source Fusion in the Era of New "INTs"

The late 1960s saw a veritable revolution in the variety of intelligence inputs—such as SIGINT, ACINT (acoustic intelligence), ELINT (electronic intelligence such as radar emissions), and increasingly specialized varieties of IMINT (imagery intelligence)—that began to become available for incorporation in the all-source fusion analyses of Navy OPINTEL. These developments continued during the 1970s, with the maturation of a number of approaches that the U.S. intelligence community had been pursuing for some time.

The ELINT Revolution

By far the most significant innovation during the 1970s was the arrival of a new ELINT collection system in the autumn of 1976. This new ELINT source—the details of which remain classified at the time of writing—provided vastly more useful information to Navy OPINTEL than had ever been possible before. Although this flood of data placed huge demands upon OSIS computerized information-processing systems, it soon allowed analysts to track virtually *all* ships and other ELINT "emitters" at sea on a near-real-time basis.[41] For intelligence officers responsible for providing finished all-source OPINTEL to operational commanders, this was an extraordinary leap in capabilities. Indeed, ELINT collection and analysis improved to such an extent that individual Soviet units could be tracked through entire deployments by following the radiation emitted by their navigation and surface-search radar sets. Before long, one participant estimated, ELINT of surface combatants constituted as much as 80 or 90 percent of the information incorporated into OPINTEL analyses.[42]

Acoustic Intelligence and HULTEC

The field of acoustic intelligence—the analysis of underwater sound recordings obtained from the seabed listening devices of the Sound Surveillance System, from air-dropped "sonobuoys," and from hydrophones carried or towed by surface ships and submarines—also made great strides during the 1970s.[43] One of NOSIC's tasks during this period was to develop a useful computerized database correlating specific sound characteristics with specific *individual* oceangoing vessels or submarines, a process that became known as hull-to-emitter correlation (HULTEC). The first phase of this program—which was considered to be "a key objective" if OSIS were "to perform as conceived"[44]— was completed in 1974.[45]

HULTEC was extremely valuable to Navy OPINTEL, for it provided a capability to track individual targets by acoustic means independent of ELINT emissions or other more conventional indicators (e.g., sighting reports or COMINT interceptions). As an alternative or an overlapping source to the new ELINT system, ACINT and HULTEC databases provided Navy OPINTEL analysts with powerful new tools— especially vis-à-vis Soviet submarines, which rarely emitted electronic signals when submerged but which always radiated at least some level of mechanical or water-flow "noise." HULTEC analysis even held out the possibility of tracking individual Soviet submarines by their acoustic "fingerprints." By 1976, for example, NOSIC and the Naval Intelligence Support Center (NISC) had completed a series of acoustic-emission "correlation studies" on the Soviet *Yankee*-class SSBN. NOSIC's Submarine Analysis Group (SAG) found these results promising enough to embark upon a program to "continue and extend this work to all classes of Soviet nuclear submarines."[46]

Merchant Ship Locators and Standardized Message Formats

In November 1975 OSIS also began to receive electronic reports of the location of all U.S.–flagged merchant vessels. Developed during the previous year by the Navy and the U.S. Maritime Administration, the U.S. Merchant Vessel Filing System (USMER) required all U.S.–flagged vessels of at least one thousand gross register tons and engaged in foreign commerce to report their at-sea positions electronically every forty-eight hours. All port arrivals and departures, as well as changes in anticipated ship schedules, were also reported. These reports—which were submitted in a message format specifically designed for automatic input to NOSIC's computers—became an important part of the Navy's operational intelligence scheme.[47]

Indeed, this methodology of requiring reporting in standardized formats was an innovation of particular importance as OPINTEL entered the age of ADP. An important prerequisite for all-source fusion in an ADP environment was the standardization of intelligence reporting and information-storage formats so that different collection systems and computer databases could share information. Without such standardization—between the U.S. military services, between the services and national agencies such as NSA, and even with the British—OPINTEL could not have taken advantage of the computer revolution.[48]

Improved Weather Data

Acoustic and ELINT tracking data were vital to OPINTEL, but sophisticated attempts to identify and explain an adversary's naval activity also require vast amounts of more prosaic information in order to put such operations into context. Among this information must be accurate reporting on weather conditions in the various fleet operating areas, since a vessel's movements might, after all, owe as much or more to storms and sea state as to deliberate operational disposition. As Capt. Robert W. Schmidt, the PACFLT N-2 (Assistant Chief of Staff for Intelligence) from 1977 to 1981, was reported to have asked about the seemingly alarming dispersal of Soviet naval vessels from an Indian Ocean anchorage in 1981, "Did anyone find out what the weather was like over there? Maybe a storm came up and they had to leave."[49]

As described in chapter 3, these NOSIC computer systems already received inputs of weather data from the Navy's Fleet Weather Central circuit, but this process was a cumbersome one. In order for information to be processed from the Navy's weather center, data tapes were hand delivered to NOSIC from the nearby Fleet Weather Facility (also at Suitland, Maryland) for batch database entry. This information was helpful, but clearly left something to be desired from the perspective of OPINTEL analysts who aspired to provide "near-real-time" support to the fleet. To improve the timely integration of weather data, therefore, NOSIC developed a direct online continuous feed of information from the National Oceanic and Atmospheric Administration (NOAA), which was also located at Suitland.[50] By 1977 such weather information entered the NOSIC databases much more quickly than before.

Information Exchange with Foreign Navies

Though not a specialized "INT" analogous to ELINT or ACINT, useful OPINTEL information also came from intelligence exchanges with foreign navies. As the commander of the Naval Intelligence Command (NAVINTCOM) put it in 1973, for example, "OSIS information exchanges with foreign navies are being actively pursued with the goal of increasing the data base in areas where U.S. tactical resources have been reduced and are unable to provide effective coverage. . . . This exchange effort is anticipated to be of great value to total OSIS effectiveness."[51] Such exchanges provided a longer-term benefit as well, by giving Navy OPINTEL professionals experience in intelligence coordination between military services with different historical backgrounds, organizational cultures, and operational perspectives. These skills would prove invaluable in the late 1980s and early 1990s as U.S. operational intelligence itself went "joint."[52]

Sanitization Issues

While it may have been true that Navy OPINTEL during this period was not *truly* "all-source" fusion, because some extraordinarily sensitive collection programs were still kept out of the OSIS system for fear of compromising them, the OSIS system functioned well as a de facto "all-source" process.[53] As such, its smooth operation required continuous attention to issues of "sanitization"—that is, the "laundering" of certain information in order to protect sensitive sources before OPINTEL products were disseminated to the fleet. FOSIF Rota, for example, depended heavily upon sensitive SIGINT from the NSA and other sources for its analysis of Soviet C^3 activity, information to which most at-sea operational commanders were not permitted access. Such information had to be carefully "sanitized" prior to distribution, and "much to the chagrin of NSA and others," the FOSIF/CSG team "sanitized freely."[54]

All in all, however, the OSIS process was marked by the development of improved, *nearly* all-source, analysis. According to former Deputy DNI Richard Haver, it had been DNI Bobby Inman's intention to create a genuinely all-source OPINTEL program. When Inman directed Haver to take charge of NOSIC in 1976, for example, it was the admiral's specific instruction that NOSIC was to develop a way to apply analytic power across a much broader spectrum of compartmented "stovepipes." "Pull it all together," Haver recalls Inman commanding him, "don't let it sit in separate bins."[55]

That such sanitization efforts worked smoothly is another testimonial to the close bonds of trust and mutual understanding that were being built up between OPINTEL intelligence staffs and fleet operational commanders. As the first commander of the CSG unit at Rota later described it, sanitization worked well in the OPINTEL environment of the early 1970s because operators trusted their intelligence officers. They cared less about where the information came from than about what it told them of Soviet naval activity and intentions. As far as he could recall, in fact, sanitized products were "never challenged by users" at any point during his time at FOSIF Rota.[56]

Technological Revolutions on the Watchfloor

Computing Power and Databases

The volume of information involved in a worldwide network such as OSIS was so tremendous that no unaided human analysts could possibly handle it. Even where analysts *could* survive this flood of information, automation still offered considerable advantages, allowing facilities to "divert personnel from manual ADP functions to areas of increased responsibilities where they are now engaged in more analytical and creative functions."[57] Consequently, it was clear from the beginning that OSIS could not survive without an aggressive effort to maintain and improve ADP equipment and related technologies. Indeed, the evolution of ADP technologies acted as a catalyst, helping drive organizational change in Navy OPINTEL, requiring the implementation of a permanent, ongoing effort at ADP modernization.[58]

It was fundamental to the concept, therefore, that an ongoing program for the "design and activation of highly sophisticated automated data handling capabilities" proceed in parallel with the establishment of the OSIS system. Indeed, it was envisioned that "NOSIC would be expected to assist the R&D [research and development] process by providing guidance to systems design and a testbed for experimental improvements in information processing and analysis."[59] To this end, NOSIC was to work with a new, operationally oriented Naval Intelligence Processing System Support Activity (NIPSSA)—which was now armed with new batch-processing computer technology—to develop new ADP and communications systems, better computerized databases, and improved user-interface equipment (e.g., user-friendly analyst consoles) optimized for OSIS support.[60]

One of the earliest fruits of this collaborative effort between NOSIC and NIPSSA was the SEAWATCH Ocean Surveillance Information Handling System, a database driven by new CDC 6400 computers designed to aid analysts dealing with the huge volume of merchant ship and fishing ship intelligence. The first phase of SEAWATCH, which utilized batch processing of received data rather than continuous online updating, became operational in March 1973 but was plagued with software problems until at least October.[61] This new equipment provided NOSIC with "a capability for on-line receipt, processing, analysis and dissemination of all-source ocean surveillance data, thereby eliminating or greatly reducing time- and resource-consuming manual handling and administration."[62]

The first NOSIC daily summary to utilize SEAWATCH processing was sent to the Atlantic Fleet in September 1972, advising operational commanders of merchant and fishing vessel activity within their area of responsibility (AOR).[63] Meanwhile, NIPSSA and NOSIC were working to develop improved graphics-driven display consoles to ease the manipulation of SEAWATCH data. To improve customer access to maritime OPINTEL, it was also planned to provide remote SEAWATCH terminals to major intelligence consumers so that they, too, would have "direct on-line access to NOSIC's current and historical data bases."[64]

Though it had begun as merely an automated means for tracking merchant shipping, SEAWATCH was soon expanding to incorporate a much wider range of inputs, gradually becoming a more all-purpose naval OPINTEL database. As Frederick Harrison has observed, highly automated systems of modern OPINTEL had their origin in ad hoc adaptation—in the ongoing development of ADP support for the demanding task of identifying and tracking merchant vessels. When SEAWATCH was shown to work well, it was decided to expand it, ultimately into the organizational core of a reporting system for all naval OPINTEL.[65]

In March 1975, for example, it was modified to accept data on Soviet naval aircraft flights over waters not contiguous to the USSR. Naval intelligence had been compiling a historical database of such information since January of that year, and its integration into SEAWATCH allowed analysts to process it just as they processed other SEAWATCH data.[66] In December 1976 NOSIC began a program to build into SEAWATCH a function that would automatically provide automated "dead reckoning" (DR) plots—that is, estimated future positions over time based upon past course information—for vessels being tracked.[67]

Another important database project got under way in 1974 as OSIS began planning how it would handle the flood of new information soon planned to arrive from the new ELINT collection system that was expected to become operational as early as 1975. In the expectation that this system would "generate a high volume of contact reports," the Naval Intelligence Command's Ocean Surveillance Information Systems Division (NAVINTCOM-42) undertook "a maximum effort . . . to have OSIS telecommunications [and databases] ready in 1975 to handle [this new system's ELINT] data.[68]

Not all of these innovations were easy, and the task of applying a new and rapidly developing technology (the computer) to OPINTEL processing was often slow. In 1975, for example, a frustrated NAVINTCOM-42 command historian noted that the developmental phase of OSIS "had reached a near-crisis state by year's end [1974] because of consistently slipped milestone accomplishments."[69] But "bugs" were gradually worked out, and OSIS emerged far more capable and effective than ever.

Databases at Sea

As noted in chapter 3, by the beginning of the 1970s the Integrated Operational Intelligence Centers (IOICs) aboard U.S. aircraft carriers had already begun to provide a degree of real OPINTEL capability to ships at sea. The cornerstone of this effort was the Naval Intelligence Processing System, "a program to provide semiautomated intelligence centers to major ship and major commands afloat and to make the databases . . . accessible to the afloat Intelligence Centers."[70] This program took another step in 1971 when a new Command Ship Data System (CSDS) and its associated file maintenance software were deployed aboard all NIPS-equipped IOICs. With this upgrade, "all IOICs [acquired the] capability to process all major NIPS Data files using this system."[71]

Since space limitations aboard ship, combined with the bulky nature of existing computer technology, still restricted the amount of "number crunching" that could be done at sea, the development of a system of Fleet Command Support Centers (FCSCs) was approved in 1972. At that point in computer development, afloat commands could not assimilate "the large volumes of data from sophisticated sensors without a concomitant loss in offensive capability to satisfy the information processing necessary for effective decision making."[72] A large experimental afloat database—the Integrated Flagship Data System (IFDS)—that embarked aboard USS *Providence* (CLG-6), for example, took up so much space that the ship sacrificed half of its missile capacity to accommodate it. In order to alleviate some of these pressures, the FCSCs were to "collate and correlate multiple types of information ashore to provide fleet commanders and units with integrated and processed data." The FCSC concept was designed to provide "an information add-on to the accepted and proven OSIS operation" for "providing timely useful information to fleet commanders and units from ashore."[73] A further development in this vein during 1973 enabled NIPS-equipped ships in the Mediterranean to receive database updates *by broadcast message,* superseding much slower and more cumbersome procedures by which databases were updated by magnetic tape flown aboard by special couriers.[74]

Connectivity

To improve the communications connectivity so essential to interanalyst coordination and the prompt dissemination of OPINTEL products, the Navy also began to link OSIS nodes by secure communications circuits capable of increasingly high rates of data transmission. As early as 1972, NOSIC possessed dedicated OSIS CROSSCOM (Cross Communication) circuits that permitted it to provide OPINTEL support to the Chief of Naval Operations and the commander of the Pacific Fleet, "as well as other Washington area intelligence agencies/offices via secure telephones."[75] The lack of secure telephone connection to facilities outside Washington, however, limited NOSIC's capacity to communicate efficiently with other parts of the OSIS system. As of late 1971, in fact, even NOSIC's secure telephone connection to the CNO's Flag Plot was not authorized to handle SI-level (special intelligence, e.g., COMINT) communications, and the NSA was not yet in the existing Defense Department telephone network at all.[76]

To remedy these deficiencies, secure data links were gradually set up between the various parts of the OSIS system during 1973. Teleprinter connections between FOSIC Norfolk, FOSIF Rota, and FOSIC London were tested at a rate of one hundred words per minute (wpm) in December 1973, which was deemed "satisfactory for current information handling" even though upon completion such linkages were expected to handle a higher data rate.[77] Though these 100-wpm linkages were extremely slow by modern standards, NOSIC officials considered them vital additions to OSIS and employed them for "exchange of ocean surveillance information and analysis with other OSIS components" and "provision of intelligence support for major user commands and agencies."[78] To help other OSIS components handle the information that such circuits could provide, new intelligence-support ADP systems were also procured, allowing "significantly improved communications handling" at sites such as the FOSIFs at Rota and Kamiseya.[79] With the various OSIS nodes now "interconnected on-line for analyst-to-analyst communications exchange," one command history concluded in 1973, "the processing, dissemination, and utilization of ocean surveillance information has been considerably enhanced."[80]

Further aiding rapid and efficient dissemination—facilitated by the proliferation of secure data links and computer processing capabilities—NOSIC and the other OSIS nodes began producing their intelligence products in electronic formats that allowed users to receive it (and themselves to process it) much more quickly. By the end of 1974, for example, NOSIC's Maritime Operations Branch was producing twenty-nine different reports on merchant shipping activity for various consumers.[81] The Geographic Intelligence Analyst Console (GIAC), a forerunner of JOTS (Joint Operational Tactical System) and other interactive workstations, was designed to take advantage of such electronic data. Developed by the Naval Research Laboratory (NRL) and field-tested at Norfolk, GIAC allowed the analyst/watchstander to work from a geographic display at the all-source level, and to create messages at the SCI (sensitive compartmented information) level or sanitized to the SECRET level of security classification for transmission on the intelligence channel of the fleet broadcast. The receiving unit could then create the same display on its own GIAC terminal.[82]

Nor was OSIS expected to be a self-contained system. Using FOSIC Norfolk as a testbed, systems were also being developed to connect OSIS to the Navy's command-and-control (C^2) system through the FCSCs.[83] With the approval of Technical Development Plan (TDP) 35–15 in July 1973, naval intelligence also set about trying to improve OSIS integration with the Antisubmarine Warfare Centers Command and Control System (ASW CCCS) "in order to maximize commonality wherever practical in the development of the two systems."[84] In 1974, in fact, responsibility for system development and management of OSIS was given to OP-942 (the Command and Control Division of OP-094, the Command Support Programs Office of OPNAV). This helped improve the coordination of OSIS's development with the Worldwide Military Command and Control System (WWMCCS), ASW CCCS, and FCSCs.[85]

An additional reason to link the OSIS OPINTEL function more closely to the overall Navy C^2 system was the growing importance, during the 1970s, of over-the-horizon targeting (OTH/T). Because new generations of long-range antisurface warfare weapons such as the Harpoon missile depended heavily upon targeting information from sources other than the firing platform, there were particular synergies to be developed in integrating OSIS-derived surveillance data to shipboard targeting computers.[86]

The increasing integration of OSIS with the Navy's operational life had far-reaching implications. Two decades before the concept of "network centric warfare,"[87] the OSIS OPINTEL nodes were taking small steps toward a degree of real interconnectivity not only with each other but also with the rest of the Navy's C^2 architecture.

Synergies of Interconnectivity

The proliferation of telecommunications technologies permitting meaningful "analyst-to-analyst communications exchanges"[88] also strengthened OPINTEL by allowing intelligence professionals to engage more easily in the kind of informal consultation and information sharing that had helped the U.S. and British submarine tracking rooms hone their analysis during the Battle of the Atlantic. Within the OSIS system, easy user interconnectivity provided important synergies, allowing analysts to improve their understanding of the operational environment through informal "back-channel" consultations, negotiations, and coordination without crossing the threshold of certainty and accountability entailed by "official" situation reports.[89] (As had sometimes happened in World War II, moreover, OPINTEL interconnectivity was so effective that operational commanders occasionally paid their intelligence staffs the compliment of using their OPINTEL circuits to relay operational communications.)[90]

Computer databases and high-speed data links did not change the basic concept of OPINTEL that had been developed during World War II. These new technologies of data storage and manipulation and communications interconnectivity, however, revolutionized the practice of OPINTEL, allowing better and faster all-source fusion, more rapid and effective dissemination of the resulting intelligence,[91] and productive analytical "value-added" through informal networking and consultations.[92] The key advances of the OSIS era lay not in these technologies themselves but in the realm of organization—that is, in the ways the Navy learned how to apply steadily advancing technologies to the OPINTEL endeavor.[93]

OSIS, in a sense, was invented in 1939, but it took the computer age to bring it to full fruition. As Richard Haver later recalled, the mechanics of "fat-fingering" data into computers had long slowed OPINTEL process, but improvements in automation that began in the 1970s helped the concept live up to its real potential: "What was created in the late 1970s and early 1980s was to make the mechanics [of the process] the analysts' friend, rather than the analysts' albatross hanging around their neck."[94] According to Haver, the process of OPINTEL automation succeeded in large part because many of the officials at NIPSSA who oversaw the technical aspects of this transformation had themselves had experience as naval intelligence analysts: "they understood what we were functionally trying to do."[95] In any event, the imaginative playing out of the OPINTEL concept with modern technologies helped make naval intelligence in the 1970s a pioneer of information management techniques that would not be well understood in much of the civilian world until the last decade of the twentieth century.

Intelligence Personnel: The Linchpin

As always, naval intelligence relied upon high-quality personnel to provide finished operational intelligence to commanders. If anything, the need for such people was more acute than ever during the 1970s, as the "INTs revolution" continued apace and the nature of ADP and communications technologies applied to OPINTEL changed with unprecedented rapidity. Fortunately, the increasingly alarming prospect of a campaign against Sergei Gorshkov's growing "blue water" Soviet navy helped ONI, and the U.S. Navy as a whole, develop its OPINTEL personnel as never before. As a career path within naval intelligence, in fact, OPINTEL came to be regarded as primus inter pares—a "fast track" career[96] in which "the best officers . . . [were] normally assigned to these [new OSIS] facilities."[97]

In 1975 the Navy also recognized the importance of enlisted personnel's contributions to intelligence work, establishing a new intelligence specialist (IS) rating on July 1 of that year by combining the photographic intelligenceman (PT) and intelligence clerk (YN-2505) ratings into one dedicated rate.[98] Training for the new IS ratings included a specialized OPINTEL subcurriculum at the Fleet Intelligence Training Centers Atlantic (FITCLANT), in Norfolk, and Pacific (FITCPAC), in San Diego. To allow them to help handle the formidable information loads of the new OSIS system, IS training also included experience on NIPS at the newly relocated Naval Intelligence Processing System Training Center Facility in Key West, Florida.[99] In 1976 a program was also begun to enlist NAVSECGRU representatives in the IS training process, reflecting the need to expose trainees to highly sensitive secure compartmented information (SCI) and begin background investigations to this effect.[100]

Naval intelligence also continued to place great emphasis upon the use of Naval Reservists in the OPINTEL system. Indeed, FOSIF Rota's initial manpower consisted of reservists and temporary active-duty (TAD) personnel; it took an entire six months to acquire a full permanent staff of seventeen at that facility.[101] In 1974 a specialist Naval Reserve Ocean Information Unit 106 was established to provide "dedicated support to [the] Current Operations Center" at NOSIC. Among these reservists' duties was setting up a desk in the Operations Center devoted exclusively to the navy of the People's Republic of China (PRC). This China desk was "manned entirely by Naval Reservists" and prepared a weekly PRC navy report.[102]

Setting the Stage for the 1980s

All in all, the various advances and innovations that came together during the 1970s helped produce a sophisticated, worldwide ocean surveillance system capable of providing Navy commanders anywhere on the planet with an integrated, "God's-eye view" of their operating environment. As a "system of aerial, surface, and subsurface systems continuously providing locating data on maritime activity," OSIS was soon regarded as "an extremely effective intelligence system that is one of the strongest aspects of naval intelligence and one of the most capable and efficient systems in the U.S. Intelligence Community."[103]

By the end of the 1980s, therefore, OSIS "provided Navy operational commanders and strategic planners with an unprecedented picture of the capabilities and disposition of current Soviet maritime forces."[104] As later recounted by Adm. William Owens,

> As Soviet submarines grew more sophisticated and quiet throughout the 1970s, the United States turned increasingly to a global, interconnected team effort to track them. We integrated information from satellites and fixed seabed sensors, which could provide warning of Soviet submarine departures from their bases, with other data, and distributed it among U.S. surface, submarine, and airborne platforms. These, in turn, coordinated their actions, maintaining a nearly constant, integrated flow of data and intelligence among the forces assigned to tracking the submarines—an approach that increasingly produced accurate, real-time location data on the submarines.[105]

As we shall see in chapter 5, without such a sophisticated worldwide monitoring system, the U.S. Navy could not have imagined—let alone hoped to carry out—the "forward-leading" and offensively oriented "Maritime Strategy" of the 1980s. By taking advantage of Owens's "integrated flow of data and intelligence" between OSIS nodes and operating forces in the effort to track Soviet submarines, moreover, Navy operational intelligence thus pioneered the concept of "network-centric warfare," which would become a major focus of strategic and operational planning in the U.S. military two decades later.[106]

Focusing and Refocusing: OPINTEL and Regional Crises

The 1970s also presaged major future developments in operational intelligence in another fashion, by illustrating the need for any such system to be able to refocus rapidly, as circumstances require, upon different potential adversaries or regional crises. This was, in many respects, an entirely new innovation in Cold War OPINTEL. The model developed by the admiralty's OIC in the late 1930s, and put into such effective practice against Germany and Japan during World War II, was predicated upon the luxury of developing a surveillance effort tightly focused upon a single, overwhelmingly important enemy. The COM-INCH and OIC tracking rooms, for example, were finely tuned machines devoted entirely to one aspect of the fight against Germany: defending against, and ultimately sinking, the U-boats. Not surprisingly, this operational model of intelligence practice translated well in the Cold War decades, being pressed increasingly into service against the Soviet submarine fleet.

By virtue of its employment by a global superpower during a prolonged period of international tensions, however, Cold War Navy OPINTEL had to be more flexible than its World War II progenitors. This was truer during the 1970s than ever before, as OSIS was increasingly called upon to maintain surveillance against Soviet naval combatants as well as other targets in a decade of great regional instability. Navy OPINTEL had been largely dismantled after the end of World War II, in fact, precisely because the initial postwar period lacked a clear, overwhelmingly important naval adversary analogous to wartime Germany or Japan.[107] It was a measure of the strength of the OPINTEL system, therefore, that by the 1970s it was able to work "third world targets" as a matter of routine.[108]

OPINTEL's most dramatic redirection toward a regional conflict came in 1972, in connection with President Richard Nixon's decision to mine the approaches to North Vietnam's Haiphong Harbor during the Vietnam War. This action prompted immediate and urgent requests from the Pacific Fleet for information on Soviet and North Vietnamese naval and air force dispositions, minesweeping force locations, and merchant shipping en route to North Vietnamese ports. This information was obviously essential to operational commanders whose job it was to plan and carry out the mining operation. OSIS, and the Ocean Surveillance Information Division at NFOIO in particular, provided a continuous flow of information on these subjects, successfully meeting the needs of Navy warfighters during this effort.[109]

The war that erupted between Israel and the Arab states of the Middle East in October 1973—the Yom Kippur war—also required rapid responsiveness from OSIS. The surveillance network was well equipped to monitor the Soviets' buildup of operating forces in the Mediterranean during this crisis. "The [OSIS] system responded quickly and efficiently to Fleet, Navy Department, and National requirements during the October 1973 Mid-East crisis and during the resulting oil embargo, thus formally establishing itself as a vital element in intelligence responsiveness."[110]

The 1973 war, however, also highlighted some weaknesses in OSIS. To begin with, the heavy information requirements of operating commanders during the crisis placed a huge strain on Navy OPINTEL's computer processing resources, underlining the pressing need for ever-improving ADP capabilities and making particularly painful the problems NOSIC was having in implementing the second phase of its SEAWATCH database system.[111] The crisis also showed an "urgent need" for timely information on the locations and intentions of U.S.–flagged merchant shipping, "primarily those located in the contiguous waters of the Middle East." This failing provided the impetus for the development of the Merchant Vessel Locator Filing System described previously.[112]

During the remainder of the 1970s, OSIS nodes—and particularly FOSIF Rota, which had the misfortune of being responsible for an especially conflict-ridden area of the world—acquired more practice in dealing with the OPINTEL needs of littoral crises. In addition to the Arab-Israeli conflict in 1973, for example, Rota provided intelligence support to Navy leaders in connection with the conflict over Cyprus between Greece and Turkey, the Lebanese civil war, and the episodes of international terrorism that became increasingly common during the 1970s.[113] For its part, NOSIC focused upon providing current intelligence on merchant shipping in the Eastern Mediterranean during the Lebanese conflict and the U.S. noncombatant evacuation operation (NEO) there. It also tracked U.S.–flagged and –controlled shipping in the Indian Ocean littoral during the Ethiopian civil war and both naval and merchant activity near Angola as Cuban and South African forces joined the civil war in that former Portuguese colony in 1975–76.[114]

This series of regional crises during the 1970s—accentuated by the increasing propensity of the Soviet Union and its Cuban proxies to become involved in third world trouble spots—helped teach Navy OPINTEL that "in an increasingly polycentric world," the Navy could not ignore "other nations and their maritime and technological developments."[115] As one command history put it, "There are recurring requirements to provide timely response to unscheduled tasks received on a near daily basis from all levels of the Department of Defense and the operating forces. Action and reaction to 'flap' situations requiring immediate response have been accepted as a way of life."[116] Such an ability to focus and refocus attention upon shifting targets of opportunity elsewhere in the world—regional crises, local wars, and other "'flap' situations"—would become particularly crucial after the collapse of the Soviet empire at the dawn of the 1990s.

World War II Foundations of U.S. OPINTEL

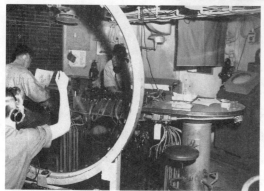

Intelligence data from multiple sources were processed, analyzed, and acted upon at the headquarters and theater levels of command, such as the submarine tracking room in the F-21 Section of the "Tenth Fleet" (top) and the Joint Intelligence Command, Pacific Ocean Area (JICPOA) (middle). OPINTEL fusion nodes also extended down to major warships, such as the Combat Information Center on USS *Guadalcanal* (bottom).

Postwar Challenges

SSB G-I Class

The Soviets built more than 450 diesel attack submarines in the decade after World War II. The Whiskey class SS (top) borrowed heavily from the design concepts of the German Type XXI sub that became operational toward the end of World War II (middle). The Type XXI's *Schnorkel* device provided an enhanced stealth capability that complicated Allied ASW efforts. During the 1950s, 235 Whiskeys were built. In 1958, the Soviets began deploying GOLF-class diesel ballistic missile submarines armed with antiship cruise missiles (bottom). The modified version of the GOLF could launch its missiles while submerged.

The First Generation of Soviet Nuclear Submarines

Soviet nuclear-powered submarines armed with torpedoes (including nuclear-tipped torpedoes) and later antiship cruise missiles served as the vanguard of an oceangoing fleet capable of challenging the West. The November SSN (top) was the USSR's first nuclear-powered submarine. Armed with torpedoes and mines, it became operational in 1958. The Echo II SSGN (middle) produced in the 1960s carried SSN-3/12 surface-launched missiles and was regarded as a primary anti-carrier threat. The Hotel II SSBN (bottom) was the first nuclear submarine capable of firing ballistic missiles while submerged.

OPINTEL Reporting

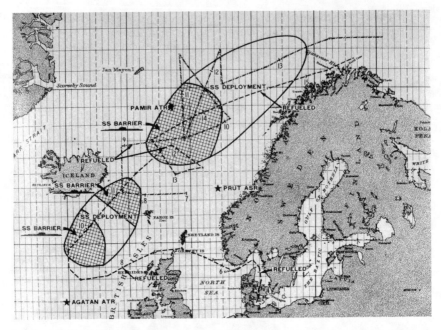

Map of a 1962 Soviet Naval Exercise in which 20 to 40 submarines and a number of surface ships participated. The vessel deployments illustrate the Soviet strategy of defense of territorial waters. Published in the DIA's *Naval Intelligence Review* (April 1963).

Growing Soviet Threat to U.S. Naval Deployments

By the late 1960s Soviet naval forces began challenging the U.S. Navy in critical overseas deployment areas. Badger and Bear long-range turbo-prop surveillance targeting and strike aircraft armed with increasingly capable long-range antiship missiles began to overfly U.S. carrier task forces, while surface ships armed with cruise missiles began to shadow the U.S. Sixth Fleet in the Mediterranean. Two F-4 Phantom fighters escort a Soviet Badger overflying USS *Kitty Hawk* (CV-63) in the North Pacific (top). A 1981 overflight of *Kitty Hawk* by a Soviet Bear bomber is escorted by two U.S. Navy F-14s (middle). A Soviet Kynda-class destroyer shadows USS *Little Rock* (CLG-4) and USS *John F. Kennedy* (CVA-67) in the Mediterranean in 1969 (bottom).

Revolution in Soviet Naval Strategy

Admiral of the Fleet of the Soviet Union Sergei Gorshkov was the most influential Cold War naval strategist. As CINC of the Soviet navy (1955–85), he saw the strategic importance of the nuclear strike mission and made it the centerpiece of the Soviet navy. By the early 1970s the Soviets deployed the first of the Delta-class SSBNs whose long-range SLBMs could strike at the heart of the United States from Soviet home waters in the Barents Sea, the Sea of Okhotsk, and the North Pacific. Much of the rest of the Soviet navy would deploy in wartime to protect these SSBNs and the Soviet homeland from attack by the U.S. Navy.

All-Source Intelligence Collection

From the late 1950s on, the United States employed increasingly capable airborne, seaborne, and overhead platforms to collect various "INTs"—IMINT, SIGINT, ELINT, and COMINT—from the USSR and its navy deployed in home waters and overseas (top right). The Galactic Radiation and Background (GRAB) satellite collected emissions from Soviet air defense radars (top left). The Corona photoreconnaissance satellite imaged Soviet bloc countries. The EA-3B Skywarrior electronic countermeasures aircraft deployed with fleet squadrons and collected tactical order of battle data from hostile radar emissions (middle). The land-based P-3 Orion long-range ASW aircraft had such advanced submarine detection sensors as directional frequency and ranging (DIFAR) sonobuoys and magnetic anomaly detection (MAD) equipment (bottom).

All-Source Intelligence Collection

The U.S. Navy's nuclear-powered attack submarines were powerful intelligence, surveillance, and reconnaissance (ISR) collection platforms. (A Permit-class SSN is shown here.) They were also major customers of U.S. naval intelligence ocean surveillance reporting from the 1950s on.

All-Source Intelligence Collection

U. S. naval intelligence was embedded in U.S. signals intelligence collection and analysis from the dawn of the Cold War onward. The "Y" Section of the Office of Naval Intelligence under the Chief of Naval Operations was located at Na-tional Security Agency headquarters at Arlington Hall (center) in Virginia. When NSA moved to Fort Meade, Maryland (bottom), in 1957 the Y Section was renamed the Navy Field Operational Intelligence Office (NFOIO) and remained at NSA through the mid-1980s.

Ocean Surveillance Information System (OSIS) Nodes

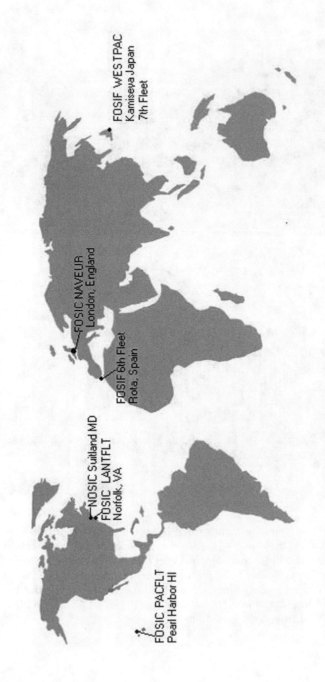

OCEAN SURVEILLANCE INFORMATION SYSTEM (OSIS) NODES

FOSIF WESTPAC
Kamiseya Japan
7th Fleet

FOSIC NAVEUR
London, England

FOSIF 6th Fleet
Rota, Spain

NOSIC Suitland MD
FOSIC LANTFLT
Norfolk, VA

FOSIC PACFLT
Pearl Harbor HI

FOSIF - Fleet Ocean Surveillance Information Facility
FOSIC - Fleet Ocean Surveillance Information Center
NOSIC - Naval Ocean Surveillance Information Facility

Ocean Surveillance Information System (OSIS) Nodes

The OSIS nodes were created in the early 1970s. The Naval Ocean Surveillance Information Center (NOSIC) was located inside the Butler Hut in the right-hand courtyard of the Naval Reconnaissance and Technical Support Center (NRTSC) in Suitland, Maryland (top). The Fleet Ocean Surveillance Information Facility (FOSIF) Rota, Spain (bottom), was located within the "bulls-eye" High-Frequency Direction Finding antenna array. FOSIF WESTPAC was similarly located within a "bulls-eye."

OSIS Culture

The OSIS nodes spawned a culture among naval intelligence officers, enlisted personnel, and civilian analysts who worked closely with the cryptologists from the Naval Security Group (NSG) embedded in each node. Keeping a twenty-four-hour watch on the Soviet navy, as well as any other threats to U.S. interests on the world's oceans, made for long hours on the watchfloors (the FOSIF Rota watchfloor in the 1970s is shown in the top photo). Getting the story "right" was critical in serving U.S. Navy operators who were the OSIS nodes' major customers. Briefing became an art form (bottom left). Advances in communications technology and automated data processing equipment put the OSIS nodes at the cutting edge in "real time" intelligence production and dissemination (bottom right).

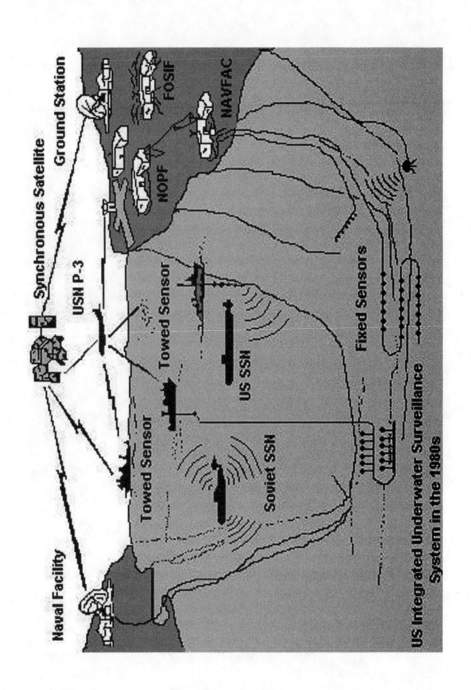

Synchronous Satellite
Ground Station
Naval Facility
USN P-3
FOSIF
NAVFAC
NOPF
Towed Sensor
Towed Sensor
US SSN
Soviet SSN
Fixed Sensors

US Integrated Underwater Surveillance
System in the 1980s

OSIS Results

PRIMARY SOVIET SUBMARINE DEPLOYMENT AREAS 1964

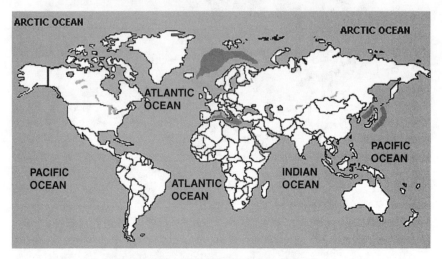

Includes all operational Soviet submarines

PRIMARY SOVIET SUBMARINE DEPLOYMENT AREAS 1984

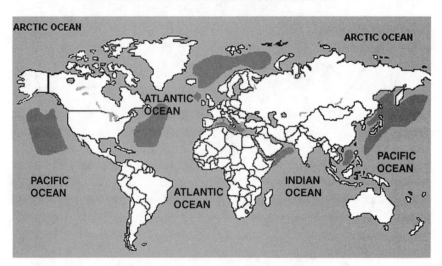

Includes all operational Soviet submarines

OSIS Results

Decades of closely watching the Soviet navy evolve—combined with improved collection, "deep penetration" sources, and sophisticated analysis—gave U.S. naval intelligence "ground truth" understanding of Soviet peacetime and wartime strategy by the early 1980s.

Current Initial Soviet Operating Areas in the Western TVDs

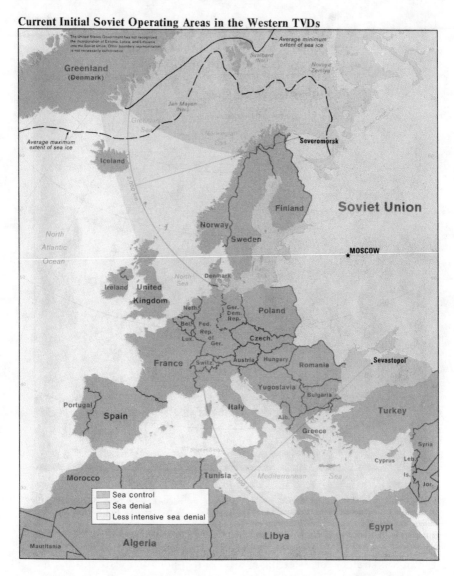

The Maritime Strategy

U. S. Naval Institute   January 1986

The new understanding of the Soviet naval threat developed by naval intelligence in the 1970s gave birth in the early 1980s to a fundamental recasting of U.S. naval strategy for deterring and fighting a potential war with the Soviet Union. Based on detailed intelligence estimates, U.S. naval war plans were changed and exercises conducted to make the Soviet Union aware of U.S. Navy understanding of its plans. The public manifestation of this recasting was known as "The Maritime Strategy," published in detail in a special January 1986 supplement of the U.S. Naval Institute's *Proceedings* magazine.

5

"High OPINTEL" in the Era of the "Maritime Strategy"

A Revolution in Understanding the Soviet Adversary

"Admirals Like Us": The Soviet Union and SLOCs

If it is the role of the intelligence professional to "know thine enemy," it is also an unfortunate human weakness to assume—as depicted in Walt Kelly's parody of Commo. Oliver Hazard Perry's 1813 dispatch from the brig USS *Niagara*—that upon meeting the enemy, he will invariably turn out to be just like us.[1] Different social and military cultures, histories, and experiences, however, can produce commanders who think and act in very different ways. Mirror-imaging the adversary— that is, assuming that his reactions in a given set of circumstances will be the same ones that one would have oneself—is thus a common analytical trap of which the prudent intelligence professional must continually be aware.

Similarly, it is also true that "any serious thinking about strategy must necessarily deal with the effect that one's forces will have on an opponent,"[2] a doubly complex task that involves not simply choosing an optimal course of action for one's own forces but choosing a course that takes into consideration how each particular enemy is likely to react. Therefore, a complex interrelationship between the intelligence and command functions exists in the strategic arena as well as that of day-to-day operations.

These dynamics were no less perplexing during the Cold War than during any other period. After all, "the military strategies of the Soviet Union, the United States, and their various allies had very different historical roots, and the institutions they maintained to educate their officers, train their soldiers, plan their wars, and procure and build their weapons and materiel differed in significant ways from one another."[3] Just as these different military cultures and operational concepts could produce weapons systems that performed differently and had different functions, so also could they produce warfighters who thought and reacted differently. Taking such differences into account at the operational and strategic levels was a challenge for both intelligence professionals and commanders.

The many triumphs of U.S. technical intelligence during the Cold War produced some remarkably good intelligence about the capabilities and status of the Soviet armed forces. Without "regular access to high-level message-like sources and a sustained effort to interpret them,"[4] however, the U.S. intelligence apparatus had great difficulty taking the intelligence art to its highest level: discovering how the enemy thinks and anticipating his plans and reactions. Thus, U.S. naval analysts and strategic planners too often assumed that Soviet admirals would act and react just as American ones would—that is, they would endeavor to bring about fleet-to-fleet actions on the high seas aimed at contesting control of crucial strategic sea lines of communication. As one naval historian described it, for years,

> the predominant view in America was one which saw the Soviets building a naval force with many capabilities similar to that which the United States Navy had developed. Most importantly, the existence of a blue-water Soviet Navy seemed to emphasize, in American minds, the capability for peacetime power projection and the capability for wartime attack on U.S. and Western naval forces and sea lines of communication, as well as a capacity for strategic nuclear strikes from the sea. . . . In short, Americans tended to view the new Soviet naval capabilities in terms of mirror-imaging and refighting World War II.[5]

As a result of such assumptions, for most of the Cold War, U.S. strategists imagined that the naval part of World War III would be a high-technology, nuclear-armed reenactment of the 1939–45 conflict.[6]

A New View Emerges

Despite such traditional mirror-imaging, however, some specialists in Soviet affairs—basing their analysis heavily upon "Soviet naval writings, naval exercises, and construction trends"[7]—gradually "began to develop an interpretation that tried to move away from an American, ethnocentric view of the Soviets."[8] In particular, Robert W. Herrick's 1968 study of Soviet naval strategy argued for an essentially defensive conception of Soviet naval doctrine.[9] Analysts such as James McConnell and others at the Center for Naval Analyses (CNA) also did influential work on this subject in the 1970s.[10]

CNA concluded, for example, that the Soviets planned to withhold their SLBM force during the conventional stages of a war with the North Atlantic Treaty Organization (NATO) and during initial nuclear strikes "in order to provide either a second strike capability or to retain a bargaining chip during [war-termination] negotiations." To this end, CNA believed that Moscow would operate its SSBNs within special "bastions" protected by naval forces dedicated to sea control missions as a means of strategic defense, thus giving the Soviet navy an important war-termination mission. This analysis led CNA analysts to suggest the need for the U.S. Navy to attack or threaten Soviet strategy by developing antisubmarine warfare capabilities in Soviet home waters that could threaten these bastions and thereby enhance the deterrent effect of U.S. naval power. This strategy, they felt, would make it more difficult for the Soviets to rely upon the underwater strategic missile reserve they believed crucial to a warfighting strategy.[11] Thus stated, this analysis encapsulates much of the thinking of the Maritime Strategy of the early 1980s.[12]

Though some of these studies clearly proved remarkably prescient, their authors were for some time prophets without honor in their own country.[13] In the end, it took a series of dramatic intelligence breakthroughs in the late 1970s to tip the intellectual center of gravity within the U.S. Navy against the traditional view.[14] It was not until November 1981, in fact, that an interagency intelligence memorandum on "Soviet Intentions and Capabilities for Interdicting Sea Lines of Communication in a War with NATO" embodied the final agreement of the U.S. intelligence community that CNA had been right all along: the Soviets regarded SLOC attack as a secondary mission. ONI prepared a similar assessment as the Navy's input to a new National Intelligence Estimate (NIE) in 1982.[15]

The intelligence breakthroughs that helped propel the Navy down this path owed much to improvements in U.S. analytic abilities, providing "a vital synergism that brought about a more holistic view of Soviet military advances."[16] Crucially, however, these analytical breakthroughs were confirmed by dramatic "deep penetrations" of the Soviet adversary, penetrations about which it is still impossible—officially, at least—to describe at anything but the most highly classified level. These successes allowed detailed studies of such things as Soviet "command and control arrangements," plans for the use of stand-by reserves,[17] and the conduct of (and after-action analysis of) naval exercises.[18]

The new intelligence sources were "predominantly SIGINT," but also included "some very significant HUMINT penetration of senior echelons of the soviet leadership."[19] These insights also revealed much about how Soviet planners viewed U.S. war planning. Perhaps not surprisingly, "how they viewed U.S. strategy in time of war . . . was about as wrong as our view of the Soviet strategy, prior to that time, had been." As such sources developed, "new classifications of 'sensitive compartmented information' [SCI] were created" for the control of this sensitive information. Handling this new information was difficult, and access was initially restricted to only a handful of high officials.[20] In 1982, in procedures that mirrored the handling of ULTRA information during World War II, small cells of indoctrinated officers were set up on each major fleet staff. With this slowly broadening access, information about the new insights into Soviet operational plans gradually spread throughout the Navy leadership.[21]

As a result, writing meaningfully about lessons from the role of intelligence in the Cold War is exceedingly difficult. The Cold War decades are "arguably the most interesting and certainly the most expensive" in the history of U.S. Naval Intelligence, but they remain heavily "shrouded in classification and . . . may be at the most risk for [historical] preservation."[22] Nevertheless, while discussion of the specifics of these breakthroughs must await future declassification, it has recently become possible to discuss the basic fact that some such "deep penetrations" occurred. It is thus possible to learn lessons about the institutions and organizational cultures that produced them and how they were able to take advantage of the insights they provided.

Regardless of their specifics, it is clear that the results of these intelligence breakthroughs were dramatic. In the late 1970s and early 1980s, several sensitive sources became available which provided us, for the first time, with highly accurate insights gleaned from the highest levels of the Soviet regime. The information derived from these sources confirmed analyses of unclassified Soviet doctrinal writings that had been going on within ONI, at the Center for Naval Analysis, and at DNI-sponsored symposia for several years. . . .

While it lasted, the insights gained from these [deep penetration] sources allowed the U.S. Navy, led by naval intelligence, to totally reassess how the Soviets would fight a war, where their strengths and vulnerabilities were, and how their perceptions and prejudices caused them to view us. This enabled naval intelligence to stimulate and participate not only in a complete rewrite of U.S. naval strategy and the war plans which governed how the U.S. would fight a war with the Soviet Union, but also to plan and conduct meaningful perception management.[23]

In the words of one participant, "We began to understand Soviet perceptions, expectations, and intentions in a possibly unique way."[24]

The combined insights of these highly sensitive "deep penetrations" and of unclassified scholarly analyses of Soviet naval doctrine helped lead the U.S. Navy completely to revise its strategic concept of operations vis-à-vis the Soviet Union, producing the so-called Maritime Strategy. Such insights helped vindicate and amplify upon the open-source insights of CNA and authors such as Herrick, and helped make possible the "slow development of an interpretation that tried to move away from an ethnocentric view of the Soviet in American terms, and began to develop an interpretation in soviet terms on the basis of the Soviet Union's values and the view, aims, and objectives of its leaders."[25]

As Adm. David Jeremiah recalls of the period,

Through a variety of sources, we learned enough about how the Russians perceived their force capability to be, so that we could be much more aggressive in the use of maritime forces. . . . We made assumptions in beginning without that information, that "you are a naval officer, [so] you are going to operate just like I operate." . . . [We assumed that] "everybody looks like me." [But] everybody *doesn't* look like me. They don't think like [me]. Different culture . . . When we understood that the Russians didn't operate the way we did, then we could take advantage of that.[26]

The rest of this chapter tells the story of this revolution—and of the Maritime Strategy's intimate interrelationship with Navy operational intelligence, both in its origin and its execution.

Soviet "Pro-SSBN" Defense-of-Homeland Strategy

As a result of these intelligence breakthroughs, the various U.S. National Intelligence Estimates published on the Soviet Union in the early 1980s were "enormously more insightful than earlier estimates."[27] But this new understanding was an awkward one, because, as two naval intelligence veterans of this period later recounted, "the intelligence that we were presenting to the leadership of the Navy was not what they expected or necessarily wanted to hear. First of all, what we were telling them about the strategy and planned operations of the Soviet Navy [was] completely antithetical to the way U.S. and other Western admirals believed that any Navy would operate."[28]

Indeed, "a new intelligence consensus on the anticipated wartime role of the Soviet Navy had concluded that the Soviets . . . would assume a defensive posture in the event of war," and would focus their efforts upon establishing and defending so-called bastions in which to protect their submarine-based ballistic missile forces.[29] The next global naval war—if it happened—would not be a 1939–45–style conflict. The Soviet fleet would not seek to reach out to interdict the SLOCs critical to the movement of American troops and materiel supporting the ground war in Europe.[30] Rather, the Soviets would seek to dominate specific areas of ocean close to their own shores, seizing and controlling the maritime "terrain" much as a ground commander might. The goal was to protect submarine-based strategic forces hidden therein and to maintain a buffer zone against airborne nuclear strikes from U.S. aircraft carriers.

This has led some to describe the Soviet approach as the conceptual work product of "a group of artillery field marshals with operations analysis degrees."[31] (The oft-cited "field marshal" formulation appears to originate with Adm. Harry Train, who reportedly declared during an intelligence briefing on Soviet naval operations planning that "My God, these [Soviet] flag officers are Army marshals in Navy uniforms!")[32] As Rear Adm. Thomas Brooks has put it, this assessment is "not far wrong, because the [Soviet] General Staff [was] permeated with ground force thinking and the Navy has always been [no more than] a deep-water adjunct to ground forces."[33]

It came to be understood that this fundamentally defensive and territorial focus of Soviet naval doctrine revolved around Soviet concepts of "the nuclear correlation of forces," which, it was believed, powerfully conditioned the outcome of even a non-nuclear conflict with NATO.[34] Where American admirals, steeped in the intellectual traditions of Capt. Alfred Thayer Mahan's sea power theories, focused upon control of the sea-lanes and bringing about decisive engagements, Soviet planners looked at naval power through the prism of "the total military power of the state." Therefore, even if a war with the United States did not involve the actual use of nuclear weapons, such a conflict would still be, "in Soviet eyes, a 'nuclear' war in the sense that the nuclear balance is constantly examined and evaluated in anticipation of possible escalation. Because of this aspect of Soviet doctrine, the Soviets placed a high priority on changing the nuclear balance, or as they term it, the nuclear correlation of forces, during conventional operations."[35] Thus, in a sense Soviet admirals did not view naval operations as having any particular independent logic of their own, but rather through the prism of how they affected the overall balance of strategic power.

This different conceptual starting point led Soviet naval doctrine in a different direction than had been expected by Mahan-schooled American naval strategists. To the Soviets, as it turned out, interdicting Western SLOCs was far less important a mission than "providing combat stability for their SSBNs [ballistic missile submarines] and defeating the West's nuclear-capable strike forces."[36] The "primary naval mission" of the Soviet navy was to favorably influence the overall East/West correlation of forces by providing Moscow with a sea-based strategic nuclear strike capability.[37] In wartime the navy's primary operational goal revolved around preserving that force and protecting the homeland against Western analogues.[38]

Specifically, according to the U.S. intelligence community's 1982 NIE on the Soviet navy, Moscow's naval priorities were, in order of importance,

1. Providing "combat stability" (i.e., protection and support) for Soviet SSBNs, principally through the creation and maintenance of submarine safe havens, or "bastions" in Soviet SSBN deployment areas;

2. Defending the USSR and its allies from NATO sea-based strike forces (i.e., aircraft carriers and Western SSBNs);

3. Supporting ground forces involved in land combat against NATO in Europe or elsewhere; and

4. Interdicting *some* Western SLOCs.[39]

The territorial focus of Soviet doctrine derived from the fact that during this period Western SSBNs were essentially immune to Soviet attack.[40] This relative Western immunity to strategic ASW effectively collapsed the Soviet navy's first and second missions into one assignment of overwhelming priority: keeping *all* NATO forces out of seas close to the Soviet Union itself. The 1982 NIE determined that the Soviet navy's objective in wartime was not to interdict Western SLOCs, but to seize and defend the Kara Sea, the Barents Sea, the northern portions of the Norwegian and Greenland Seas, the Sea of Japan, the Sea of Okhotsk, and the Northwest Pacific Basin. The Navy would then extend "sea denial" operations out to a distance of perhaps two thousand kilometers, in order to protect the homeland against Western carrier-based nuclear strikes.[41]

The shift in the U.S. Navy's understanding of Soviet naval doctrine may be seen from the following chart, which contrasts public statements made in the Department of the Navy's periodically revised pamphlet *Understanding Soviet Naval Developments* between 1978 and 1991. (See facing page.)

Evaluating the New Intelligence and Its Implications

As with much really valuable intelligence, the remarkable new intelligence sources that began providing information in the late 1970s about how Soviet admirals actually planned to fight the Third World War did not yield their bounty to casual intelligence analysis. Indeed, it was some time before the U.S. Navy was able to evaluate it properly and began to understand its profound implications. One of the Navy's first steps in evaluating this information was to establish special teams to study it with the requisite depth and intensity.

The Director of Naval Intelligence, Rear Adm. Sumner ("Shap") Shapiro, chose civilian analyst Richard Haver to lead the analytical work being done by OP-009J within the Office of Naval Intelligence,

The U.S. Navy's Understanding of Soviet Naval Strategy:

**Tracking an Intelligence Revolution through
Illustrative Public Statements**

1978 Assessment	1985 Assessment	1991 Assessment
Office of the CNO, U.S. Department of the Navy, *Understanding Soviet Naval Developments* (3rd ed., January 1978).	Office of the CNO, U.S. Department of the Navy, *Understanding Soviet Naval Developments* (5th ed., 1985).	Office of the CNO, U.S. Department of the Navy, *Understanding Soviet Naval Developments* (6th ed., July 1991).
"The Soviets are firm believers in the old adage that 'the best defense is a good offense.'"	The Soviet navy is "for the first time in its history . . . capable of conducting hostile and aggressive operations if it should desire." It has become "a modern, oceangoing, 'blue water' Navy . . . increasingly capable of accomplishing the full range of naval tasks. . . . The Soviets are employing their Navy in much the same way as the United States, Great Britain and other naval powers."	The principal Soviet navy wartime role is strategic strike. The top priority for non-SSBN forces, therefore, is to provide SSBN forces with "combat stability" by protecting them against attack.
The Soviet navy is focusing increasingly upon fighting a long, conventional conflict with NATO, and is increasingly "challenging the United States in all aspects of maritime activity."		To this end, SSBNs are increasingly deployed in "bastions" surrounded by layered antisubmarine and antiship defenses.
"The Soviets are employing their navy in much the same way as the United States and Great Britain, . . . [and the Navy can now] perform most of the traditional functions of a naval power in waters distant from the Soviet Union."	Nevertheless, the Navy's top two missions are strategic offense and strategic defense. In the defensive mission, great emphasis is placed upon countering NATO antisubmarine warfare in order to protect Soviet ballistic missile	The priority mission for the Soviet Atlantic and Pacific Fleets is to ensure SSBN survival and keep U.S. carrier battle groups as far as possible from the Soviet homeland.
		In time of war, much of the Atlantic and Pacific Fleets would be devoted to the protection of

The U.S. Navy's Understanding of Soviet Naval Strategy:

Tracking an Intelligence Revolution through
Illustrative Public Statements (continued)

1978 Assessment	1985 Assessment	1991 Assessment
Interdicting NATO sea lines of communication (SLOCs) is "one of the most important of the Navy's missions."	submarines (SSBNs). The aim is to "exercise their own type of sea control and hence to provide maritime security for their submarines . . . particularly in those waters considered critical by the Soviet leadership." SLOC interdiction has long been a mission of the Soviet navy, but it is only the fourth of the five main Soviet navy missions.	SSBN bastions. The main mission of most Soviet navy forces, therefore, is primarily defensive. Interdicting SLOCs is a low-priority mission. The only forces that would be available for this in wartime would be those not needed for higher-priority missions such as protecting SSBN "bastions."
The Soviet Navy as Our Deep-Sea Antagonist	Transition Period: Offensive Capabilities but Defensive Mission	The Soviet Navy as a Primarily Defensive Force

reporting directly to Shapiro himself. Dr. Alfred Andreassen—the chief civilian scientist at the Directorate of Naval Warfare (OP-95)—was subsequently also brought into this endeavor as the head of "Team Charlie." That group was populated mostly by line officers whose job it was to assess the implications of the new ideas being developed by Haver's OP-009J.[42] In 1978, under CNO Adm. Thomas Hayward, the Navy also established a Strategic Studies Group (SSG) at the Naval War College, which reported directly to the CNO and worked heavily upon many of these issues of Soviet naval doctrine.[43] Finally, the Strategic Concepts Branch (OP-603), staffed by "line officers who were part of the navy's political-military planning brain trust," played an important role in developing new strategic approaches in conjunction with allied NATO naval commanders.[44]

The "board of directors" for this overall assessment and evaluation effort was something called the Advanced Technology Panel (ATP), an institution established by the Chief of Naval Operations in 1975 and consisting of several senior flag officers under Vice CNO Adm. William Small and his successors.[45] The ATP's official mission—stated in understandably vague terms given the sensitive nature of the project—was to advise the CNO on "issues identified through insights provided by highly sensitive intelligence, future warfighting capabilities available through advanced technology, and innovative strategic thinking."[46]

Over time, as OP-009J's analysis matured, the ATP shifted focus from evaluating Soviet capabilities in light of the new intelligence to devising approaches for acting on this information.[47] Given across-the-board access to even the most sensitive new intelligence, the ATP was able to provide an unmatched, truly "all"-source analytical perspective that helped it understand Soviet perceptions, expectations and intentions in new ways.[48] Issues related to "the Soviet defensive employment issue" represented only "a very small part of the ATP agenda,"[49] but the panel was nonetheless to play an important role in the process that gave rise to the U.S. Navy's new operational approach in the early 1980s.

Selling the New Ideas and Changing the Navy

This focused effort to evaluate and assess the implications of Soviet naval planning helped revolutionize American naval doctrine by giving U.S. commanders a far better understanding of their likely adversary and enabling them to devise strategies and approaches based not upon mirror-imaging but upon genuine insight. Ultimately, the late 1970s and early 1980s represent one of the very few instances in history where the acquisition of intelligence helped lead a nation to completely revise its concept of military operations. In the words of two participants, this period thus stands as an example of "how good intelligence, well-analyzed and well-applied by teams of Intelligence Officers and Line Officers working together, enabled the U.S. Navy to devise a strategy and a set of war plans which would have helped ensure victory, should we have had to fight a war with the USSR."[50]

The fruits of these labors were not fully publicly revealed until January 1986, in CNO Adm. James Watkins's famous article in a special supplement to the U.S. Naval Institute's *Proceedings* magazine, "the nearest thing to a British-style 'White Paper' . . . that we are likely to encounter in the American political system."[51]

As Watkins's effort suggests, the public dissemination of the Maritime Strategy was in part the culmination of a broader effort begun in mid-1981 to develop "an intelligence and persuasive exposition of why we need a Navy . . . a public relations effort aimed at members of Congress, the media and the American public . . . [that] could be drawn upon for internal purposes as well."[52] This has led some to suggest that the Maritime Strategy itself was no more than a cynical public rationalization for larger Navy budgets and Navy Secretary John Lehman's dream of a "600-ship Navy."[53] The Maritime Strategy, however, made its first public appearance only in 1985, when President Ronald Reagan's defense buildup had already passed its peak.[54] Long before this—when these issues were wrapped in the tightest secrecy within the Navy Department and could therefore have no impact upon public opinion—the U.S. intelligence breakthroughs that began in the 1970s had already left their mark upon U.S. naval doctrine in the development of the "Maritime Strategy."

That new intelligence information could be acquired is itself a remarkable tale that owes much to the planning, foresight, and willingness to take risks shown by the Navy's senior leadership during the 1960s and early 1970s, without which these vital "deep penetrations" of the Soviet Union could not have occurred.[55] That the acquisition of such information could lead to wholesale doctrinal revisions, however, is in some ways an even more remarkable story. The institutional history of this Navy "sea change" must be told elsewhere, but in some respects the Navy was simply lucky: the service's leaders were fortunate that these intelligence windfalls could be whispered into ears that were willing to listen.[56]

Not everyone was equally willing to listen, of course. Though one might have expected the Navy's submarine community to grasp Soviet pro-SSBN "nuclear correlation of forces" concepts more quickly than admirals with surface warfare or aviation backgrounds,[57] Admiral Small remembers that U.S. submariners were "not in favor of anti-SSBN concepts."[58] The submarine community's resistance to new strategic thinking about submarine operations, however, apparently did not long survive the retirement of Adm. Hyman Rickover, the founding father of the U.S. nuclear Navy, in 1982.[59] According to Small, it was the Navy Secretariat itself that became the locus of much resistance to the Maritime Strategy, apparently because "the new view of Soviet operations did not support the 600 ship Navy requirement" as strongly as Secretary John Lehman would have preferred.[60]

Operator/Intelligencer Trust and Credibility

The Navy was ultimately willing to listen for several reasons. To begin with, Navy intelligence professionals were themselves fortunate in that they were able to draw upon a considerable reservoir of operator trust and credibility. This illustrates the continued importance of the operator/intelligencer relationship: if senior Navy leaders had not learned to trust intelligence advice and respect those who offered it, the new insights into Soviet war planning would have been worthless. As one former DNI recalled, the Navy's leadership "at the three- and four-star level are people who grew up side by side with intelligence. They understand its importance. It was operationally relevant to them when they were in operational billets." As a result, they learned to trust intelligence as a basis for operational planning thereafter.[61] This was a crucial element in convincing operators to accept ONI's "new thinking" in the late 1970s and early 1980s: "the key was . . . the credibility of the ONI leadership that was presenting this case to the unrestricted line Navy."[62]

By bringing operators and intelligence professionals together to help assess Maritime Strategy–era "new thinking," Team Charlie further improved the already close relationship between the two communities. So successful did this model prove, in fact, that the Navy subsequently institutionalized it through the creation of analytic groups that brought together both intelligence professionals and operators into analytical groups to analyze an adversary's doctrine and tactics. Team Charlie thus provided the model for present-day ONI organizations such as SWORD (Submarine Warfare Operations Research Division, which does submarine analysis), SPEAR (Strike Projection Evaluation and Antiair Research, which assesses air and strike operations), and SABER (Surface Analysis Branch for Evaluation and Reporting, which analyzes surface warfare).[63]

Institutional Dynamics

Senior leaders' receptivity to the new ideas also derived in part from a series of bitter internal debates over Navy spending and force structure in the early and mid-1970s driven by the budget pressures of the post-Vietnam era. As a result, by the late 1970s the search was on for a clear guiding theory around which to build Navy programming. The Navy was forced to think strategically about force structures in order to prioritize its mission planning in an environment of scarce resources. Crudely put, it needed a cognitive guide to program triage, and their search for a grand strategy helped make Navy leaders more receptive to new ideas.[64]

Also crucial to the Navy's receptiveness was the growing interest of senior commanders such as Pacific Fleet commander (and later CNO) Adm. Thomas Hayward in developing Navy operational plans that did not revolve exclusively around the nuclear war envisioned by the national Single Integrated Operational Plan (SIOP). They wanted more flexibility, and sought approaches that might help the United States win a conventional war against the Soviet Union as well.[65] This, too, helped predispose the Navy leadership toward "new thinking" of the sort that naval intelligence and the new operational study groups began to provide.

This new strategic thinking was preached within the Department of the Navy by analysts such as Richard Haver, whom one historian, quoting Rear Adm. Tom Brooks, describes as having been "the Saint Paul of the movement, going forth among the Gentiles (read unrestricted line) and preaching the gospel."[66] Such proselytizing was not without setbacks, most notably the distinctly chilly reception it received from Hayward and from Deputy CIA Director Adm. Bobby Inman when first presented by then-Capt. Thomas Brooks to a conference of fleet CINCs in October 1981.[67] Over time, the movement acquired increasing numbers of influential converts.

Moreover, despite having its origins in times of budget pressures, this interest in more strategic program planning continued into the 1980s, when money flowed more freely for the Navy, and helped improve the process of making strategic thinking an integral part of overall Naval planning. Vice CNO Adm. William Small, for example, in 1982 insisted upon careful strategic appraisals before implementing the annual Program Objective Memorandum process. No longer, he hoped, would the Navy be able to avoid considering strategy when it formulated its plans for ship and weapon construction.[68]

Indeed, Small believes that the primary initial motivation for the new strategic thinking that ultimately became the Maritime Strategy derived from such "programming issues" unrelated to new intelligence information. As he describes it, the strategic ferment that gave birth to the Maritime Strategy grew out of an effort to "make people at all levels of the Navy think about current and future threats, capability and to illuminate and test contentious issues. . . . It was also important to bring reality to the Navy programming and budgeting process and help eliminate parochialism, particularly among platform sponsors."[69] These efforts led to, as Small put it at the time, a push for "rational force employment against realistic threats" rather than "exotic responses to extreme requirements."[70] This, he believed, would produce a more realistic understanding of "how naval forces will be employed in wartime,"[71] and would help end the Navy's "confusion about strategies and analysis related to force *acquisition,* and *strategy* for *winning wars.*"[72]

Thus the Navy's senior leadership found itself particularly interested, during the late 1970s and early 1980s, in finding out "what 'grand tactics' [should lie] behind these [force] employments in meeting U.S. commitments and security needs."[73] This receptivity to new "big picture" strategic planning vis-à-vis the Soviet Union made the Navy especially willing to listen to its intelligence professionals in this regard just at the time when new intelligence insights were helping give ONI a new picture of how Moscow would fight the Third World War. This coincidence of analytical progress and leadership receptivity had dramatic consequences, inasmuch as it made it much easier for the Navy's push for future force-structure thinking to be "properly coupled" with ONI's "growing awareness of Soviet defensive strategy."[74] It also made it easier for this coupling to produce a radical revision of U.S. Navy operational doctrine.

Validation through War Gaming

Another crucial factor in the acceptance of the new ideas was their validation in practice—or at least "virtual" practice—through extensive war gaming. These efforts brought operators and intelligence professionals together to test their theories in something approximating "real life," and proved invaluable in developing ways for the U.S. Navy to counter the operational plans that it now understood the Soviets to have. From the beginning, the Navy leadership chose war gaming as "one of its key analytical tools," and, with the ATP's sponsorship, a series of war games were conducted from 1982 onward, supported by "all-source" intelligence information at the "code word" (SCI) level, to validate key concepts of the Navy's new theoretical approach.[75]

To be sure, according to one participant, the validation of Maritime Strategy concepts "took considerably less than five percent of the ATP's time over the course of the 1981–83 period." In fact, according to Adm. William Small, the ATP itself never "agreed, espoused, or recommended, at least through 1985, that the U.S. Navy embrace an anti-SSBN strategy. . . . Advocating a concept of U.S. naval operations was not within the ATP's purview, particularly on a contentious fleet matter, and the CNO at a subsequent CINC Conference, specifically tabled the issue."[76] Nevertheless, the ATP's support was vital to the SSG wargaming efforts—and thus, albeit indirectly, to the validation of Maritime Strategy concepts.[77]

Through their seamless integration into Navy war gaming, OPINTEL professionals played an important role in testing and validating the new analytical conclusions that underlay the Maritime Strategy. NFOIO established a specialized detachment at the Naval War College at Newport, Rhode Island, in August 1977, dedicated specifically to providing OPINTEL support for war games conducted by the Center for Advanced Research (CAR) there. In its first year, this "Newport Detachment" participated in nine major war games and several minor games and demonstrations.[78] In 1979 the Secretary of the Navy updated this program to the status of a full shore activity, for the purpose of providing "operational intelligence support on Soviet Naval matters and U.S. Navy Operational Intelligence Systems" to the CAR and the War College's Center for War Gaming.[79]

Officially organized as NFOIO-05, the Newport Detachment not only provided OPINTEL support for Naval War College war games but also "worked closely with the Strategic Studies Group" over the next several years in helping produce and verify the assessments of Soviet strategy and doctrine that underlay the Maritime Strategy.[80] The Strategic Studies Group (SSG) was established in 1981 by the CNO, Adm. Tom Hayward. Eight to ten highly regarded post-command Navy line officers from the air, surface, submarine, and later the special warfare communities were specially chosen each summer, along with one or two senior Marines, to go to the Naval War College in Newport. There, away from the pressures of the fleet and Washington, they were given a yearlong assignment to extensively analyze a specific strategic or operational problem or problems. Through the late 1980s, those problems addressed issues arising from ATP deliberations or fleet operations related to the evolving Maritime Strategy. Each SSG reported its findings to the CNO the following spring. SSG veterans of the 1980s rose to occupy a significant number of the Navy's top flag leadership positions in the 1990s and beyond.

Taking advantage of their OPINTEL-derived expertise in seeing the battlespace through Soviet eyes, the NFOIO Detachment formed the nucleus of the "Red" force opposition in Naval War College and SSG war games,[81] thereby also allowing U.S. operational commanders to develop and validate new approaches to gaining advantage over the Soviet fleet. The cadre of OPINTEL professionals at Newport was thus able to play an important role in helping the SSG "examine the strengths and weaknesses of the Maritime Strategy."[82]

Though much of this war gaming focused upon submarine—or more specifically, potential antisubmarine—campaigns, it also played an important role in developing new approaches to surface operations, especially for aircraft carrier battle groups.[83] As John Hattendorf has written, ATP-sponsored war gaming validated the use of U.S. carriers as a kind of "'tactical nuclear reserve,' . . . a nuclear bargaining chip." The carriers tied down Soviet air assets in northern areas while remaining just outside their reach "until that point in a war when it became necessary to negotiate with the Soviet Union whether the war could be terminated or would escalate into a nuclear war."[84] As one participant recalls, such "highly classified all-source war games" helped sell surface and air operators on ONI's new ideas and provided "probably the largest contribution that ONI made to war fighting since World War Two."[85]

The Maritime Strategy

Strategic Concepts

This new understanding of Soviet naval doctrine was the critical element in the Navy's decision to adopt a new "doctrinal foundation [for] U.S. naval power"—an "avowedly offensive maritime strategy toward the USSR in the early 1980s, discarding plans for the kind of [SLOC-focused] defensive barrier strategy that had been put forward in the 1960s and 1970s."[86] This offensive strategy took its cue from the ancient Chinese military theorist Sun Tzu's maxim that "the highest realization of warfare is to attack the enemy's plans" and his advice to attack "what they love first."[87] In what has been described as the fourth and final phase of postwar U.S. planning for conflict with the USSR, the period from the late 1970s through most of the 1980s was marked by "new approaches based on the concept of attacking Soviet military strategies and operational practices, as perceived and understood by military planners in the West, rather than just [attacking] Soviet forces."[88]

This new American approach took various shapes across the spectrum of military activity during the 1980s, showing its face in the U.S. Army's "AirLand Battle" theory, in NATO's "Follow-On Forces Attack" (FOFA) doctrine, and in the defensive strategic nuclear ambitions of the Strategic Defense Initiative (SDI).[89] Its naval incarnation, however, was the Maritime Strategy: having, it seemed, finally understood what Soviet war plans would really look like, U.S. naval strategists set about devising ways to disrupt them.[90]

To be sure, the Maritime Strategy always remained something of a work in progress and never acquired a definitive final form. Rather, it developed over time, being periodically modified according to approaches suggested by the fine-tuning of intelligence analyses and extensive war gaming.[91] Nevertheless, throughout this period the Maritime Strategy revolved around a basic conceptual core firmly rooted in the "new thinking" about Soviet war plans that can be traced to CNA's analyses of the late 1960s and the dramatic intelligence insights of the late 1970s.

Soviet naval doctrine stressed the protection of ballistic missile submarines in order to preserve a favorable "correlation of forces," so the Maritime Strategy sought to hold SSBNs at risk through an aggressive approach to antisubmarine warfare—even beneath the polar ice caps and in Moscow's vital SSBN "bastions."[92] Soviet naval doctrine also stressed keeping U.S. carrier battle groups well beyond the launch points from which carrier-based aircraft could launch nuclear strikes against the Soviet homeland. U.S. commanders therefore staged aggressive exercises in which U.S. carriers surged forward in operations clearly designed to contest the control of the very northern seas they knew Moscow deemed essential to Soviet planning.[93] U.S. submarine force commanders even sent well-publicized surges of attack submarines toward Soviet waters and reportedly staged practice "sinkings" of Soviet SSBNs beneath the polar ice caps in order to demonstrate an ability to threaten these prized assets at will.[94] By such means, the Maritime Strategy sought to "attack the preferred strategy of the Soviet Navy for a general war at sea."[95]

A vital part of the new understanding of Soviet doctrine by U.S. intelligence analysts was the assessment, as embodied in the 1982 NIE, that the Soviet navy's territorially focused defensive operational concept would almost wholly preoccupy it in the event of war. Protection of vital northern waters, it was believed, would occupy "virtually all" of the Soviet navy's two most powerful operational flotillas, the Northern Fleet and the Pacific Fleet, as well as perhaps two-thirds of the attack submarines so feared by Western admirals.[96] In short, "the Russians would assign their most capable air, surface, and subsurface forces to this mission."[97]

The Maritime Strategy thus sought to help make victory possible in a war against the USSR in three principal ways: (1) through destroying as many Soviet SSBNs as possible, thus reducing the strategic nuclear threat to the United States; (2) by launching strikes upon Soviet targets from U.S. carriers; and (3) by tying down the Soviet fleet in static, defensive operations in the far north and thereby preventing it from causing mischief elsewhere. As President Reagan himself put it in a January 1987 strategy document, the Maritime Strategy "permits the United States to tie down Soviet naval forces in a defensive posture protecting Soviet ballistic missile submarines and the seaward approaches to the Soviet homeland, and thereby to minimize the wartime threat to the reinforcement and resupply of Europe by sea."[98] An aggressive forward-focused naval strategy, it was hoped, would also "divert Soviet forces . . . [from] using [naval aviation] air power directly on the Central Front" in Europe.[99] In this fashion, American admirals hoped to help seize the initiative in any general war, allowing NATO to fight and win the kind of war it preferred to fight in Europe.

Conversely, if Western forces in wartime did not move north to threaten Soviet submarine bastions and the USSR itself, more Soviet naval aviation assets would be free to join the battle in Europe and more Soviet attack submarines would be free to move against the vital NATO SLOCs. The Maritime Strategy must therefore be viewed in context with its alternative: the traditional Cold War "defensive barrier" approach to protecting the NATO sea-lanes. Ironically, if indeed ONI now correctly understood Soviet naval doctrine, threats to the transatlantic SLOCs would *increase* the more NATO directly focused upon trying to protect them.

This new U.S. naval doctrine was thus designed to win a war against the Soviets if need be, but its conceptual touchstone was deterrence[100]— that is, trying to prevent the Third World War by demonstrating to Soviet naval commanders that their strategy in it would be a resounding failure. By "denying the Soviets their kind of war" and holding their most cherished assets at risk,[101] U.S. naval strategists hoped to move beyond mirror-imaging and direct their deterrent strategy "not [at] a collection of American theoreticians and scholars, but a Soviet naval leadership that constantly calculates the nuclear correlation of forces and uses those calculations in the decision-making process. By making it clear at the outset that Soviet SSBNs will be at risk in a conventional war, the strategy alters Soviet correlation of forces calculations and thus enhances deterrence."[102]

Some observers criticized the new strategy as being dangerously prone to escalation in crisis, fearing that it might tempt Soviet leaders to use their submarine-based missiles earlier in a crisis than they might otherwise have contemplated, lest by waiting they lose them to U.S. hunter-killer submarines.[103] Nevertheless, U.S. naval leaders embraced it as the best way for NATO to persuade Moscow—whether or not this was, in fact, the case—that a naval war could only be a net loss to the USSR.

Perception Management: Provocation or Deterrence?

The importance of such deterrent dynamics may suggest why the ATP's initial Soviet strategy study group in 1982 and the subsequent larger working group of junior admirals and senior captains formed in 1984 to support the ATP in deterring Soviet strategic options for war focused so much of its attention upon "perception management." This included likely Soviet reactions to American anti-SSBN operations and the effects of command, control, and communications countermeasures (C³CM)—that is, the disruption of Soviet battle-management capabilities.[104] The aim of much of the Maritime Strategy, as one ATP Soviet strategy working group member put it, was to "continuously reinforce in the Soviet mind the perception that it could not win a war with the United States, both *before* a war, to enhance deterrence, and at all phases of the war should it occur. . . . The key point is that the desired prospect must be *as perceived and measured in Soviet terms*."[105] The ATP hoped that if faced with aggressive moves that threatened their control of the Norwegian Sea and other northern areas, "the Soviets would seek war termination prior to increasingly intensive assaults by Marines and CVBGs [carrier battle groups] on the Soviet flanks and without risking nuclear war."[106]

Some commentators have suggested that during a real international crisis with the USSR, the U.S. civilian leadership would not actually permit the Navy to embark upon the contemplated initial moves of
the Maritime Strategy for fear of provoking unwanted escalation.[107]
Nevertheless, even if such moves were at root no more than an extraordinary strategic bluff—perhaps not unrelated to contemporaneous
efforts to create the appearance of dramatic progress toward the Strategic Defense Initiative's avowed aim of constructing a workable defense
against Soviet ballistic missiles[108]—the aggressive U.S. naval exercises
and publicly announced forward-focused war planning of the Maritime
Strategy era might still hope to do much good by "proving" what Soviet
admirals' own doctrinal presuppositions about the correlation of forces
already led them to expect and fear. If the "overriding purpose" of the
Maritime Strategy was to "influence the Soviet strategic mindset" during peacetime,[109] there was reason for U.S. admirals to encourage the
diversion of resources to the far North by playing upon Soviet fears even
if U.S. commanders never expected actually to execute their plans.

In any event, Admiral Small recalls that "the uniformed Navy
never really took a position" with regard to precisely where the line lay
between aggressive Maritime Strategy deterrent actions and destabilizing provocation. "No one knew or should have tried to really know
whether such a strategy would be destabilizing or a good/bad idea. It
was simply an option that needed to be considered at an appropriate
time."[110] Small also cautions that most of "the ATP perception management effort" had "nothing to do with SSBNs of either side"—but
that it is not possible to elaborate further in an unclassified setting.[111]

OPINTEL and the Maritime Strategy

Ability to Refocus upon Regional Crises

Despite its overwhelming focus upon the Soviet adversary, the U.S.
Navy's operational intelligence system continued to display, as it had
during the 1970s, an ability to redirect its attention to various regional
or local trouble spots as the need arose. As events heated up in the
Middle East, following the overthrow of the Shah of Iran by Islamic
militants in 1979 and the outbreak of the Iran-Iraq war in September
1980, the Navy Field Operational Intelligence Office set up a special
task force within the Navy Ocean Surveillance Information Center to

produce daily reports on Iranian and Iraqi naval affairs. NOSIC's Merchant Operations Branch also began producing a multisection support message on all merchant shipping in the Persian Gulf, the Gulf of Aden, the Gulf of Oman, and the Western Arabian Sea; this message was incorporated into situation reports given to national-level U.S. leaders and fleet commands.[112]

As the diffusion of high-technology naval strike systems such as antishipping cruise missiles made third world navies increasingly able to threaten first world capital ships, NFOIO established a World Navies analysis branch out of what formerly had been a panel focused entirely upon Asian navies. Organized in recognition of "the increasing need for operational intelligence on the many high threat and high interest navies of the world *other than* those of the Soviet Union and other Warsaw Pact members," this new branch was designed to provide background information that would enable working OPINTEL analysts to put observed activity into its proper context.[113]

Support for the Maritime Strategy

Antisubmarine OPINTEL

The most important mission of Navy OPINTEL, however, remained that of tracking the Soviet navy itself. Potential Soviet naval activity remained an important target in a regional context. During the tense period surrounding the declaration of martial law in Poland in a crackdown on the trade union Solidarity, for example, NOSIC also began delivering a daily situation report on the USSR's Baltic Fleet—the naval force that might be called upon to support a Soviet invasion should the Polish Communist Party prove unable to crush the popular movement on its own.[114] With the development of the Maritime Strategy, however, OPINTEL's mission became more crucial than ever in a strategic context.

This was particularly true, during the 1980s, for the tracking of Soviet ballistic missile submarines—targets that the Maritime Strategy sought to threaten even in their well-defended "bastions" in Soviet home waters. As one intelligence veteran has noted, detecting a submarine at sea is difficult, and holding it at risk for long periods of time without making it aware of such a threat is very difficult indeed.[115] Yet this was precisely what the Maritime Strategy demanded of U.S. Navy

OPINTEL. This focus upon continuous real-time monitoring of Soviet submarine forces required a huge investment in and emphasis upon operational intelligence of the most challenging sort.

This, then, is the contribution of OPINTEL during the period of the Maritime Strategy. The strategy would have been unimaginable from the outset had the Navy not already possessed an enormously sophisticated and effective operational intelligence system, and the adoption of that strategy required that OPINTEL reach and remain at a level of unprecedented capability. As Vice Adm. Mike McConnell has recounted, after much work and learning, the Navy responded well to these challenges, ultimately succeeding consistently even against targets as uncooperative as Soviet nuclear-powered submarines.[116] The Maritime Strategy thus required more, better, and more difficult operational intelligence than ever before—and got it. This was, perhaps, the apogee of the art.

Because operations to hold Soviet SSBNs at risk pursuant to the Maritime Strategy would require going after them in their defended "bastions," the depths of Moscow's home waters became a major focus of OPINTEL attention. From 1976, as an adjunct to its operational intelligence activities, therefore, NFOIO's "Special Projects" Detachment (NFOIO-06) had been providing "unique support" through in-depth analysis of "various topics relating to U.S. security, Soviet ASW technology and Soviet underwater reconnaissance programs, as well as threat assessments in support of sensitive National intelligence collection programs."[117] Also in keeping with the Maritime Strategy's emphasis upon the threat posed by Soviet naval aviation, NFOIO established a twenty-four-hour Soviet air watch and increased its emphasis upon the Soviet Naval Aviation Readiness Evaluation (SNARE) program.[118]

By July 1980 NFOIO had replaced its prior daily reports on submarine activity by geographic area with a more focused daily message on Soviet "in-area/local area submarine operations and . . . Soviet submarine readiness."[119] Whereas previous Submarine Activity Report (SAR) messages had emphasized Soviet out-of-area submarine deployments, this new "Summary Evaluation of Nuclear Submarine Operational Readiness" (SENSOR) report was designed to exploit "improvements in both the quality and quantity of incoming data" in order to "more fully address the status of the Soviet SSBN force" in its local home-water operational areas.[120] This was anti-SSBN Maritime Strategy OPINTEL at its most focused.

Reorganization

The most important institutional change in the world of Navy OPIN-TEL during this period, however, was the reorganization of NFOIO and NOSIC and their collocation under a single administrative aegis in the federal complex at Suitland, Maryland. The resulting Navy Operational Intelligence Center (NOIC, aka NAVOPINTCEN) was dedicated to providing, among other things, "current operational intelligence on a continuous watch basis, reporting all-source information on foreign naval/naval air movements and operations in progress."[121]

Active-Duty and Reserve Augmentation

With the increased activity and the increased emphasis placed upon OPINTEL during the period of the Maritime Strategy came increased resources. Increases in the number of personnel billets assigned to NFOIO in fiscal years 1981 and 1982, for example—combined with the increasing power of automated intelligence processing—allowed it to take "giant steps toward increasing the amount of intelligence provided to the fleet and other users."[122]

Nor was the additional support during this period limited to active-duty personnel. To meet the OPINTEL and other intelligence needs of the Maritime Strategy period, NAVOPINTCEN received increasing support from Naval Reserve intelligence professionals. By 1985 this reserve support consisted of 127 officers and 28 enlisted members in five dedicated support units within the Naval Reserve Intelligence Program (NRIP)—not including support received by twelve other reserve units, including one attached to the FOSIC serving the Commander of U.S. Naval Forces in Europe (CINCUSNAVEUR).[123] The NAVOPINTCEN reserve support program expanded rapidly during the mid-1980s, with augmentations focusing particularly upon "OPINTEL watchstanding to meet ongoing commitments as well as to achieve adequate training to meet mobilization requirements." By 1986 the program had expanded to 213 officers and 125 enlisted, and reservists played "a vital role" in day-to-day intelligence support for "submarine warfare, surface ship tactics and operations, Soviet naval air activity, and the increasingly complex merchant shipping problem."[124] In 1987 the program reached 221 officers and 131 enlisted, and in 1988—entering a "period of stabilization after . . . enormous growth"—it totaled 224 officers and 107 enlisted.[125]

ELINT and Cryptology

More intensive efforts were also made during the early 1980s to properly exploit the new ELINT source that had become available in the mid-1970s, with the assignment in November 1981 of an ELINT analyst to NOSIC's twenty-four-hour "indications and warnings" watchfloor.[126] This full-time exploitation of ELINT as an OPINTEL source was institutionalized with the creation of an OPELINT (operational ELINT) Analysis Branch within NFOIO. In 1982 NFOIO allocated civilian ELINT specialists to each of the NOSIC real-time watch stations and began testing new Naval ELINT Analysis Tool (NEAT) computer hardware and software.[127]

At the same time that Navy OPINTEL came to include such full-time OPELINT specialists, it was also moving to strengthen its relationship with the National Security Agency and the rest of the U.S. cryptologic community. Because "recent developments in SIGINT related to the Soviet Navy" had "reemphasized the importance of the analytic relationship between NFOIO and NSA," Navy leaders took steps to preserve this relationship despite NFOIO's relocation from Fort Meade to Suitland. Shortly before the move, arrangements were made for NSA to provide a GS-15 civilian employee to serve as technical director at the new NOIC.[128] This official was made responsible for "providing the overall operational intelligence direction and guidance required in conceiving, planning, developing, executing and evaluating the Command's programs and projects and for ensuring appropriate all-source intelligence support to the Department of the Navy as well as effective liaison with NSA." This NSA detailee's principal mission was to help Navy OPINTEL analysts with "the Soviet Navy SIGINT problem."[129]

Technological Developments

The information demands of Maritime Strategy–era OPINTEL placed enormous demands even upon the rapidly developing information technologies of the 1980s. Sophisticated analytical work being done by the Submarine Analysis Group and the Soviet Combatant Readiness Evaluation (SCORE) programs at NOSIC, for example, required massive computerized databases of past Soviet activities against which to compare current operations. As the Navy moved into the 1980s, however, such data storage and manipulation technologies were still comparatively primitive. Command histories from the period warned that "the volume and complexity of information is growing and automation supporting the analytical process is urgently needed,"[130] and that the Naval Intelligence Command had experienced "increasing demands for more sophisticated tools to process data from currently existing sensors as well as an increasing volume of data from new sensor systems."[131] Naval intelligence programmers and systems engineers struggled to meet the challenge.

To help handle this information, a second-generation SEA-WATCH analyst console system was developed in the late 1970s, with full-time watch operations using this new graphic-driven terminal beginning in early 1980. A new automated "dead reckoning" system—that automatically predicted the progress of maritime contacts based upon position data previously reported by the Ocean Surveillance Information System—was also incorporated as a standard SEAWATCH II subsystem.[132] Internal information connectivity was also improved at NAVOPINTCEN through the installation of an electronic Automated Message Handling System (AMHS) to direct message traffic to particular divisional elements.[133]

In a pattern that has since become familiar in the highly automated business world, Navy OPINTEL began a process of near-continuous technological improvements. By 1983 NAVOPINTCEN had developed the Integrated Automated Intelligence Processing System (IAIPS), through which was installed a local area network (LAN) connecting the center's various computers in such a way as to allow analysts to access "any number of applications, regardless of [in] which host processor the application resided."[134] Though commonplace in today's world of server-driven workplace LANs, this was a remarkable innovation in 1983.

Work on a general upgrade to technology employed at OSIS nodes—the OSIS Baseline Upgrade (OBU)—had begun at least as early as 1983,[135] and teleconferencing between NAVOPINTCEN and fleet commands at the SCI level commenced in 1985, beginning with the Commander, Pacific Fleet (CINCPACFLT).[136] Another important step was the development of a new Developmental Unified ELINT Testbed (DUET), a computerized system that automated the receipt and correlation of ELINT intercepts and kept an extensive database of emitter tracks for "subsequent display and analysis."[137] Use of DUET for ELINT processing was "routine" by 1986, at which point it was already providing "correlated output products electrically to SEAWATCH II."[138]

Further steps were also taken to devolve OPINTEL functions to afloat units, thus allowing intelligence staffs directly attached to commanders at sea to have a greater role in the sort of all-source fusion analysis that once had been possible only at the national level. Computer software for a new Naval Intelligence Processing System database was completed in 1984, and was first installed aboard the *Independence* (CV-62) and the *Dwight D. Eisenhower* (CVN-69) later that year. This constituted the first database containing "red, white, and blue data"—that is, information on Soviet/Warsaw Pact navies, neutral naval forces, and U.S., NATO, and other allied fleets—to be distributed to the fleet.[139]

Meanwhile, however, older systems were rapidly being overcome by the torrent of incoming OPINTEL information. By the middle of the decade, SEAWATCH II was already essentially obsolete. Its operations were possible only at "marginal levels from a throughput, performance, timeliness and capability point of view," and the Navy had already been working on a SEAWATCH III for two years.[140] The era of the "continuous upgrade" had arrived.

Additional Intelligence Inputs

The high-level OPINTEL fusion that allowed the Maritime Strategy's aggressive focus upon ASW in Soviet home waters was thus made possible in part by the U.S. Navy's high-technology integration of command, control, computers, and intelligence (C^3I) systems to create a satellite-linked, highly informed hunter-killer network.[141] Also important, however, was the continuing development of additional intelligence sources and their integration into this interconnected scheme. SOSUS inputs of acoustic intelligence locator and identification data,[142] for example, were supplemented during the 1980s by information from Surveillance Towed Array Sensor System (SURTASS) ships—vessels that trailed long hydrophone sets through northern waters and that uplinked semiprocessed acoustic intelligence to OSIS nodes via satellite link.[143] In addition, information also came from Rapidly Deployable Surveillance System (RDSS) units that could be dropped to the ocean floor on very short notice to produce semipermanent mini-SOSUS beds.[144] Such multiple-source ACINT, in fact, provided "the vast majority of information on [submarine] units in deployed status, filling the space between the bookends of national sensors [e.g., satellites] which could accurately report the departure and return of the Soviet SSBNs from their homeports."[145]

Improvements in the analysis of oceanographic phenomena also helped ACINT analysts improve their techniques for finding Soviet submarines attempting to hide in the ocean depths.[146] On a more prosaic note, efforts to track worldwide merchant shipping also came to benefit in 1981 from routine inputs of worldwide shipping data from the maritime insurance giant Lloyd's of London, which were transmitted to NOSIC via AUTODIN (Department of Defense Automatic Digital Network) terminal from December of that year.[147]

Conceptual Work on the Maritime Strategy

In addition to providing the informational predicate for the Maritime Strategy—the real-time battlespace awareness that was necessary for U.S. carrier and submarine admirals to "take the fight to the enemy"—the Navy's OPINTEL legacy was vital to the analytical understanding of the Soviet navy upon which the Strategy was based. To be sure, the intelligence analysis that produced the Maritime Strategy was not *itself* OPINTEL analysis. The deep strategy and doctrine insights into Soviet naval operations of the late 1970s and early 1980s that gave rise to the Maritime Strategy, however, were possible in large part only because so many of the experts who reached such new conclusions were products of the Navy OPINTEL system.

The "OSIS culture" that had begun to develop in the mid-1960s, and that had come to full fruition by the mid-1970s, produced a generation of naval intelligence professionals who possessed an unprecedented wealth of personal and institutional experience of watching the Soviet navy from close range. They also had an enormously close and productive relationship of mutual trust and understanding with U.S. operating commanders whose vessels (and fates) they had shared when maneuvering against the Soviet fleet. By the time the new "deep penetration" sources of the late 1970s began to produce information about the Soviets, this generation of intelligence professionals had already acquired an unequaled peacetime education in Soviet operations.

The new analytical insights that produced the Maritime Strategy were, in effect, a triumph of learning to "get outside's [one's] own preconceptions, in short as well as long-term analysis" and see the world "through the target's viewpoint."[148] The OPINTEL-trained professionals tasked with analyzing the new information that became available in the late 1970s and early 1980s already understood their enemy well. They thus needed far less of a "push" from the new sources than other analysts might have required in order to solve the final riddles of Soviet operational behavior.

OPINTEL as a Weapon

By the mid-1980s, at which point the Maritime Strategy was firmly ensconced as U.S. naval doctrine, OPINTEL had emerged as a tool of extraordinary effectiveness at the strategic level of U.S.–Soviet competition. The methodology of all-source fusion—first adopted by the Navy during World War II and now updated and developed into the age of computers and satellites—allowed OPINTEL analysts to wield a variety of collection systems almost as one. Grist for OSIS's fusion mill came from dozens of underwater listening arrays around the world, an extensive network of ocean-surveillance SIGINT stations, and a system of oceanwide ELINT collection. Other radar detection, merchant ship locator data, visual reports, and electronic collection from platforms at sea provided a vast number of inputs. Combined with a variety of inputs and analytical support from other parts of the sprawling, multibillion-dollar U.S. intelligence community, these torrents of information were knit together via a number of data processing facilities and intelligence analysis centers connected by satellite communications links. All together, this information provided a coherent, real-time operational picture for U.S. naval commanders.[149]

The Maritime Strategy was possible only because the vast and sophisticated OPINTEL system gave U.S. naval commanders an unprecedented picture of their adversary. "For the first time, navy planners and commanders could follow the movements of an enemy navy both theater-wide and globally on a day to day basis, providing a great sense of confidence in analyzing Soviet naval operations."[150]

This was particularly true with regard to antisubmarine warfare. One cannot strike a target one cannot see, and during this period submarines at sea were effectively invisible *unless* one possessed the ability to cross-correlate such far-reaching and diverse information sources with "near-real-time" rapidity. As Adm. David Jeremiah later recalled, antisubmarine OPINTEL became extremely effective:

> When Mike McConnell was my N-2 at CINCPACFLT . . . he had unique stuff that he could use to identify by hull number the identity of Soviet subs, and therefore we could do a

body count and know exactly where they were. In port or at sea. If they were at sea, N3 [Assistant Chief of Staff for Operations] had an SSN [nuclear-powered attack submarine] through SUBPAC [Commander, Submarine Force, U.S. Pacific Fleet] [on them], so I felt very comfortable that we had the ability to do something quite serious to the Soviet SSBN force on very short notice in almost any set of circumstances.[151]

With the OPINTEL concept having been brought to technological maturity, American antisubmarine warfare could pose a very real threat to the naval assets most prized by Soviet strategists—ballistic missile submarines—thus making intelligence-driven ASW a strategic military asset.[152] Because the Soviets lacked an equivalent OPINTEL capability, however, their ASW could present NATO with no countervailing threat. As suggested by Moscow's view of ultimate outcomes hinging upon the strategic nuclear "correlation of forces," the Soviet navy's "most critical defensive task" was the destruction of enemy SSBNs before they could launch their missiles at the Soviet homeland.[153] The Soviets certainly tried to emulate U.S. OPINTEL capabilities in some respects, deploying limited ocean surveillance hydrophone arrays, land-based SIGINT stations, satellite-based ELINT and radar satellites, and ocean-going intelligence-gathering ships (AGIs) and reconnaissance aircraft.[154]

To maintain this comparative advantage in OPINTEL capabilities, U.S. intelligence analysts spent much time and effort assessing and monitoring the "at-sea ASW threat" posed by Soviet naval forces and by Soviet research and development efforts in both acoustic and nonacoustic detection systems.[155] U.S. Navy OPINTEL professionals engaged in a continual operational duel of wits with Soviet naval commanders, who during the early 1980s continually probed and tested the limits of U.S. battlespace awareness and operational responsiveness. The early 1980s were thus heady days for OPINTEL. As Comdr. J. R. Reddig remembers, for example, the summer of 1983 was in some ways the "ultimate experience" for OSIS professionals.[156] At that time, in an effort to threaten the U.S. mainland in response to NATO's deployment of ground-launched cruise missiles (GLCMs) and Pershing II intermediate-range ballistic missiles (IRBMs) in Europe, Soviet SSBNs lurked in unprecedented numbers off each American coast. At the same time, Soviet nuclear-powered attack submarines conducted operations near the U.S. SSBN bases at Kings Bay, Georgia, and Puget Sound, Washington. It was an enormous challenge for OSIS to monitor these deployments and provide useful operational intelligence to U.S. ASW commanders.

Thanks to the efforts of the OSIS watchfloors, it was clear to the American authors of the 1982 National Intelligence Estimate on the Soviet navy that while U.S. OPINTEL provided NATO navies some chance to conduct effective ASW work, the Soviets "probably recognize . . . that there is a wide gap between the importance of this task and the capability of their current forces to carry it out. . . . They probably also recognize . . . that they do not now have the capability to detect U.S. SSBNs operating in open ocean areas or to maintain contact or trail if a chance detection occurs."[157]

The advent of longer-ranged U.S. Trident submarine-launched ballistic missiles carried aboard *Ohio*-class SSBNs in the 1980s made the Soviets' ASW task even more difficult by greatly expanding the area of ocean where U.S. submarines could operate while still holding Soviet land targets at risk.[158] All in all, Moscow's attempt at real-time, all-source intelligence fusion lagged far behind U.S. Navy OPINTEL and lacked "any significant capability to detect deployed submarines, especially in open-ocean areas such as the central Atlantic or Pacific."[159] Any strategic naval war between East and West, it was therefore hoped, could have only one outcome.

OPINTEL during the era of the Maritime Strategy thus demonstrated how good intelligence can be used, in effect, as a weapon of war—one that helped the U.S. Navy develop the capability to "bring the Soviet Navy to their knees."[160] The imbalance of OPINTEL capabilities between the United States and the USSR provided NATO a potentially decisive advantage over the Warsaw Pact in the event of war. It allowed the U.S. Navy to threaten the only strategic nuclear assets Moscow might expect to survive attacks upon land-based strategic systems (missile silos and bomber bases) while U.S. SSBNs remained essentially invulnerable. As Vice Adm. Thomas Wilson recalls, "The knowledge that the Soviets had [was] that we were very good at our OPINTEL mission and therefore good at our operational mission of war at sea—ASW, protecting our carriers, projecting power. . . . [Eventually,] they realized we were good at finding them, [and] attacking them if necessary. You saw OPINTEL and operational ability contributing to the strategic environment that was developed."[161]

If indeed it was "the main objective of the [Maritime] Strategy . . . to enhance deterrence by attacking the Soviet strategic mindset before war began,"[162] Navy OPINTEL was perhaps one of the West's most powerful weapons and may have contributed in important ways to NATO's victory in the Cold War.[163]

6

Transition, Refocus, and the Future

A New Strategic Environment

Diminished Soviet/Russian Threat

By making possible the Maritime Strategy of the 1980s, U.S. Navy operational intelligence performed its last great service of the Cold War. With the collapse of the Warsaw Pact in 1989, the disintegration of the Soviet Union itself by the end of 1991, and the ensuing period of organizational confusion and financial austerity for the Russian armed forces, U.S. naval intelligence—and its operational component—entered a new era.

To be sure, the threat posed during the Cold War by the Soviet navy, now flying solely Russian colors, did not disappear. Despite the maintenance of a sea-based strategic nuclear force and a number of increasingly quiet and capable attack submarines, however—and Moscow's long-delayed acquisition of a conventional aircraft carrier (ultimately christened the *Kuznetsov*)—Russia's fleet was reduced to a shadow of its former self. Moscow remained America's most powerful potential adversary, but by the early 1990s it had become merely one potential adversary among others in a world that now seemed to contain few threats of any real immediacy. Particularly after the United States' remarkably easy triumph in destroying the Soviet-supplied and train-ed Iraqi armed forces in the Gulf War, the perceived military and political threat from Moscow reached perhaps its lowest point since the Bolshevik coup of October 1917. Geopolitically speaking, the 1990s ushered in an entirely new world.

These changes had an enormous impact upon U.S. Navy operational intelligence. With an organizational and theoretical genealogy running directly back through the strategically polarized Cold War years to Allied efforts to combat the German U-boat threat in the Atlantic, Navy OPINTEL had been extraordinarily well adapted to the task of maintaining a comprehensive, real-time picture of a single, overwhelming foe. Able to spend entire careers dedicated to understanding the Soviet fleet, the Navy's intelligence professionals were able to base on-the-spot operational assessments upon a tremendous base of accumulated personal and institutional knowledge and experience with Soviet naval operations.

Certainly, Navy OPINTEL repeatedly proved able to adapt to the imperatives of providing time-urgent intelligence support during various regional crises (e.g., during the mining of Haiphong Harbor or the Yom Kippur war). Throughout the Cold War, however, the fundamental focus of all OPINTEL efforts remained the Soviet Union. As Michael Herman has written, "Modern intelligence got its peacetime form through the Cold War. The Soviet target (and its substantial Warsaw Pact allies) dominated most Western efforts. 'It is difficult to exaggerate how thoroughly the gathering of information on the Soviet Union, and especially its military power, dominated U.S. intelligence operations since the Cold War began.'"[1]

In the 1990s, however, no such obvious and overwhelming adversary presented itself, and intelligence professionals no longer had the luxury of having decades in which to learn the nuances of their adversary's behavior. In intelligence as in other spheres, where the international order of the Cold War had previously "provided a focal point for Free World policies," the Cold War's clarity of focus was quickly "blurred by a whirlwind of historic change."[2]

According to DNI Rear Adm. Edward Sheafer, the stable bipolar strategic alignments of the Cold War were quickly replaced with complex, shifting multilateral alliances, with global competition and global relationships recast along geoeconomic and ethnic lines in an environment of high uncertainty and low predictability. In fact, he believed that the basic criterion of national security had shifted from one focusing upon national *strength* (in a clear competition with a global adversary) to one revolving around national *vulnerability* (of a dominant power to a variety of shifting and complex lesser challenges).[3] These changes produced significant new challenges for Navy operational intelligence.

Shifting Regional Challenges and Littoral Warfare

The loss of an active and powerful single enemy at sea proved profoundly disorienting to the OPINTEL community. As the Director of Naval Intelligence (DNI) himself wrote in 1993, "The changed world poses new challenges for the intelligence community. For over four decades, we in intelligence were able to focus most of our attentions on a very clearly defined, unambiguous threat from the Soviet Union and could comfortably treat all other threats more or less as lesser involved cases. . . . That Soviet force and those underlying assumptions no longer pertain."[4]

The U.S. intelligence community's continuity of effort and focus upon the USSR was shattered by the events of 1989–91. According to former CIA Director Robert Gates, some 50 to 60 percent of Central Intelligence Agency resources were directed against the Soviet Union and its allies during the Cold War. By 1993, however, only some 13 percent was reportedly directed against the countries of the former Soviet Union.[5]

In the 1990s, in place of the Soviet threat, the United States entered a complex and shifting geopolitical environment in which it was confronted with a dizzying succession of varied and much weaker adversaries du jour. These ranged from fanatical militiamen in Somalia, semiorganized bandits loyal to the deposed dictator in Haiti, scattered Iraqi air defense units during a long struggle of aerial attrition in the Gulf, and various military and paramilitary units in Bosnia-Herzegovina and Kosovo. In a broader sense, in DNI Sheafer's words, this may have represented less a wholly new world than "a *reversion* to historic national roles" such as that played by the early U.S. Navy in suppressing the Barbary pirates.[6] Nevertheless, the institutions and practices of Navy OPINTEL—born during the all-out fights against Germany and Japan and raised on a diet of superpower competition—had never encountered such ever-shifting and formless threats.

Only once in the 1990s did U.S. naval forces ever come close to confronting an adversary of more than local power—during the tense period in March 1996 when Beijing fired "test" ballistic missiles into waters off Taiwan. And in the end this proved no more than a small distraction from the Clinton administration's policy of "strategic partnership" with the People's Republic of China. For the most part, the OPINTEL community could only prepare itself for rapid shifts between different targets in relatively short cycles of "thunderburst violence" around the world.[7]

In some respects, naval OPINTEL confronted a post–Cold War variation of the dilemma that confronted more predictive politically and economically focused American intelligence components with the globalization of the U.S.–Soviet rivalry during the age of decolonization beginning in the early 1960s. In 1963, for example, CIA Director Allen Dulles had written that it was no longer possible "to predict where the next danger spot may develop. It is the duty of intelligence to forewarn of such dangers so that the government can take action. No longer can the search for information be limited to a few countries. The whole world is the arena of our conflict. . . . To meet this threat we will need to mobilize our assets and apply them vigorously at the points of greatest danger and in time."[8]

During the 1960s, this challenge still occurred within an overall context in which the ultimate adversary—the USSR—was clear. Moreover, the CIA's Cold War challenge was largely met simply by an expansion of budgets and manpower. During the 1990s, however, Navy OPINTEL was expected to adjust to even more sweeping environmental changes during a period of budgetary and personnel contraction.

Nor was it simply that the post–Cold War world made it difficult to acquire an intimate knowledge of the adversary's operations. The Navy faced additional difficulties because the world of the 1990s presented challenges to U.S. military power, primarily in coastal areas. Rather than pitched battles with the Soviet fleet on (and under) the high seas of the far north, U.S. admirals now prepared for conflicts with highly diverse opponents in littoral areas around the world.[9] This presented unique challenges, because operations in shallow waters presented not only the "normal" threats confronting "blue water" navies but also threats from land-based aircraft, surface-to-surface missiles, small boats, naval mines, coastal defense artillery, and even waterborne special operations forces. Even in areas of OPINTEL's Cold War strengths, such as antisubmarine warfare, littoral combat presented new problems, as the Royal Navy had discovered in the Falklands when chasing Argentina's German-made Type 209 diesel-electric submarine, the *San Luis*. Shallow-water ASW is enormously difficult for even the best-trained naval forces.[10]

To cope with these new potential areas of interest and operations, the various components of the naval intelligence system set about trying rapidly to improve their knowledge base in nontraditional areas of the world. To give just two small examples noted in command histories from the period, the secretive Joint Intelligence Research Office (JIRO)—dedicated to "sensitive source exploitation, database efforts, and analysis coordination/production programs"—"dramatically expanded" its efforts to "cover rest-of-world (ROW) issues."[11] Similarly, the detachment of ONI intelligence professionals supporting the Strategic Studies Group and naval war-gaming efforts at the Naval War College in Newport, Rhode Island, expanded its activities to include non-Soviet scenarios. During 1990, for example, Newport Detachment members "broadened their expertise by participating in games requiring them to play or control the actions of Third World nations and international terrorist organizations"[12] and "stressing littoral operations by naval forces."[13]

This kind of adaptation was the bread and butter of naval intelligence as the Navy moved into the 1990s, and fortunately so. As luck would have it, the February 1990 war game at the Naval War College revolved around a (then) fictional Iraqi invasion of Kuwait and Saudi Arabia. The lessons learned during this scenario proved very useful later that year, when a *real* Iraqi invasion of Kuwait occurred—thus setting the stage for the Gulf War of January–February 1991.[14]

Unprecedented Challenges

All in all, the new strategic environment of the 1990s presented Navy OPINTEL with an unprecedented challenge. It now faced a shifting, unfocused, and unpredictable world of "enormous uncertainty in regions critical to our national interests."[15] This new environment required, as U.S. military authorities saw it, "a more diverse, flexible strategy which is regionally oriented"[16] and "swift to respond, on short notice to crises in distant lands."[17] Since this new strategy emphasized the increased forward deployment of U.S. naval forces in unstable areas—"with the objectives of *preventing* conflicts and *controlling* crises"[18]—the question was: How could OPINTEL adapt to meet these challenges in an era of significantly reduced military budgets and manpower?

Post–Cold War Developments in Navy OPINTEL

OPINTEL Goes "Purple"

JICs and JACs

Following the Goldwater-Nichols Bill of 1986, which restructured the U.S. military command structure into a series of worldwide joint-service regional and functional commands, the OPINTEL community was also restructured, albeit gradually. In particular, the major development of the late 1980s and early 1990s in operational intelligence was the creation of joint (or "purple" in military jargon) intelligence watchfloors at the joint-command level. Thus, Navy organizations such as the Fleet Intelligence Center Pacific (FICPAC) and Fleet Ocean Surveillance Information Center Pacific (FOSICPAC), both at Pearl Harbor; the Fleet Intelligence Center Europe and Atlantic (FICEURLANT) and the Fleet Ocean Surveillance Information Center Atlantic (FOSICLANT) in Norfolk; and the Fleet Ocean Surveillance Information Center Europe (FOSICEUR) in London were folded into new joint-service fusion centers such as the Joint Intelligence Center Pacific (JICPAC) at Pearl Harbor, the Atlantic Intelligence Command (AIC) (which subsequently by the end of the decade became the Joint Forces Intelligence Command [JFIC]), and the Joint Analysis Center at Molesworth, England (JAC Molesworth).[19]

Functioning as the OPINTEL specialists for their commander's area of responsibility, theater-level JICs provided information both "up" to national-level commanders and "down" to various service components, as well as performing their primary duty of supporting the theater commander.[20] Except for the unorthodoxy of conducting all-source intelligence fusion in analysis centers staffed by personnel from various services—which cut against the grain of longstanding service-focused parochialism—there was nothing conceptually new about these centers. The development of the JICs (Joint Intelligence Centers) and JACs (Joint Analysis Centers) was nothing more (and nothing less) than an extension into the joint-service arena of the OPINTEL concept pioneered by the Navy in the 1960s and 1970s. The JICs and JACs were "OSIS by another name."[21] Though its origins were as a naval art deriving from the peculiar operational intensity of day-to-day U.S.–Soviet maneuvering at sea, the concept of OPINTEL "knows no service boundaries" and was soon "being practiced on joint-service watchfloors" around the world.[22]

The drive toward "jointness" was often a rocky one. Even the Navy—which had pioneered the node-based OSIS model followed by the new JICs and whose DNI spearheaded the effort to ensure that Navy OPINTEL drove the JIC concept—was reportedly less than enthusiastic about developing a truly "purple" intelligence culture. By one account, in fact, the Navy's support for the JIC project derived largely from nothing more principled than a fear of budget cuts. The OSIS system, for example, was funded by the General Defense Intelligence Program (GDIP) at the national level, whereas Army and Air Force intelligence budgeting was done largely at corps level or below. The specter of GDIP reductions, therefore, held special dangers for Navy OPINTEL that it did not for the other services, and may have increased the Navy's willingness to welcome the Army and Air Force into "joint" operational intelligence.[23] Nevertheless, "jointness" moved slowly ahead, drawing in important ways upon Navy OPINTEL practice.

The Navy Leads the Way

Understood in this light it is not surprising that in establishing the basic organization and working relationships of the new joint-service JIC/JAC structure, Navy OPINTEL played a crucial leadership role. The Navy's success during the OSIS period with integrating all-source intelligence production into the fabric of operational decision making had already begun to be followed by the other services independently.[24] In the JIC/JAC era, these various efforts all came together at the joint-service level.

Because Navy OPINTEL had no real analogue in the other services,[25] however, it fell to veterans of the OSIS system to help build the mechanisms for all-source intelligence fusion on the new "purple" watchfloors.[26] As one former DNI noted in 2000, "If you look today . . . you'll see [that] a number of people occupying key positions at the Joint [Intelligence] Centers and on Joint Staffs throughout the world are frequently Naval Intelligence professionals, and Intelligence enlisted specialists as well, because of the experience our people have in dealing with operational intelligence and developing the capabilities and procedures that evolved into OSIS and are now evolving in the Joint arena."[27] As one OPINTEL veteran remembers, "When the world fell apart [at the end of the Cold War], and the Navy went 'joint,' the Navy wanted to inculcate the idea of OPINTEL [fusion] to the Air Force and Army folks."[28] Navy intelligence professionals hoped that the "ethos of the OSIS era would help educate the other Services in the fusion intelligence art."[29]

Inculcating an OPINTEL culture in the other U.S. services required some tact. In a bow to rival services' sensibilities, for example, former DNI Jake Jacoby has emphasized that the key to the Navy's credibility in this regard was not "preaching the 'Navy way'" but rather "demonstrating the operational relevancy of the way we do business to the operators. And if you do that, it's sort of like the ballfield out in the middle of Iowa [in the motion picture *Field of Dreams*]: 'If you build it, they will come.'"[30] Fortunately, the OPINTEL model proved compelling enough to win converts in other branches, and before long "a lot of Army and Air Force seniors [began] asking for Navy J2s and Navy commanders in their JICs."[31]

The process did not always run smoothly. During the Gulf War of 1991, for example, Army intelligence professionals had far more difficulty than their Navy counterparts in integrating all-source national sensor inputs into their intelligence products, and took some time to become proficient in this aspect of the fusion process.[32] Even as late as 1996, in fact, former Deputy Director of the Central Intelligence Agency, NSA Director, and DNI Adm. William O. Studeman declared that the other services were only "just beginning" to catch on.[33] Indeed, by some accounts, quality OPINTEL support in the early "jointness" period suffered markedly from the integration of the other services. As Capt. J. R. Reddig recounted it, for example, the Navy clearly pulled the other services "up" less than they pulled the Navy "down."[34] Nevertheless, joint OPINTEL gradually improved as the various services learned to work with one another, and as advances in high-speed satellite communications and computer workstation interconnectivity made it ever easier for information and analyses to be shared.

By the late 1990s, however, the new system was functioning well, and OSIS-type organization had become firmly entrenched as the prototype of the joint watchfloor.[35] Interestingly, the all-source fusion model was increasingly adapted elsewhere in the U.S. intelligence community as well. In the late 1980s and early to mid-1990s, for example, the CIA developed a series of "fusion centers" designed to achieve "community-wide intelligence fusion" on high-interest subjects— specifically, counterterrorism, counternarcotics, counterintelligence, and nonproliferation.[36] In late 1999, moreover, the Federal Bureau of Investigation (FBI) also announced plans to reorganize its analytical offices to create an overall Investigative Services Division. The new unit would handle a wide array of intelligence-related and criminal investigative information in an effort to provide fused multisource analytical support for the bureau's various investigative and operational components.[37]

The OPINTEL analysis pioneered within OSIS clearly seemed to have a future in the post–Cold War world. Some of the more arcane analytical techniques pioneered by Navy OSIS analysts, in fact, proved useful during the Gulf War. This was particularly the case during the U.S. military's frantic efforts to find and destroy Iraqi SCUD missiles that threatened to draw Israel into the conflict and tear apart the international coalition so painstakingly built by President George H. W. Bush. As Richard Haver recounted, in frustration at its lack of success in "SCUD hunting," the U.S. intelligence community turned in desperation to analysts at the Submarine Desk at the Naval Operational Intelligence Center. The NOIC sub hunters provided important analytical strengths to the SCUD hunters by virtue of their long experience in finding hidden adversaries—or at least narrowing areas that need to be searched. This was based less upon positive identification of a stealthy and noncooperative target than upon the skillful use of negative information and inferences based upon probabilities of detection within a given search zone. Ultimately, however, their efforts produced few results, because the brief war concluded just as their new analytical approaches to "SCUD hunting" were beginning to bear fruit.[38]

As it turned out, the OSIS organizational model also returned to its country of origin. Just as U.S. Navy OPINTEL during World War II had been based on a model developed by the British Admiralty, by the end of the century British and Australian watchfloors were equipped with the American-made OSIS Baseline Upgrade system.[39]

Organizational Changes at the Office of Naval Intelligence

ONI Consolidation

The Office of Naval Intelligence also went through its own period of reorganization in the early 1990s. With the theater JICs now providing day-to-day OPINTEL support to the theater commanders in chief (CINCs) who now had operational control over the Navy's regional fleets (and all other U.S. forces in their AOR), ONI's role evolved into that of "providing basic and background maritime intelligence for the JICs."[40] Pursuant to an OPNAV directive of October 1991, therefore,

ONI disestablished its separate national-level OPINTEL centers and merged its operations into a single, overall analytical command—the Naval Maritime Intelligence Center, aka NAVMIC or sometimes NAV-MARINTCEN.[41] NAVMIC contained the consolidated components of the three naval intelligence commands previously based at Suitland, Maryland: CTF 168 (which handled certain human intelligence issues), the Naval Technical Intelligence Center (NTIC), and the Navy Operational Intelligence Center (NOIC).[42] Within NAVMIC, the Current Operations Division within the Navy Maritime Operations Center (NMOC) of the Directorate of Intelligence still maintained a twenty-four-hour watchfloor. At the same time, NAVMIC's OPINTEL Branch also "continued its unique effort in support of local consumers."[43] Still, with the joint JICs firmly in place, it was clear that the primary locus of OPINTEL for both the Navy and the U.S. military as a whole had devolved to the theater-level commands.[44]

In 1993 this consolidation process took another step, bringing the three principal remaining naval intelligence components under the same roof by pulling together NAVMIC, the Naval Intelligence Activity (NAVINTACT), and the second-echelon headquarters of the Naval Intelligence Command into a single ONI framework.[45] In October of that year the consolidated ONI began moving into a new building in Suitland, the National Maritime Intelligence Center (NMIC), where it remains today as a management headquarters activity organized into various directorates.[46] Except for the war gaming and Strategic Studies Group support performed by the renamed ONI vice NFOIO or NOIC Detachment at the Naval War College in Newport, Rhode Island,[47] and the Naval Security Group at NSA, all of the Navy's varied intelligence-related components had been brought under the same roof.

Reserve Utilization

Like the rest of naval intelligence, the reserve program went through great changes with the end of the Cold War. In 1989 some 229 officers and 131 enlisted personnel supported ONI—organized into ten regular units and one specialist cryptologic unit—and progress continued in giving reserve units access at their drill sites to facilities certified for secure compartmented information.[48] The Iraqi invasion of Kuwait in August 1990 and the American-led multinational military buildup that made possible Iraq's expulsion in early 1991 required the Navy to take unprecedented advantage of its intelligence reservists. Reservists were mobilized for the war on an individual basis, but in considerable numbers, making 1990 "the most significant year in the history of NAVOPINTCEN's Reserve Program." Reservists augmented naval intelligence activities in virtually all areas, including OPINTEL: among other things, reservists helped staff the Persian Gulf–focused ONI Crisis Action Team (CAT) watchfloor.[49] During the course of Operations Desert Shield and Desert Storm in 1990–91, more than four hundred naval intelligence reservists were called up to augment intelligence staffs in Washington and the Middle East.[50]

After the Gulf War, however, the Intelligence Reserve followed the rest of the Navy in facing considerable personnel and budget reductions. Over the course of 1994, for example, reserve intelligence billets nationwide—including personnel supporting ONI as well as other Naval and joint components—were cut by 81 officer and 111 enlisted positions, reducing the program total from 1,171 to 979.[51] By the end of 1995, further cuts had brought the total reductions since January 1994 to 335 billets.[52] The pace of these reductions did not continue, and by the end of the twentieth century ONI had nearly 800 reservists assigned to it, but the drawdown of the mid-1990s left the program significantly smaller than in its halcyon days of the late 1980s. This made it more difficult for the reserve units to focus upon the increasingly novel and complex "rest of world" littoral threats with which it had little prior experience.

Technological Changes

While all of this was going on, important developments in communications and computing technology were revolutionizing the capabilities of shipboard all-source OPINTEL fusion. Perhaps most important of all was the Navy's rapid progress in pursuing the "holy grail" of warfighting in the information age: communications bandwidth.[53]

During the Gulf War, U.S. combatants had experienced difficulties receiving the high-volume electronic communications that were coming to typify "joint" warfighting. To the Navy's embarrassment, for example, its aircraft carriers did not have the ability to receive satellite transmissions of the huge Air Tasking Order (ATO) generated by joint (though largely Air Force) mission planners, and thus had to fly it aboard each day on spools of magnetic tape. By the mid-1990s, however, the development of the high-capacity CHALLENGE ATHENA satellite receiver gave Navy carriers and command ships unparalleled communications power.

Improvement of Older Systems

The rapid pace of information system development in the 1980s had rapidly made earlier variants of Navy OPINTEL systems such as SEA-WATCH II obsolete. In an attempt to keep up with the computer revolution, for example, ONI developed a SEAWATCH III system in the late 1980s.[54] In such an environment of rapid technological change, making new systems compatible with the comprehensive historical databases ONI had been accumulating since the 1960s was not easy. SEAWATCH III conversion was extremely difficult and required that over four million data points be manually reviewed before the archived data tapes could be successfully read by the new computers.[55] Nevertheless, database conversion had been completed by January 1990 and the transition to SEAWATCH III completed soon thereafter,[56] though it was apparently not fully up to speed until at least late 1991.[57]

To improve the interconnectivity of various intelligence centers and allow the better exploitation of such new systems, ONI also continually upgraded the personal computer (PC) workstations employed by intelligence analysts and watchstanders.[58] New automated data processing equipment was also deployed to OSIS nodes such as FOSIF Rota, FOSIF WESTPAC, and FOSIC LANT.[59] E-mail links were established between ONI, the Pentagon, and the Defense Intelligence Agency (DIA) in 1992, and the Coast Guard and the National Military Joint Intelligence Center (NMJIC) were both given remote access to SEAWATCH III.[60] In 1993 analysts' online access to information was improved still further, with the completion of an "INFONET" CD-ROM-driven database of "open-source" intelligence information and the implementation of electronic access to "numerous classified and unclassified databases such as INTERNET and FEDWORLD."[61] Upgrades were also made in the WHARFMAN system at ONI in 1994, improving ONI's ability to electronically transfer SIGINT information directly from the National Security Agency—a vast improvement upon the old method of transferring tape spools by courier.[62]

By the end of the 1980s, ONI had also begun an "ambitious training and education program" for ONI personnel "in an attempt to keep pace with the new technology which has been introduced in many areas of the Command."[63] ONI considered this "aggressive educational agenda" employing "formal, informal, and on-the-job sources" necessary in part because the technology was changing so fast: the new computers that were becoming available were quite powerful, but personnel "required significant training and dedicated support to achieve the promised result" of "better analysis" using these new capabilities.[64]

New Systems: JDISS and INTELINK

Nor did the pace of change slow at all during the 1990s. Indeed, in May 1997 the Navy saw initial delivery of components for SEAWATCH-R, a new system designed to replace the venerable SEAWATCH architecture completely.[65] This new scheme, based on the new Joint Maritime Command Information System (JMCIS), was itself viewed as only a temporary expedient, being deemed merely a "migration system for functions performed by SEAWATCH III" and "an intermediate step" toward more comprehensive global information systems to come.[66]

More dramatically, in this era of joint-service intelligence centers and theater-level OPINTEL watchfloors, intelligence information systems—as the JMCIS acronym suggests—were themselves going "purple."[67] The most successful "joint" information system, by the end of the 1990s, was the Joint Deployable Intelligence Support System (JDISS). This program, spearheaded by ONI as the executive agent for the Defense Department in this regard, began in 1993 as a relatively small program to provide 53 units to various theater-level unified commands and to DIA. It was so successful, however, that it rapidly expanded to become the ubiquitous intelligence support console for OPINTEL in the information age.[68] By the end of 1993 some 120 units had been installed, and by the end of 1995 this number had mushroomed into the thousands.[69] A number of JDISS units were even installed with foreign allied navies, forming "the technical core of a permanent . . . intelligence-sharing architecture with ONI." By the end of 1995 foreign users or soon-to-be-purchasers of JDISS included Canada, France, Spain, Japan, Britain, Italy, Norway, Australia, and the NATO Communications and Information Systems Agency.[70]

Essentially an Internet-based PC workstation, JDISS allowed access to the remarkable new global INTELINK network—a classified intelligence information web analogous to the unclassified Internet/World Wide Web that revolutionized global connectivity in the civilian world during the 1990s. JICs and national-level intelligence agencies had merely to upload information onto their home servers in order to give anyone in the system access to *any* of it— including e-mail and video teleconferencing (VTC) interaction with the authors—in real time.[71] It was gradually integrated into the Global

Command and Control System (GCCS), the more Navy-specific JMCIS, the Army's All-Source Analysis System (ASAS), and the Linked Operations-Intelligence Centers Europe (LOCE) system. JDISS tied together the entire U.S. national security community and helped "break down traditional barriers of demarcation between strategic and tactical intelligence production and dissemination systems."[72] JDISS soon became "the primary intelligence support tool" for U.S. military operations during the 1990s.[73]

Impact of Technological Change

This availability of unprecedented communications "bandwidth" to ships at sea and the interconnectivity of virtually all major intelligence production and dissemination systems via INTELINK and JDISS brought remarkable—even revolutionary—new capabilities. As one veteran of this period recalled,

> The technical change that transformed intelligence support to afloat units was as profound as those that had changed the shore environment in the late 1960s. . . . With SCI connectivity [aboard ships], it was possible for the intelligence community afloat to leverage the resources of the JICs ashore, and balance the take with that of the national agencies. Liberated from the oppression of the 9800 baud circuit, it was now possible to provide as much tailored intelligence to the operators afloat as it was ashore. The change was so profound as to be unimaginable only a decade before. Where the small communications pipe has isolated the ship, now the Challenge Athena satellite dish brought CNN to the commander's desk. In the 1980s it took most of a night watch (and the dedication of the admiral's privacy circuit) to transfer a single national image through the Fleet Imagery Support Terminal (FIST). Now, the imagery take could be tailored to take all available imagery to support a mission, with everything loaded to a central server by the JICs and available on a "pull" basis.[74]

The turnaround from the low-bandwidth days of Desert Storm was remarkable. By early 1997 it was calculated that a single aircraft carrier in the Western Pacific was sending fifty-four thousand e-mail messages every month. This single-ship volume was equal to about half of the message traffic that would have been expected in the entire theater prior to the arrival of CHALLENGE ATHENA.[75] During the Desert Strike operations against Iraq later in the decade, in fact, the carrier USS *Carl Vinson's* (CVN-70) intelligence team provided national imagery support to the NAVCENT (U.S. Naval Forces, Central Command) commander ashore.[76]

In the emerging era of military strategies of "information dominance"—in which wars seemed likely to be won not by "beating the other guy by dint of firepower alone, but also because you know more and you know it faster"[77]—these changes were revolutionary. As discussed in previous chapters, it had always been important to have the analytical process performed as close to the operator as possible in order to maximize intelligence professionals' intimate understanding of the needs of the warfighter they were supporting. As we have seen, the ultimate extension of this principle, the colocation of commander and operational intelligence aboard ship, had first begun to appear during World War II, when Adm. William Halsey embarked a Radio Intelligence Unit aboard his task force flagship in early 1942.[78] Important steps took place during the 1960s and 1970s with the deployment of 1630-designated officers and rudimentary computer databases aboard aircraft carriers and command ships. Limitations of data management technology and fleet communications bandwidth, however, precluded the development of real at-sea, "OSIS afloat," all-source fusion for many years.[79]

The bandwidth and interconnectivity revolution of the early 1990s changed all that and made full-service afloat OPINTEL a reality for the first time. Only at this point, in fact, could it really be said that the OPINTEL model had fulfilled the potential inherent in the British Admiralty's original 1939 concept. Within the regional theater-based command structure established by the Goldwater-Nichols legislation, these new technologies permitted two essentially new modes of fused, all-source operational intelligence support: first, the forward deployment of a "node" of the theater-level JIC in times of crisis, locating them as close as possible to the local warfighters; and, second, full-fledged OPINTEL carried out aboard a command ship, aircraft carrier, or amphibious ship in support of local combat operations. Plans for the forward deployment of a partly staffed theater-level JIC, for example, were developed by the U.S. Central Command (CENTCOM), which planned to send such a unit to the Middle East in the event of a regional crisis.[80]

Meanwhile, by the late 1990s it was recognized that "it was now possible to provide as much tailored intelligence to the operators afloat as it was ashore."[81] By that time intelligence professionals serving in genuinely operational posts were no more necessarily restricted in their access to information than were national-level OPINTEL specialists at the Pentagon. They had equal ability to consult in real time with scores of subject-matter specialists and database support systems at ONI, the Defense Intelligence Agency, or elsewhere. Indeed, provided that the requisite communications linkages could be maintained in the face of enemy denial efforts and ordinary hardware or software "glitches," such fin-de-siècle technologies made the very concept of a colocated intelligence center in some respects somewhat obsolete.[82] "Split-based" JIC staffing, in which members of the same staff occupied interconnected workstations perhaps thousands of miles apart, became increasingly feasible.[83] Thus did the concept of the Internet "chat room" revolutionize the original British concept of the "Intelligence Center": the age of the "virtual node" was dawning.

By the end of the twentieth century, therefore, naval intelligence—indeed, now joint-service U.S. military intelligence—had managed to "harness the *process* of fusion of the past for the *power* of fusion in the information age."[84] With the admixture of JDISS-driven INTELINK interconnectivity—tying analysts, watchstanders, and databases together as never before even conceivable—the process of OPINTEL developed by the British Admiralty in the late 1930s reached its most mature form.

Lessons Learned and Challenges for the Future

OPINTEL as a Process

Veterans of Navy operational intelligence during the Cold War and the 1990s agree upon the importance of understanding OPINTEL not as a product or a specific set of organizational forms or information-management systems but as a *process* adaptable to circumstances as threats and technologies change over time.[85] There was no OPINTEL "master plan." Rather, the Navy's operational intelligence architectures evolved over time under pressure from events: the changing threats posed by America's adversaries and the developing technological possibilities of collection and information processing.[86] So unpredictable was this evolution, in fact, that one former DNI has described it as "truly a two-steps-forward, one-and-a-half-back" process that seemed neither easy nor logical to its participants.[87]

But the fundamental ideal of OPINTEL remained in many respects unchanged even as the ways in which the Navy was able to live up to this ideal changed radically over time. As one former DNI has emphasized, the OSIS system to which the OPINTEL concept gave rise in Navy usage during the Cold War was "as much a process as it was a specific organizational and technological system. It was a way of approaching operational intelligence for the warfighter. Initially, data processing and communications technology limited its potential. As a refinement of the idea of operational intelligence, however, OSIS has enormous vitality. Ultimately, all military branches learned a great deal from the Navy's experience and the concept thrives on our joint watchfloors today."[88] To be sure, the scheme first developed for the needs of the U-boat war in 1939 changed radically in form when adapted to the needs of Cold War tracking of the Soviet fleet and the capabilities of modern sensors, communications bandwidth, and high-speed computers. It did not, however, change in *concept.*

This illustrates both the promise and a major challenge of OPINTEL for the twenty-first century. Navy (and joint-service) experiences from the Cold War and the immediate post–Cold War era strongly suggest that the OPINTEL/OSIS concept is a sound and a vital one. This same history demonstrates, however, that no *specific* fixed model of OPINTEL organization or technology can long survive in a world where threats and technologies change constantly. It is therefore the paradoxical and continuing challenge of OPINTEL to keep the concept alive through constant innovation—continually changing its execution so as to maximize the benefits it provides to operational commanders.

One of the few certainties about the mechanics of OPINTEL is that however well-organized and -adapted present forms may be, we will have to modify or abandon them soon. Therefore, a prerequisite for providing good OPINTEL support to the warfighter over time is an enormous degree of flexibility and an ability to innovate and adapt. Military intelligence organizations in the modern world are large and bureaucratic environments not normally known for encouraging such flexibility, but their OPINTEL components will require this for their very survival.

All-Source Fusion

One of the enduring strengths of the OPINTEL process has been its emphasis upon the "fusion" of information from all available sources of information. In the U-boat war in the North Atlantic, this meant the incorporation of everything from merchant ship spotting reports to enormously sensitive ULTRA decrypts. During the Cold War, the arsenal of information and sensor inputs increased enormously, to include new detection systems built around underwater hydrophone arrays, satellites, aircraft, and other systems, all tied together in "real time" via satellite communications and increasingly powerful computer processing. Future "all-source" intelligence will surely incorporate even more exotic inputs.

Nor are today's potential threat areas limited to particular known or anticipated sections of ocean—for example, the GIUK gap upon which NATO naval strategy focused during the 1960s and 1970s, or the northern-ocean Soviet SSBN "bastions" targeted during the Maritime Strategy period of the 1980s. Today's joint-service operations, carried out on a regional basis by the various unified commands established by Goldwater-Nichols, may literally occur anywhere, requiring in effect the establishment of a global OPINTEL network of unprecedented breadth and granularity.

With the proliferation of modern sensor inputs and the expansion of the geographic areas for which warfighters need (and expect) their intelligence staffs to provide quality all-source fusion analysis, of course, come huge and interrelated challenges. More inputs and more geographic area—not to mention more and more varied potential threats—mean more information to be analyzed, greater burdens upon information-management technologies, more demands upon analytical staffs, and greater strains upon communications architectures. Because the objective is *all-source* fusion, the increased use of exotic sensor technologies creates new challenges for "sanitization" as well. As illustrated by debates over the use of ULTRA information during World War II, it has always been a major challenge for all-source fusion analysis to draw a sensible line between rapid dissemination of highly sensitive information to the warfighter and the protection of intelligence sources and methods. The tension between the security of "black" special access programs (SAPs) and operational commanders' "need to know" what the enemy is doing is very real, and is likely only to increase in the years ahead.[89]

There is, of course, no formulaic way to approach sanitization: solutions to particular sanitization challenges will depend upon the specific nature and characteristics of the information in question. Nevertheless, the Navy's experience with OPINTEL since the beginning of World War II suggests that sanitization challenges in operational intelligence are most easily overcome where operators trust intelligence professionals to give them the information they need to know without asking too many questions about sources. In turn, intelligence professionals will trust operators to safeguard the confidences that must necessarily be shared.[90] It will no doubt continue to be true that without all-source knowledge, the "tyranny of the stovepipes . . . will produce the wrong answer."[91]

Ties to the Operators: Knowing "Blue" as Well as "Red"

As the importance of intelligence/operator trust and credibility in sanitization matters illustrates, a recurring theme in the history of Navy OPINTEL during the Cold War is "the paramount importance of cultivating close relationships of understanding, respect, and trust between intelligence professionals and their operational customers."[92] Traditionally a Navy strength—built upon the fact that naval operators and intelligence professionals often literally inhabit their weapons platforms and maneuver in them on a daily basis against their adversaries[93]—the intimacy of the operator/intelligence relationship is a fundamental prerequisite for good OPINTEL in the joint-service environment as well. Consequently, the good intelligence professional is an expert not only on "Red" (adversary) forces but on "Blue" (friendly) ones: to provide good, tailored intelligence support, he must understand the needs and responsibilities, capabilities and weaknesses of his *own* side as well as those of the enemy.[94] As former DNI Rear Adm. Jacoby has phrased it, "intelligence professionals need to become experts on friendly as well as potential enemy forces. They need an intimate understanding of the needs of their customer as well as a detailed knowledge of the adversary, and they must speak the language of operations. In short, it is vital for an intelligence professional to penetrate not just the enemy but also the customer."[95]

Knowing one's customer—as well as knowing the adversary—is crucial to the craft of intelligence, because the adversary does not act in a vacuum. In part, the enemy's activities are responses to one's own, and "Red" actions cannot be fully understood without knowledge of "Blue" ones.[96] As Sun Tzu wrote, "One who knows the enemy and knows himself will not be endangered in a hundred engagements."[97]

Good intelligence professionals, Jacoby argued, must also be "evangelists for their craft," aware of both the capabilities and the limitations of intelligence and aggressive in "preaching the gospel of intelligence to the operational community."[98] Vice Adm. Tom Wilson preferred a different metaphor. Reasoning that "an evangelist tells you how you are supposed to live your life," Wilson suggests that an intelligence professional should aspire to the analogy of a social worker, "who does the meals on wheels and gets out and interacts with the customer and delivers the goods—*that* is really going to create trust and confidence and a desire to get more from the [intelligence] systems."[99] For their parts, former DNI Rear Adm. Shapiro and former Deputy DNI Richard Haver prefer the image of intelligence professionals as salesmen.[100]

Regardless of which is the most apt analogy, however, it is clear that intelligence professionals must develop and maintain close ties of respect and trust with operational commanders. Perhaps most of all, what distinguishes a good intelligence officer from a great one is the degree to which great ones "are very close to their bosses, and have achieved an ability to know what their boss is thinking, and what they're going to think next."[101] This kind of intimate knowledge is developed only over time, and through a very close relationship. By the same token, it is also important for operators to know their own limitations. As Admiral Jeremiah has noted, the operator often "is not a very qualified evaluator" to tell intelligence professionals precisely what pieces of information are needed. Nevertheless, it is vital that the operator keep his intelligence staff apprised of his mission and intentions. Intelligence analysts must "understand what [information] is important to the commander . . . in order to carry out the mission."[102]

The development of the Maritime Strategy in the late 1970s and early 1980s illustrates the potential strengths that can derive from a strong operator/intelligence relationship. The crucial "deep penetration" successes achieved against the Soviet adversary would have meant little had not the naval intelligence community been able to make its case based upon these insights to operators who trusted them and were willing to make great changes based upon the new information. Moreover, the process worked both ways: it is difficult to imagine that the Maritime Strategy could have developed as it did if intelligence officials and operators *together* had not been intimately involved in the intelligence assessment and the operational planning processes symbolized by the Advanced Technology Panel and the Strategic Studies Group. This close relationship, in turn, would be difficult to imagine if the Navy had not already developed a strong tradition of close operator/intelligence relationships rooted in the decision to allow 1630-designated officers to serve at sea during the early 1960s. The Maritime Strategy, in other words, was grounded in intelligence insights and the remarkable capabilities of "high OSIS" OPINTEL, but it was a journey that operators and intelligence professionals took together from the outset.[103]

The importance of developing and maintaining such a close relationship is hard to overestimate and must rank as one of the most formidable challenges of OPINTEL in the joint-service environment. But the relationship is essential, and essential to the credibility upon which an intelligence professional's success depends. As Rear Admiral Jacoby put it, "If your boss isn't going to listen to what you say and use it for part of the basis for decision, you might as well not be there. [If] intelligence, then, is not relevant to the situation and the decision-making . . . then we are wasting our time. So how do you develop credibility? It's based on professional integrity. . . . [The intelligence professional must have] established a personal relationship [with the operators] and that credibility and reliance that so often is part and parcel of the commander's relationship with his intelligence officers."[104] As Richard Haver put it, "If we don't have the trust of the customer, we're dead . . . [and] we've lost the essence of what we're here for."[105]

Today, operators and intelligence professionals may often lack the intimacy of the naval relationships built of shared operational experience at sea in daily maneuvers against the Soviet fleet. In today's system of unified theater-level commands and truly "joint" task force operations the operational commander and his intelligence chief may not have such a common background of shared experiences, understandings, and vocabulary; they may not even have been from the same branch of service. This hardly precludes the provision of good OPINTEL support, but it provides an additional challenge that will have to be met in the twenty-first century. Not incidentally, the centrality of close operator relationships to good operational intelligence support is another reason why computer processing power and communications bandwidth will never be able to replace the intelligence analyst.[106]

Know Thine "INTs"

In an era of proliferating sensor technologies and "all-source" information inputs to the intelligence process, an important corollary to the significance of the operator/intelligence relationship is the need for intelligence professionals to maintain close relationships with the various specialized "INT" communities—for example, SIGINT, MASINT, IMINT, ELINT, and ACINT—that feed the fusion process. In the history of Navy operational intelligence, this is most clearly seen in the close relationship between Navy OPINTEL staffs and the SIGINT community. During World War II, Navy OPINTEL in the Pacific was virtually synonymous with radio intelligence (SIGINT), and this close relationship continued into the postwar period with the attachment of a small group of analysts to Naval Security Group headquarters in Washington, D.C. This colocation of all-source analysts and cryptologists, in turn, laid the groundwork for years of invaluable work by the Navy Field Operational Intelligence Office (NFOIO) and by the Cryptologic Support Group cadres stationed at OSIS nodes such as FOSIF Rota, where they worked so closely with Navy OPINTEL staffs "that they were nearly indistinguishable."[107]

But close relationships with the "INT" community went beyond SIGINT, as important as this was, and also came to include each new discipline as it came along. This was especially the case with acoustic specialists of the Navy's ACINT community who ran the SOSUS network and the radar analysts of the overhead ELINT system pioneered by the revolutionary GRAB satellite of 1960. In the OPINTEL world of the twenty-first century, in which intelligence will surely have to deal with an increasingly bewildering constellation of supporting "INT" architectures, it will be more important than ever for intelligence professionals not only to understand the technological capabilities and limitations of collection systems but also to "speak the language" of the men and women who run them.[108]

The Role of Technology

The development of OPINTEL has always been inescapably linked to the development of communications and information-management technologies, from the Navy's initial acquisition of IBM keypunch machines in the 1930s, to the first deployment of Radio Intelligence Units aboard aircraft carriers during World War II, to the beginnings of computer-driven OPINTEL automation in the first SEAWATCH system for tracking merchant shipping, and to the development of global interconnectivity via JDISS, satellite data links, and an intelligence-focused analogue to the World Wide Web. The OPINTEL concept may not have changed fundamentally from the British Admiralty's first operational intelligence center of 1939, but its execution has been repeatedly revolutionized as technologies have made possible new organizational forms and practices.[109]

Yet the increasing technological sophistication of OPINTEL is not really the story of hardware innovations. Rather, "the real advances occurred in establishing the system into which new hardware was integrated—that is, in the realm of organization. In other words, operational intelligence prospered as technologies matured because a sound foundation had been laid first."[110]

The development of new technologies did not change what OPINTEL *was* as much as they permitted this to be accomplished better, and in more sophisticated forms.[111] As former Sixth Fleet commander Vice Adm. David Richardson put it in the late 1990s, for example, after visiting a state-of-the-art aircraft carrier intelligence center, "We now appear to have installed what we moved so slowly to get in the late '60s, and into the '70s and '80s. . . . We had the collection and analysis [then], but information distribution and presentation for command decision was constrained by communications capabilities and printed messages."[112] The evolution of processing and communications technologies often acted as a catalyst for changes in the Navy's OPINTEL scheme, but the crucial changes were related less to hardware than to *organization*—the conceptual and practical development of the system through which such hardware was used and integrated into a functional whole.[113]

The strengths of OPINTEL could be brought out in new and innovative ways as technologies matured, but for the most part these strengths were inherent in the model. This also suggests an important lesson for applying new technologies to intelligence in the future: "Strive to automate not what you do now—but what you want to be able to do."[114] Future innovations will likely come from a continued ability to adapt new technological possibilities to the challenges of providing the kind of fused, all-source, operator-tailored support that has been fundamental to the OPINTEL art since before World War II.

The Importance of People

Despite the enormous sophistication and remarkable capabilities of the OSIS system developed by the Navy operational intelligence community—and which has since become the model for today's joint-service system of OPINTEL "nodes" at the national, theater, local, and (increasingly) platform level—it never had a "master plan." Rather, it was "created from scratch and out of necessity, under pressure from events" and through the incorporation of new technologies and organizational forms as they were gradually developed, from 1939 through the end of the century.[115]

The nature of this ad hoc evolutionary history has important implications, in that it suggests that no "master plan" for OPINTEL of the future will be possible either. It will continue to be difficult to predict the nature of future threats, especially in a post–Cold War environment at least temporarily lacking obvious, overwhelming adversaries of the sort that galvanized the development of OPINTEL during World War II and NATO's long global standoff with the Soviet Union. It will surely be essentially impossible to predict future technological developments of the sort that might further revolutionize the sensor, information-management, or communications systems upon which modern OPINTEL relies so heavily. What today's planners *can* do, however, is to work to ensure a continued supply of the ingredient most important to OPINTEL's development to date: high-quality, highly motivated intelligence professionals—full-time active-duty service members, TAD personnel, and reservists[116]—who are capable of "thriving in . . . a changing environment by virtue of creative flexibility and on-the-job training."[117]

This is no mean challenge. During World War II and the Cold War, naval intelligence did a superlative job of attracting quality personnel, and the OPINTEL staffs within that community traditionally attracted some of the best among them. During these two periods of global conflict, U.S. intelligence professionals were also notable for their powerful "sense of *mission,*" what Michael Herman described as an enormously impressive feeling "that the safety of the free world depended on them."[118] This sense of threat and noble challenge helped attract and retain the sort of personnel needed to make OPINTEL work, and to permit it successfully to change and adapt continually to its environment.

After the Cold War—although this has been somewhat mitigated by the post-2001 war on terrorism—the job of attracting and retaining such people is perhaps more difficult than ever, because "we face shifting, nontraditional threats that can lack the Cold War sense of urgency and purpose that for many years helped motivate and retain first-rate intelligence professionals."[119] Moreover, attraction and retention in the 1990s had to be done in an environment in which—at least for the moment—a booming civilian economy made it difficult for the military to compete with the private sector *without* such powerful sense of national security urgency.[120] (As one naval intelligence flag officer noted in 1998, as real as post–Cold War threats are, they compete poorly with the sense of urgency created by the prospect of spotting a Soviet submarine's periscope behind one's ship.)[121] OPINTEL's history suggests that unless such challenges are met, it will be difficult to sustain the record of innovation and adaptive evolution that has brought operational intelligence to where it is today.

Focus and Refocus in a Shifting World

The dramatic changes in the international environment that flowed from the collapse of the Soviet Union in 1991 posed a considerable challenge to operational intelligence. OPINTEL was both born and came to maturity during times of global strategic crisis in which the overriding imperative was to provide military intelligence support to operational commanders faced with actual or potential hostilities with a single, obvious, and overwhelming adversary.[122] Whether facing Hitler's U-boats in the North Atlantic, the Imperial Fleet in the Pacific, or the Soviet Northern or Pacific Fleets in the GIUK gap or the far northern oceans, Navy OPINTEL had always known exactly who its collection target is. Indeed, during the Cold War, intelligence professionals had the luxury of being able to spend entire careers becoming experts in Soviet naval operations and thinking. They could thus advise U.S. commanders in wartime by developing the sort of intimate understanding of Soviet thinking that was possible only through years of focused and sustained observation and analysis.

Since the end of the Cold War this has no longer been possible. The obvious enemies of World War II and the Cold War have been replaced by a shifting constellation of less powerful but far more diverse adversaries. This has allowed far less sustained study of any single potential opponent and made it more difficult for intelligence professionals to "know their enemy" in the way they had become accustomed to and had come to expect.[123] These challenges have been little diminished with the advent in 2001 of global counter-terrorist operations, which—apart from certain interdiction functions—generally do not involve Navy units apart from special forces. The post–Cold War environment, and the new joint-service institutional context in which OPINTEL must now operate, requires of U.S. intelligence "more breadth and greater depth of coverage than ever before," which "spreads resources thinly, creates difficulties in long-range planning, and makes setting priorities difficult."[124] In effect, it requires "both depth and breadth simultaneously," thus creating important challenges to "risk management" as intelligence staffs attempt to place resources where they are likely to be most needed while maintaining enough "flexibility and agility" to adjust quickly if they guess wrong.[125] It is a continuing challenge to provide high-quality, all-source, tailored intelligence support to the warfighter even as the target of intelligence analysis shifts rapidly from adversary to adversary in an era of bubbling regional conflicts.[126]

Interestingly, though the other U.S. services may have much to learn from Navy OPINTEL, the contemporary Navy may also be able to profit from Army and Air Force approaches. Specifically, Vice Admiral Wilson has suggested that the other services' emphasis upon "doctrine and tactics and techniques and procedures in the exercise world" may provide a way to "help keep [our] OPINTEL skills up" in an environment that lacks a clear adversary.[127]

Information Overload: Balancing Collection and Analysis

In the popular imagination it is the perennial focus of the intelligence officer to acquire ever better and more reliable information about the enemy. In reality—at least in today's world of satellite, aerial, surface, and subsurface collection by a huge variety of sensors all integrated into a global near-real-time information processing and dissemination net-work—it might be more accurate to say that the challenge is often coping with having *too much* information about the enemy or being uncertain which bits of data are the *right* information.[128] Intelligence professionals provide perhaps their most important "value added" in the intelligence process by applying their experience and analytical expertise to the difficult task of sifting through the torrent of information available to identify the crucial information the war-fighter needs to know.

As it has always been, good intelligence work in many ways resembles a jigsaw puzzle, with analysts working to see the relationships and make the right connections between fragmentary data points. Today, however, this process is complicated still further by the increasing difficulty of identifying the fragmentary puzzle "pieces" in the first place—that is, by the need to cut through an ever-larger blizzard of information "noise" in order to identify the crucial "signals" that require analysis. When done properly, in fact, analysis can provide intelligence "value-added" equivalent to possessing an entirely new sensor system.[129]

Keeping the "Expert in the Loop"

This "signal-noise" problem emphasizes the importance of maintaining a balance between collection and analysis in intelligence work.[130] As one former DNI has suggested, this poses a major challenge to modern intelligence managers and planning staffs: "No matter how good the communications and how large the data bases, there is no substitute for analysis. The value added by trained specialists capable of discerning how the enemy thinks and understanding him through his own eyes is incalculable. Collecting raw data is crucial to the operational intelligence process, but it is the thought process that makes this information really useful."[131]

The remarkable developments that led to the Maritime Strategy in the early 1980s, for example, underscore the point that although the acquisition of information from multiple sources is important to the process of all-source fusion, the most critical element is that of analysis. Ultimately this includes the value added by analysts capable of discerning how the enemy thinks and understanding him through his eyes.[132]

Automation is thus helpful to the extent that it enables the analyst to make profitable use of more data than ever before, but machines cannot replace the "expert in the loop." As Richard Haver describes it, this is because it is the ultimate aspiration of OPINTEL to tell the operator what the target is likely to do next, "and *that* has to be created by the human mind. Computers can help. . . . But at the end of the day, I still think we're going to rely on grey matter packed inside skullbone to figure out what it all means, and why. And that's the essence of the job."[133]

Frequently, said former DNI Shapiro, "what really counts is applying human judgment . . . [and asking] 'Does this really make sense?' 'What does it mean, and is this what I want the boss to know?' 'Is this what he *needs* to know?'"[134] (This returns us to the crucial point that no matter how good the technological support, "the quality *people* in organizations are the key to success.")[135]

Without maintaining a firm distinction between raw data and analysis, "the recipient will often be deluged with information that cannot usefully be employed."[136] When in a crisis the vast resources of the U.S. intelligence-collection machine are swung into action against a particular target, "People on the scene are inundated with intelligence support, which gets in the way of perishable intelligence and often throws a lot of chaff into the equation."[137]

Indeed, the central importance of *analysis* to intelligence production is such that it is in some respects artificial to draw a distinction between information and intelligence in the first place. As Michael Herman has observed, "Intelligence is evidence-driven, but most of the evidence emerges from processing of some kind; it does not have separable elements of 'facts' and 'interpretation.' A give-and-take between the two takes place at all stages."[138]

The importance of analysis is well understood, but it may be more difficult than ever to bring such analysis to bear—that is, to turn mere *information* into useful *intelligence*[139]—in tomorrow's wars, because technology is blurring the line between operators' combat information systems and intelligence collection and dissemination systems.[140] Improved data links, for example, can now potentially provide raw sensor information directly to pilots in their cockpits in real time. Military planners also boast of the new "sensor-to-shooter" information architectures they are now developing—programs driven by the memory of "SCUD-hunting" difficulties during the Gulf War and exemplified by the deployment of the Rapid Targeting System (RTS) during U.S. military operations in Bosnia.[141]

These new capabilities, however, also entail risks, for as one commentator has suggested, modern computer and communications tools tempt the warfighter to act on an ad hoc basis as his own intelligence officer.[142] At worst, these technologies threaten to "eliminate the human analysis formerly associated with intelligence."[143] "Too much emphasis upon pumping raw information directly from 'sensor to shooter,' in fact, can be confusing and dangerous. . . . Rather than supplying as much information as possible, the true measure of success is providing as little information as possible—that is, only the right information at the right time. Operational intelligence is more than speedy, technology-driven collection and transmission. The crucial element is thought, and this can be accomplished only by people."[144] As former NSA Director Vice Adm. Mike McConnell colorfully put it at an OPIN-TEL "Lessons-Learned" conference in 1998, analysis is vital, because "bullshit at the speed of light is still bullshit."[145]

Even the Navy's foremost exponent of high-technology, information-driven twenty-first-century warfighting, Vice Adm. Arthur K. Cebrowski, the "founding father of . . . network-centric warfare,"[146] admitted that future wars could easily "provide enough information to overwhelm decision-makers," and that "it will do us no good to accelerate bad decisions."[147] And as former DNI Rear Admiral Sheafer has noted, it is a challenge for U.S. Naval Intelligence to "facilitate the integration of own-force, neutral, environmental intelligence and other relevant data into coherent pictures delivered to operational units with improved timeliness . . . [but also to] effectively compensate for the increased processing time which such command-level integration implies."[148] Preserving some balance between collection and analysis in OPINTEL support, therefore, will be a huge challenge in "the fast-paced, information-flooded battlespace of the [twenty-first] century"[149]—in which wars are more likely to resemble the continuous, integrated movements of soccer more than the preplanned, episodic movements of American football.[150]

The challenges of timeliness in the modern battlespace are not unique to the realm of operational intelligence, of course. Nonetheless, they are far more acute there than with regard to finished intelligence of a noncurrent nature (e.g., capabilities studies, tables of organization and equipment, biographical studies, and strategic intentions assessments). In any event, it seems clear that the balance between collection and analysis *is* a balance. As Rear Admiral Jacoby and Vice Admiral Wilson have both observed, "sensor-to-shooter" architectures can be valuable but are dangerous if overused.[151]

The persistent need for intelligence analysis returns us, therefore, to the critical importance of *people* in the OPINTEL scheme.[152] Real analysis is something that can be done only by real people, stepping back from the raw data to make sense of it.[153] Timely analysis of incoming information in volume sufficient to meet the demands of such an information-flooded future battlespace can be accomplished only if one maintains "the critical mass of experienced watchstanders [needed] to interpret the flood of available information."[154]

This is perhaps one of the defining challenges of OPINTEL for the twenty-first century. It is worth remembering, however, that these dilemmas are in many respects not wholly new ones for Navy operational intelligence. The range of sensor systems from which "all-source" information is to be compiled has been steadily increasing since the first OPINTEL watchfloor was established at the British Admiralty on the eve of World War II. Similarly, the automated data processing power with which intelligence professionals can approach their analytical functions, and the communications technologies with and through which they can disseminate their product, also steadily advanced during OPINTEL's first six decades. Thus, to some extent it has *always* been the challenge of OPINTEL organization to keep a professional intelligence "expert in the loop." Today, just as then, the key is providing effective analytical value within the narrowing time horizons imposed by the ever-increasing range and speed of weaponry and the capabilities of command and control systems.

Nevertheless, while these difficulties were somewhat implicit in the OPINTEL model for more than half a century, it is only in recent years that they have become acute as collection and communications technology steadily turned the flow of information into a torrent and the torrent into a flood. While this very technological maturity is a major strength of modern OPINTEL—making all-source fusion possible on a scale and with a sophistication never before conceivable—it is thus also forcing the U.S. military to confront organizational challenges of unprecedented complexity.[155]

OPINTEL and "Network-Centric Warfare"

In this sense, one might even go so far as to argue that OPINTEL's organization—both in concept from the very beginning in 1939 and in increasingly sophisticated execution during the course of the Cold War—was a vital institutional forerunner of modern notions of "network centric warfare." This term has been used to describe a paradigm of information-age warfighting in which previous notions of "platform-centric" warfighting are being replaced by "network-centric" approaches.[156]

The military planners developing these approaches envision the sophisticated, "effects-based" coordination of joint-service military assets built around a "warfighter's Internet" containing integrated intelligence, surveillance, and reconnaissance (ISR) products[157] in a "high-capacity, multimedia network of sensors, shooters, and commanders . . . [forming] a seamless information grid which provides high-speed information transfer."[158] Empowered by "dominant battle-space knowledge" and thus at least somewhat freed from the "fog of war," it is argued, commanders will be able to "operate within an opponent's decision and reaction cycle" and defeat him.[159]

This comprehensive, interlinked global information network, they anticipate, is supposed to provide "an evolving, but consistent Common Tactical Picture of the battlespace"[160] that will let future warfighters take advantage of World Wide Web–style connectivity in the comprehensive and efficient coordination of military power.[161] "Speed of command," it is hoped, will "turn a superior information position" into an unbeatable military competitive advantage.[162] Since this requires being able to "make more sense, faster, out of the information we are able to collect," however, the blizzard of information available in modern conflict requires shifting information management from a process of fitting pieces of information together to one of *excluding* extraneous information to the greatest extent possible.[163]

If these notions sound familiar, they should. "Network-centric warfare" is in many respects a recapitulation of and an elaboration upon the OPINTEL concept developed by naval intelligence into the OSIS system beginning in the 1960s. It is a globe-spanning, interlinked information collection, processing, and dissemination network for battlespace awareness built around state-of-the-art computer and communications technologies and evolving along with these technologies into ever more sophisticated institutional forms.[164]

To be sure, the primordial OPINTEL model of the British Admiralty had only one real intelligence fusion "center," and even the early U.S. Navy OSIS scheme relied upon a system of discrete, fixed "nodes" such as FOSIF Rota. As technological capabilities improved over time, however, the locus of all-source OPINTEL "fusion" became more widely distributed. Ultimately, with the development of INTELINK connectivity, fusion came to take place simultaneously at essentially *all* points in the system, from national-level watchfloors all the way down to the individual JDISS console operator afloat.

As we have seen, under pressure from the requirements of high-technology OPINTEL,[165] the Navy developed—and the joint-service world adopted—a sophisticated approach to managing information overload by "distributing it among the interconnected forces that, working together, could solve" complex problems.[166] "Network-centric warfare" will undoubtedly come to involve technological advances far beyond what OPINTEL had achieved by the end of the twentieth century. In conceptual terms, however, the "network-centric" scheme is really no more than the creation of an analogous Web-based command-and-control network and its integration into the information grid pioneered by the OPINTEL community. This was already visible in the

Navy's OSIS organization for a generation before the term "network-centric" warfare came into vogue.

Learning Lessons: The Importance of OPINTEL Meta-Analysis

A final lesson that might be drawn from the history of OPINTEL during World War II through the end of the twentieth century relates to the "lessons learned" process itself—of which this text itself is one small part. As the most effective intelligence professionals have always understood, "intelligence history is important"[167] because it allows practitioners the chance not only to avoid the mistakes of the past but also to build upon its successes.[168] Indeed, it may be "the most important lesson of all . . . that how well an organization learns from its past is a crucial index of its capacity to survive challenges in the future."[169] It is thus vital, as the Navy and the U.S. military as a whole move into the twenty-first century, that intelligence professionals and warfighters alike take time to step back from the day-to-day pressures of their work to review what has come before and to plan for the future.[170] The "lessons learned" process itself, therefore, must be seen as an important ingredient for OPINTEL's future progress.

Nor are the lessons of OPINTEL's past significant only for the future of the intelligence community because the joint-service operational community itself has moved increasingly to OPINTEL-style distributed information-management networks for core battlespace-management tasks. In the coming era of "network-centric warfare," an understanding of OPINTEL's history and evolutionary development during the last sixty years may suggest important insights into how to continue moving forward in the mature information age. Mindful of Byron's observation that "the best of prophets of the future is the past,"[171] it is the authors' hope that this work will help us approach the future on a sounder footing, learning lessons from OPINTEL's past in order to build upon its rich legacy in the years to come.

Notes

Chapter 1: OPINTEL and Its Origins

1. Rear Adm. Lowell E. Jacoby, "Operational Intelligence: Lessons from the Cold War," U.S. Naval Institute *Proceedings* (September 1999): 102. Michael Herman observes a similar distinction, preferring, however, to speak of "intelligence" (static, planning intelligence) and "tactical intelligence" (OPINTEL). See Michael Herman, *Intelligence Power in Peace and War* (Cambridge: Royal Institute of International Affairs, 1996), 121–24. As discussed herein, the U.S. Navy also observed a distinction between planning and operational intelligence during World War II, with the Office of Naval Intelligence engaged exclusively in the former and the War Plans Division assuming responsibility for the latter.

2. Capt. Wyman H. Packard, *Century of U.S. Naval Intelligence* (Washington, D.C.: Department of the Navy, 1996), 215; see also Bruce Watson, Susan Watson, and Gerald Hopple, eds., *United States Intelligence: An Encyclopedia* (New York: Garland, 1990), 421.

3. Jacoby, "Operational Intelligence," 103; see also Frederick Harrison, presentation to Office of Naval Intelligence Symposium, "U.S. Navy OPINTEL: Lessons Learned from the Cold War" (September 12–13, 1998) [hereafter referred to as ONI OPINTEL "Lessons Learned" Symposium], describing the quality of timeliness as being a distinguishing characteristic of OPINTEL.

4. Packard, *Century of U.S. Naval Intelligence,* 220.

5. For example, Adm. Horatio Nelson used fast frigates—communicating via coded hoists that were readable with help from the new Royal Navy signal book developed by Sir Home Popham—to help keep him informed of the movements of the French fleet. Fast British

frigates would approach as close as they dared to major French ports in order to ascertain the status of the fleet, while picket ships communicating by signal would be used to patrol key sea transits where the French were likely to pass. (As a countermeasure to Nelson's port surveillance, the French sometimes tried to sortie just after the end of gales—hoping to make good their escape before the British patrol could resume station.) A small network of such vessels, for example, helped Nelson shadow the French fleet on the night before the battle of Trafalgar. See Steven E. Maffeo, *Most Secret and Confidential: Intelligence in the Age of Nelson* (Annapolis, Md.: Naval Institute Press, 2000), 43, 46–47, 71, 73–75, 77, 95, 100–103, 154; see also John Keegan, *The Price of Admiralty* (New York: Penguin, 1988), 17.

6. General Order Number 292 (Washington, D.C.: Department of the Navy, March 23, 1882). Assistant Navy Secretary Franklin Delano Roosevelt similarly circulated a letter in 1919 declaring that Naval Intelligence officers should have as their first duty in wartime "the collection and compilation of prompt, reliable, and accurate information concerning the approach, arrival, movements, and position of enemy naval forces . . . [and] the prompt dissemination of [the] above information." See Packard, *Century of U.S. Naval Intelligence,* 215.

7. See, e.g., J. C. R. Colomb, "Naval Intelligence and Protection of Commerce of War," *Royal United Services Institute Journal* 24, no. 112 (1881).

8. See Office of Naval Intelligence, "Our Story," in Program for Dedication of National Maritime Intelligence Center (October 20, 1993), 12, 14, which notes that the advent of shipboard radio "revolutionized the distribution of intelligence to naval operating forces and ultimately provided another source of intelligence."

9. Packard, *Century of U.S. Naval Intelligence,* 215.

10. Robert M. Grant, *U-boat Intelligence, 1914–18* (Hamden, Conn.: Archon Books, 1969), 10, 166–67.

11. Ibid., 9, 17.

12. James Bamford, *The Puzzle Palace* (New York: Penguin, 1983), 66; F. W. Winterbotham, *The Ultra Secret* (New York: Harper and Row, 1974), 2 (quoting letter of July 1945). One former Naval Intelligence flag officer and director of the National Security Agency estimates that COMINT shortened the war by eighteen to twenty-four months. Vice Adm. John M. McConnell, USN (Ret.), presentation to ONI OPINTEL "Lessons Learned" Symposium.

13. See Bamford, *Puzzle Palace,* 66.

14. Winterbotham, *Ultra Secret,* 175.

15. Ibid., 188.

16. John Prados, *Combined Fleet Decoded* (New York: Random House, 1995), 73.

17. Ibid., xxii.

18. Watson et al., *United States Intelligence,* 399.

19. Douglas Porch, *The French Secret Services* (New York: Farrar, Strauss, and Giroux, 1995), 112.

20. The French Deuxième Bureau during World War I, for example, was justifiably proud of its efforts to integrate intelligence information obtained from such diverse sources as aerial reconnaissance, cryptology, radio direction-finding (radiogoniometry), prisoner-of-war interrogations, captured documents and equipment, postal censorship, and message "traffic analysis" (Porch, *French Secret Services,* 112). All-source intelligence fusion was pioneered—at least in U.S. practice—by no less a figure than Gen. George Washington himself, who personally took reports during the Revolutionary War from spies as well as cavalry and individual scouts. The first recognizably modern institutionalization of all-source fusion may have been in the Bureau of Military Information, established under Col. George H. Sharpe in the Union Army in 1863 by Gen. Joseph Hooker. The high-quality intelligence analysis provided by this bureau incorporated the results not only of its own spying and interrogation efforts but also of cavalry reconnaissance, balloon observations, Signal Corps observation stations, flag-signal interception, the examination of Southern newspapers, and intelligence reports arriving by telegraph from neighboring Union Army commands. See Edwin C. Fishel, *The Secret War for the Union* (Boston: Houghton Mifflin, 1996), 298–99.

21. Brig. Gen. Joseph A. Twitty, Assistant Chief of Staff for Intelligence, U.S. Pacific Fleet, Memorandum on "Report on Intelligence Activities of the Joint Staff, CinCPac-CinCPOA" (October 15, 1945) [declassified], 4, 37. Copy courtesy of Rear Adm. Donald M. Showers, USN (Ret.).

22. The term "ULTRA" has become accepted as a shorthand for high-grade cryptanalysis during World War II. As Patrick Beesly and others have pointed out, however, ULTRA was actually just a marking applied to some of the decrypted COMINT known as "Special Intelligence." See

Patrick Beesly, *Very Special Intelligence: The Story of the Admiralty's Operational Intelligence Centre, 1939–1945* (London: Greenhill, 2000), 100; see also the introduction by W. J. R. Gardner, vii–viii.

23. Herman, *Intelligence Power,* 95–98. Herman believes that the strength of all-source analysis lies in allowing analysts to become subject-matter specialists by providing them with information from a great many different sources. Analysts who are expert simply at one specific type of collection technique, by contrast, seldom acquire expertise in the actual adversary. See Herman, 43.

24. See, e.g., Prados, *Combined Fleet Decoded,* 242, noting that "a synergism existed between different kinds of intelligence reporting, [such] that a multidimensional intelligence effort would be greater than the sum of its parts."

25. See Allen Dulles, *Great True Spy Stories* (Secaucus, N.J.: Castle, 1968), 291–92.

26. Beesly, *Very Special Intelligence,* 222, 223, and 226.

27. Rear Adm. Edwin T. Layton, USN (Ret.), *"And I Was There": Pearl Harbor and Midway—Breaking the Secrets* (New York: William Morrow, 1985), 21.

28. Prados, *Combined Fleet Decoded,* 352–53 and 412–14.

29. Layton, *"And I Was There,"* 357. (Adm. Chuichi Nagumo commanded the Japanese Imperial Navy's First Air Fleet during the surprise attack upon the U.S. Pacific Fleet on December 7, 1941.)

30. Modern theorists of "nonlinearity" in military affairs have often remarked upon the complexity of warfare as an interactive process characterized by complicated feedback loops between intelligent, adaptive players who are each reacting, simultaneously, to their perceptions of the other's actions. See generally, e.g., Alan D. Beyerchen, "Clausewitz, Nonlinearity, and the Unpredictability of War," in *Coping with the Bounds: Speculations on Nonlinearity in Military Affairs,* Tom Czerwinski, ed. (Washington, D.C.: Institute for National Strategic Studies, 1998), 161, 180–81; Robert Jervis, "Complex Systems: The Role of Interactions," in *Complexity, Global Politics, and National Security,* David S. Alberts and Thomas J. Czerwinski, eds. (Washington, D.C.: Institute for National Strategic Studies, 1999), 45–60. This dynamic, however, is particularly important to OPINTEL analysts, who are required nonetheless to understand and predict enemy behavior in such an environment.

31. Packard, *Century of U.S. Naval Intelligence,* 216; see also, e.g., Alan Harris Bath, *Tracking the Axis Enemy* (Lawrence: University Press of Kansas, 1998), 76, recounting careful efforts of U.S. and British operational intelligence tracking rooms during World War II to plot both own forces and those of the enemy; Layton, *"And I Was There,"* 124, noting efforts of Comdr. Arthur McCollum during war to discern U.S. movements by reading decrypted Japanese intelligence reports when denied such information by U.S. operations staffs.

32. Layton, *"And I Was There,"* 55 (emphasis added).

33. A parallel to this dynamic in the world of operational intelligence may be seen in "revolutionary" jumps in naval combat power. As Karl Lautenschläger has recounted, for example, "important advances in naval weaponry" more commonly come less from "the introduction of spectacular new technology" than from "the integration of several known, often rather mundane, inventions." Karl Lautenschläger, "Technology and the Evolution of Naval Warfare," *International Security* 8, no. 2 (Fall 1983): 173, 174.

34. See Adm. William O. Studeman, USN (Ret.), interview by then–Lt. Comdr. David A. Rosenberg, USNR, and then–Lt. Comdr. William R. Hunt, USNR (August 17, 1996), discussing power of "analysis as a sensor"; see also Adm. William O. Studeman, USN (Ret.), presentation to ONI OPINTEL "Lessons Learned" Symposium, making a similar point.

35. See, e.g., Herman, *Intelligence Power,* 12.

36. Bath, *Tracking the Axis Enemy,* 47.

37. Herman, *Intelligence Power,* 25. Herman contrasts this British focus upon integrated intelligence to the practice that was obtained in Germany and Japan during the war, in which service baronies each attempted to provide their own independent intelligence information.

38. Bath, *Tracking the Axis Enemy,* 47.

39. Beesly, *Very Special Intelligence,* 1, 5–7; see also 157, contrasting Room 40 and OIC.

40. Bath, *Tracking the Axis Enemy,* 13.

41. Beesly, *Very Special Intelligence,* 14.

42. Bath, *Tracking the Axis Enemy,* 19; Beesly, *Very Special Intelligence,* 17–18.

43. Bath, *Tracking the Axis Enemy,* 19 and 92. The Mediterranean OIC's principal mission was to monitor Italian activity. See John Winton,

ULTRA at Sea (New York: William Morrow, 1988), 10. After the fall of Singapore, the British Far East fleet received similar intelligence support from Station Anderson in Ceylon (Sri Lanka). See Prados, *Combined Fleet Decoded,* 409. Similarly, shortly before the Normandy invasion in 1945—when it was believed to be vital to supply the best possible operational intelligence to naval commanders who would be leading the Allied invasion force across the channel—the OIC set up a sort of "satellite office" of its tracking room at the naval base at Plymouth. Rodger Winn himself was dispatched to ensure that this new center provided the best possible support to the invading forces (Beesly, *Very Special Intelligence,* 242).

44. Bath, *Tracking the Axis Enemy,* 22. Interestingly, Godfrey also emphasized the importance of ensuring that the operational intelligence system remained in close contact with the national-level cryptologic community (in Britain's case, the famous "ULTRA" code breakers at Bletchley Park). This focus upon close relations with the signals intelligence (SIGINT)/cryptologic world would be paralleled in postwar American practice. As Winn's example suggests, throughout World Wars I and II the British seem to have had considerable success in recruiting excellent operational intelligence officials from nontraditional demographic pools. During the 1914–18 conflict, Britain's top intelligence expert on German U-boats was the fleet paymaster. Indeed, according to one study in 1919, "The most striking feature in the expansion of the Intelligence Division [of the British Admiralty] was the introduction of civil ability with the object of gaining the help of experts of all kinds. Men of science and letters, eminent scholars, lawyers and linguists, and travelers acquainted with all countries were brought into the Service. This was, perhaps, the boldest and most successful thing done by Admiral Hall" (Grant, *U-boat Intelligence,* 11, 16). As we will see later, Winn's American counterpart in 1942, Lt. Comdr. Kenneth Knowles, was also a somewhat nontraditional naval officer. This tradition of supplementing homegrown naval abilities with talent recruited from the civilian world lives on today in the Direct Commission Officer (DIRCOM) Program of the U.S. Naval Reserve Intelligence Program (NRIP).

45. Bath, *Tracking the Axis Enemy,* 18. In fact, the OIC's effectiveness was initially hampered, during the first year of the war, by the paucity of intelligence information susceptible to analysis. Nevertheless, it was well organized and proved itself "ready to shift into top gear as soon as

more fuel in the shape of first class information could be fed into it" (Beesly, *Very Special Intelligence,* 41; see also Beesly, 26–27).

46. Bath, *Tracking the Axis Enemy,* 76–77. Winn started as a civilian assistant in the OIC's tracking room (its submarine plot), but was subsequently commissioned in the Royal Navy Volunteer Reserve. Before the end of the war, he had received the Order of the British Empire and had been promoted to the rank of captain (Beesly, *Very Special Intelligence,* 57, 108, and 236).

47. Bath, *Tracking the Axis Enemy,* 18–19.

48. Beesly, *Very Special Intelligence,* 253.

49. Bath, *Tracking the Axis Enemy,* 35 and 59.

50. Ibid., 63.

51. Layton, *"And I Was There,"* 98.

52. Packard, *Century of U.S. Naval Intelligence,* 225. Anderson made this recommendation in 1939, in conjunction with his Army counterpart, the assistant chief of staff for Intelligence.

53. See Bath, *Tracking the Axis Enemy,* 48, 70–71, and 93–94; see also Capt. Richard W. Bates, USN (Ret.), presentation to ONI OPINTEL "Lessons Learned" Symposium. This is not to suggest that Britain was entirely free of interservice rivalries that inhibited efficient coordinated use of intelligence information, though the British system seems to have done better in this regard than the American system. Winterbotham, for example, recounts that the Royal Navy resisted efforts to jointly exploit ULTRA-derived intelligence and kept the use of intelligence derived from the German naval ULTRA system largely to itself. See Winterbotham, *Ultra Secret,* 19, 23–24, 83, and 175. Such squabbles, however, seem relatively tame compared to the antics of the U.S. services, who could resolve their feud over the control of ULTRA and MAGIC cryptologic traffic only by agreeing to alternate months in providing such intelligence to President Roosevelt at the White House. Indeed, at one point interservice coordination proved so dysfunctional that no one managed to inform the president of ULTRA or MAGIC information for approximately a month. See Layton, *"And I Was There,"* 117.

54. Packard, *Century of U.S. Naval Intelligence,* 204.

55. Prados, *Combined Fleet Decoded,* 353.

56. Admiral King reputedly picked the awkward moniker "COMINCH" because the previous reference to the Commander in Chief, U.S.

Fleet—CINCUS—sounded too much like "sink us." See Layton, *"And I Was There,"* 354–55.

57. Packard, *Century of U.S. Naval Intelligence,* 204.

58. Bath, *Tracking the Axis Enemy,* 103–4.

59. Beesly, *Very Special Intelligence,* ix (from the introduction by W. J. R. Gardner); see also 68, describing the admiralty as reserving the right to take operational control—and frequently exercising it, even down to the tactical level.

60. Ibid., 106 and 186–87.

61. Bath, *Tracking the Axis Enemy,* 76; Beesly, *Very Special Intelligence,* 110 and 187.

62. Bath, *Tracking the Axis Enemy,* 71; see also 79.

63. Prados, *Combined Fleet Decoded,* 354; see also 543, describing ONI during the war as having "a mere library function, to service requests from combat intelligence and COMINCH operations planners."

64. The first U.S. Navy radio intercept station had been set up in the U.S. consulate in Shanghai, China, in 1924, to be followed a year later by a station in Peking (Beijing), the target of which was Japanese diplomatic radio traffic, and a temporary listening post at Wailupe, east of Honolulu, Hawaii. Fleet radio intelligence units were established at Guam and Olongapo, Philippines, in 1927. The nerve center for the Navy's radio intelligence intercept operations was "Station Negat" in Washington—its name deriving from the phonetic alphabet "N" of the Navy Department building—with Stations "Hypo" (Honolulu) and "Cast" (Cavite, Philippines) functioning as Negat's satellite offices and engaging similarly in decryption and traffic analysis (Layton, *"And I Was There,"* 52, 56–57, and 102).

65. Packard, *Century of U.S. Naval Intelligence,* 205–6, 216–18.

66. Ibid., 204, and David Kohnen, "F-21 and F-211: A Fresh Look into the 'Secret Room,'" in *New Interpretations in Naval History: Selected Papers from the Fourteenth Naval History Symposium,* ed. Randy Carol Balano and Craig L. Symonds, (Annapolis, Md.: Naval Institute Press, 2001), 288, 304, and 309–18. Like Winn, Knowles was something of an anomaly within his service. He suffered from physical disabilities that had forced him from the service in 1936, but later rejoined it after acquiring a reputation as an intellectual and writer on naval issues while working in Brooklyn.

67. "Traffic analysis" is the intelligence term for information derived from enemy communications intelligence (COMINT) short of actually breaking the encryption used to protect message contents. Traffic analysis seeks to derive useful information from an understanding of such things as messages' address headers, transmittal precedence (e.g., "urgent" versus "routine"), routings, lengths, regularity, points of origin, and recipients. See generally Norman Polmar and Thomas Allen, *Spy Book* (New York: Random House, 1997), 555; Watson et al., *United States Intelligence,* 569.

68. Bath, *Tracking the Axis Enemy,* 101–2; see also Packard, *Century of U.S. Naval Intelligence,* 205.

69. Packard, *Century of U.S. Naval Intelligence,* 205.

70. Bath, *Tracking the Axis Enemy,* 101.

71. Packard, *Century of U.S. Naval Intelligence,* 204–5.

72. Ibid., 217–18. Interestingly, one of the Navy's new operational intelligence specialists was a young lieutenant named Byron White. A football star and future Supreme Court Justice, White served during the war as part of the OPINTEL section of the intelligence center for the Commander, South Pacific Area (COMSOPAC). See Packard, *Century of U.S. Naval Intelligence,* 409.

73. Prados, *Combined Fleet Decoded,* 403–5; Layton, *"And I Was There,"* 465.

74. Prados, *Combined Fleet Decoded,* 596.

75. Twitty, "Report on Intelligence Activities," p. 2, para. 13.

76. Rear Adm. Donald M. Showers, USN (Ret.), videotaped interview by Comdr. Stephen W. Scalenghe, Suitland, Md., (January 8, 2000).

77. Layton, *"And I Was There,"* 470; see also Bath, *Tracking the Axis Enemy,* 194, who contrasts the genuinely "joint" Nimitz staff with the Army-dominated intelligence structure under Gen. Douglas MacArthur. Captain Packard describes JICPOA as "a unique organization . . . the only U.S. agency in which Military and Naval Intelligence were formed into a single comprehensive organization servicing all the needs of ground, air, and naval forces of a theater command" (Packard, *Century of U.S. Naval Intelligence,* 32). Interestingly, the term "Central Intelligence Agency" was apparently first used in U.S. intelligence practice in connection with the establishment of this Pacific theater OPINTEL all-source fusion scheme. According to Thomas Troy, this term was

used in a March 24, 1942, memorandum from the Marine Corps commandant to COMINCH Admiral King. This memorandum proposed creating a "Central Intelligence Agency" to serve as "a clearing house" for the "Advanced Joint Intelligence Centers" then being planned for the Pacific theater. See Thomas F. Troy, *Donovan and the CIA: A History of the Establishment of the CIA* (Frederick, Md.: Aletheia Books/CIA Center for the Study of Intelligence, 1981).

78. Layton, *"And I Was There,"* 471; Bath, *Tracking the Axis Enemy,* 186.

79. Bath, *Tracking the Axis Enemy,* 186; see also Packard, *Century of U.S. Naval Intelligence,* 234.

80. Layton, *"And I Was There,"* 470.

81. Bath, *Tracking the Axis Enemy,* 186.

82. Packard, *Century of U.S. Naval Intelligence,* 229 and 235; Prados, *Combined Fleet Decoded,* 403–5 and 409; U.S. Pacific Fleet, *Report of Intelligence Activities in the Pacific Ocean Areas* (October 15, 1945) [declassified], 52, copy courtesy of Rear Adm. Donald M. Showers, USN (Ret.).

83. See Bath, *Tracking the Axis Enemy,* 153 and 180.

84. Prados, *Combined Fleet Decoded,* 353.

85. Winston Churchill, quoted in James F. Dunnigan and Albert A. Nofi, *Dirty Little Secrets* (New York: William Morrow, 1990), 189–90.

86. See Winterbotham, *Ultra Secret,* 84. "Those in the know would agree that Ultra was the hub of the whole Atlantic battle. Nowhere was it more vital than in the battle between the German U boats and the convoys of merchant ships and their escort vessels whose supplies were vital to Britain's survival throughout the first years of the war, not to mention their role in supplying the troops and arms for the eventual Allied victory." As Beesly recounts, intelligence-driven rerouting of transatlantic convoys worked remarkably well. Between May 1942 and May 1943, some 60 percent of the 174 scheduled convoys were diverted, with only 16 convoys losing more than four ships each (Beesly, *Very Special Intelligence,* 185).

87. Admiral Nimitz described the U.S. victory at Midway as "essentially a victory of intelligence," for as Gen. George C. Marshall put it, without good intelligence, "we almost certainly would have been some 3,000 miles out of place." See Jeffrey T. Richelson, *A Century of Spies*

(New York: Oxford University Press, 1995), 183. Midway has entered the lore of intelligence, in particular, because of the clever ruse employed by U.S. cryptologists to confirm the destination of the embarked Japanese invasion force. In order to confirm that the target designation "AF" appearing in decrypted radio traffic was in fact Midway Island, U.S. Navy intelligence officers in Hawaii arranged (via secure underwater cable) for the U.S. garrison there to broadcast an unencrypted radio message announcing problems with its desalinization plant. Japan's own radio intelligence service obligingly picked this up and reported to Tokyo—in messages that were quickly broken and read by U.S. cryptologists, as had been expected—that "AF" had water problems. See Richelson, *Century of Spies,* 182; Prados, *Combined Fleet Decoded,* 318–19.

This story of the confirmation of "AF" has become such stuff of intelligence legend that it is often overlooked that the cryptologists at Pearl Harbor apparently already believed that Midway was the Imperial Fleet's target. Apparently, the "AF" trick was principally a symptom of internal Navy bureaucratic rivalries. The cryptologists in Washington, D.C., disagreed with naval cryptologists in the Pacific, concluding that "AF" was a communications designator and not a geographic one. By this account, therefore, the famous "AF" deception was really designed for U.S. Navy consumption—to convince Washington that Station Hypo at Pearl Harbor and the Melbourne station had all been correct in identifying "AF" as Midway and that OP-20-G at the Navy Department mistaken. See Layton, *"And I Was There,"* 421; Frederick D. Parker, *A Priceless Advantage: U.S. Navy Communications Intelligence and the Battles of Coral Sea, Midway, and the Aleutians,* United States Cryptologic History, Series IV, World War II, vol. 5 (Ft. Meade, Md.: National Security Agency, 1993), 43 and 50–51.

88. Winton, *Ultra at Sea,* 196.

89. See Robert Louis Benson, *A History of U.S. Communications Intelligence during World War II: Policy and Administration,* U.S. Cryptologic History, Series IV, World War II, vol. 8 (Ft. Meade, Md.: National Security Agency, 1997), 21.

90. Indeed, "it was impossible for Allied code breakers to furnish information derived from cryptologic sources for many months of the war." During these periods, when enemy codes were not broken, the tracking rooms had to rely upon other location methods. See Kohnen, "F-21 and F-211," 317.

91. See generally Capt. John Q. Edwards, USN (Ret.), and Rear Adm. Donald M. Showers, USN (Ret.), presentations to ONI OPINTEL "Lessons Learned" Symposium, where they discuss the role of ULTRA/ Enigma in revolutionizing OPINTEL.

92. Winton, *Ultra at Sea,* 33–39.

93. Ibid., 76.

94. Ibid., 105–6.

95. Bath, *Tracking the Axis Enemy,* 106–7; Winton, *Ultra at Sea,* 86. The Germans blamed their U-boat losses on Allied superiority in radar and direction finding, not guessing that it actually stemmed from a combination of superior organization, training, tactics, and code break- ing. See generally Holger H. Herwig, "The Failure of German Sea Power, 1914–1945: Mahan, Tirpitz, and Roeder Reconsidered," *International History Review,* x, no. 1 (February 1988): 1, 102; see also Bam- ford, *Puzzle Palace,* 66, where he recounts the German attempt to blame losses upon Allied possession of an (imaginary) super-sophisticated direction-finding device.

96. Bath, *Tracking the Axis Enemy,* 107.

97. The term is Vice Adm. Francis Low's. Low was Chief of Staff to Fleet Adm. Ernest J. King, Commander of the Tenth Fleet. See Packard, *Century of U.S. Naval Intelligence,* 216.

98. See Marc Milner, "The Battle of the Atlantic," *Journal of Strategic Studies* 13, no. 1 (March 1990): 45, 46; Winterbotham, *Ultra Secret,* 85.

99. Sir John Slessor, foreword to Winterbotham, *Ultra Secret,* xii.

100. Beesly, *Very Special Intelligence,* 88; see also 95.

101. Ibid., 238.

102. Winton, *Ultra at Sea,* 94–95, 112, and 114; Beesly, *Very Special Intelligence,* 145.

103. Winton, *Ultra at Sea,* 132. The chief of the German U-boat arm was titled the *Befehlshaber der U-boote* (BdU). See Winton, 197.

104. See Winton, *Ultra at Sea,* 83, 103, 105, and 124.

105. Beesly, *Very Special Intelligence,* 52–53.

106. See Marc Milner, "The Dawn of Modern Anti-Submarine Warfare: Allied Responses to the U-Boats, 1944–45," *Royal United Services Institute Journal* 134, no. 1 (Spring 1989): 61, 66–67.

107. Prados, *Combined Fleet Decoded,* 727. Layton suggests that Japan suffered enormously for lack of any analogous capability. Indeed, Adm. Isoroku Yamamoto did not even have a full-time intelligence officer on his staff until after the Battle of Midway. Instead, Imperial Navy leaders relied only upon on-the-spot estimates by operational commanders—supplemented by inputs from a radio intelligence system that consisted of a series of listening posts running from the Kurile Islands south to Formosa (Taiwan) and east across the Mandates (e.g., Marianas) (Layton, *"And I Was There,"* 102 and 361).

108. John Adams, Letter to Jonathan Sewall, October 1759, quoted in David McCullough, *John Adams* (New York: Simon and Schuster, 2001), 53.

109. Michael Howard, *War in European History* (Oxford: Oxford University Press, 1976), 134, quoted in Herman, *Intelligence Power,* 23.

110. Layton, *"And I Was There,"* 22.

111. Herman, *Intelligence Power,* 45.

112. Winton, *Ultra at Sea,* 47.

113. Twitty, "Report on Intelligence Activities," p. 2, para. 17.

114. Showers, videotaped interview.

115. Comdr. J. R. Reddig, USN, "The OSIS Culture: Intelligence Support to Naval Operations from Cold War to New World Order," unpublished paper prepared for Maritime Strategy elective class at the National War College, February 2, 1998, 16. Reddig, for example, quotes Comdr. Michael McConnell—who would later become a vice admiral and the director of the National Security Agency (NSA)—as saying to a submarine analyst in 1982, "OK, you know it. Have you told anyone?" (Reddig, 12).

116. Marshall N. Wright, "Battlespace 2000: Intelligence Communications or Deployed Naval Forces," *American Intelligence Journal* (1997): 59, who discusses the importance of rapidly getting information "from the source (i.e., sensor) to quickly determine the tactical situation, and get the 'battlespace picture' as seen by the [carrier battle group or amphibious ready group] commander."

117. See, e.g., Gen. A. M. Grey, USMC, *Warfighting: The U.S. Marine Corps Book of Strategy* (New York: Doubleday, 1995), 77. ("By our actions, we seek to pose menacing dilemmas in which events happen unexpectedly and faster for the enemy than the enemy can keep up with

them."); see also generally Ens. Christopher A. Ford, USNR, "Dinosaur's Dilemma," U.S. Naval Institute *Proceedings* (September 1996), 78–80, discussing application of cybernetic theory to warfare and the application of Colonel John Boyd's concept of the "observe-orient-decide-and-act" command cycle.

118. As Marshall Wright indicates, the continual drive for improved technological solutions obtains across all parts of the OPINTEL process: "The present and future demands for on-time delivery of ISR [intelligence, surveillance, and reconnaissance] products to the Battle Group Commander in support of the warfighter requires revolutionary approaches to the handling of sensor information, encompassing collection, processing and dissemination of the ISR products" (Wright, "Battlespace 2000," 59).

119. Packard, *Century of U.S. Naval Intelligence,* 243.

120. Prados, *Combined Fleet Decoded,* 78–79.

121. Layton, *"And I Was There,"* 46–47.

122. Frederick D. Parker, *Pearl Harbor Revisited: United States Navy Communications Intelligence, 1924–1941,* United States Cryptologic History, Series IV, World War II, vol. 6 (Ft. Meade, Md.: National Security Agency, 1994), 32.

123. Layton, *"And I Was There,"* 410 and 144.

124. Ibid., 361–62 and 394–95.

125. Ibid., 394–95. As a rule, according to one veteran of World War II submarine operations and post–World War II Naval Intelligence, the average operational junior officer had little knowledge of or appreciation for the value of intelligence. Rear Adm. Maurice H. Rindskopf, USN (Ret.), presentation to ONI OPINTEL "Lessons Learned" Symposium.

126. Showers, videotaped interview.

127. Prados, *Combined Fleet Decoded,* 353.

128. Beesly, *Very Special Intelligence,* 169.

129. Bath, *Tracking the Axis Enemy,* 103. This tension between operational utility and the protection of "intelligence sources and methods," of course, was not new. During World War I, the British Admiralty had chafed at what they considered to be the unseemly willingness of both American and French naval commanders to act upon sensitive radio intercepts. The admiralty restricted its *own* responses to U-boat dangers in 1914–18 when no other plausible reason for patrol activity

could be found, and on at least one occasion was apparently willing to let a French cruiser unknowingly risk sinking rather than risk disclosing British code-breaking successes by taking obvious precautions. See Grant, *U-boat Intelligence,* 19, 158, and 161–62.

130. Adm. David Jeremiah, videotaped interview by Comdr. Stephen W. Scalenghe, Suitland, Md., February 4, 2000. As Francis Dvornik has recounted, there is a historical relationship between effective long-range communications systems and intelligence services. This connection dates back to ancient Assyria—where government-run road systems and a series of fire-signal towers proved indispensable to imperial intelligence organization as well as command and control. Francis Dvornik, *Origins of Intelligence Services* (New Brunswick, N.J.: Rutgers University Press, 1974), 16–18 and 23.

131. F. W. Winterbotham, for example, recounts the story of American commanders' initial desire immediately to sink all of the Germans' so-called *Milch Cow* at-sea submarine-replenishment ships when their locations were revealed by ULTRA. See Winterbotham, *Ultra Secret,* 86. Patrick Beesly's "insider" history of the admiralty OIC provides a broad discussion of British worries about sanitization, "need-to-know" issues, and operational security in connection with Special Intelligence—as well as their worries about American handling of cryptanalysis information from Bletchley Park. See Beesly, *Very Special Intelligence,* 89, 98–100, 189–90, and 279.

132. Kohnen, "F-21 and F-211," 304, 327–29.

133. See Herman, *Intelligence Power,* 92.

134. Winton, *Ultra at Sea,* 148; see also Winterbotham, *Ultra Secret,* 86, recounting that British officers persuaded the Americans to sink the German ships only gradually, so as not to alert the Nazis to the compromise of their most sensitive communications.

135. R. V. Jones, *The Wizard War* (New York: Coward, McCann, and Geoghegan, 1978), 204; see also Bates, presentation.

136. Bath, *Tracking the Axis Enemy,* 79; see also Herman, *Intelligence Power,* 44.

137. See generally, e.g., Robin W. Winks, *Cloak and Gown* (New York: William Morrow, 1987), 271.

138. Winton, *Ultra at Sea,* 4.

139. Bates, presentation. For an account of the SSO system, see Benson, *U.S. Communications Intelligence,* 41–43.

140. Showers, presentation. The former officer aboard the wartime submarine USS *Drum* recounts the amusing story of acquiring a reputation for prescience because of the remarkable accuracy of the ULTRA-derived information he received, the source of which could not be revealed. See Rindskopf, presentation.

141. See, e.g., Winton, *Ultra at Sea,* 4. Winton believes that this was done only imperfectly and that in fact a serious actuarial study of Allied operational moves against German assets would have revealed that the Enigma machine had been compromised. Nevertheless, throughout the entire war, the Germans always assumed the Enigma was secure and found other excuses to explain Allied successes. See generally Winton, 38–39, 89–90, 104, and 181–95; Beesly, *Very Special Intelligence,* 90, 196, and 281–84.

142. Kohnen, "F-21 and F-211," 305, 330.

143. Francis F. Low, *A Study of Undersea Warfare,* TOP SECRET Annex, "United States Administrative Histories of World War II, Appendices Collection," Draft submitted January 1, 1946 (declassified). U.S. Naval Historical Center, Operational Archives, Command Files. Quoted in Kohnen, "F-21 and F-211," 331–32.

144. Layton, *"And I Was There,"* 81.

145. Ibid., 91, 120, and 139.

146. Benson, *U.S. Communications Intelligence,* 47.

147. Ibid., 379, and Bates, presentation.

148. Showers, videotaped interview.

149. Showers, presentation.

150. Winton, *Ultra at Sea,* 1.

151. Studeman, presentation.

152. Bath, *Tracking the Axis Enemy,* 234.

153. Watson et al., *United States Intelligence,* 399.

154. Showers, presentation.

155. U.S. Pacific Fleet, *Report of Intelligence Activities,* 46.

156. Rear Adm. Sumner Shapiro, USN (Ret.), videotaped interview by Comdr. Stephen W. Scalanghe, Suitland, Md. (January 8, 2000).

157. U.S. Pacific Fleet, *Report of Intelligence Activities,* 3.

158. Twitty, "Report on Intelligence Activities," p. 3, paras. 29–31.

159. U.S. Pacific Fleet, *Report of Intelligence Activities,* 4.

160. Twitty, "Report on Intelligence Activities," p. 2, para. 14.

161. U.S. Pacific Fleet, *Report of Intelligence Activities,* 3.

162. Ibid.

163. Twitty, "Report on Intelligence Activities," p. 3, para. 31.

Chapter 2: The Postwar Years

1. Showers, videotaped interview.

2. David A. Rosenberg, "The History of World War III, 1945–1990: A Conceptual Framework," in *On Cultural Ground: Essays in International History,* Robert David Johnson, ed., Imprint Studies in International Relations, 1 (Chicago: Imprint, 1994), 97, 198.

3. See generally Rosenberg, "History of World War III," 201–4.

4. See Norman Polmar and K. J. Moore, *Cold War Submarines: The Design and Construction of U.S. and Soviet Submarines* (Washington, D.C.: Brassey's, 2004), 49–70; and Karl Lautenschläger, "The Submarine in Naval Warfare, 1901–2001," *International Security* II, no. 3 (Winter 1986–87), 238, 268, and 273.

5. Polmar and Moore, *Cold War Submarines,* 85–114; and Lautenschläger, "The Submarine in Naval Warfare," 268–69.

6. See George W. Baer, "U.S. Naval Strategy 1890–1945," *Naval War College Review,* no. XLIV (Winter 1991): 6, 26–27.

7. Breaching NATO antisubmarine warfare barriers and using the growing Soviet submarine fleet to disrupt the maritime links between North America and Europe was indeed, during this period, the major focus of Moscow's naval strategy. See Capt. 2nd Rank V. Dotsenko, "Soviet Art of Naval Warfare in the Postwar Period," *Morskoy Sbornik,* no. 7 (1989): 22, 28.

8. The beginnings of ONI's Cold War–era focus upon the Soviet Union can be seen as early as February 1950, when field collection agencies were strengthened within countries contiguous to the USSR. This effort included the creation or augmentation of listening posts, interrogation sites, stepped-up training of Russian linguists, increased efforts to obtain Soviet publications, increased reliance upon reporting from friendly merchant ships and commercial aircraft, and the development of more precise collection requirements vis-à-vis the USSR. See Packard, *Century of U.S. Naval Intelligence,* 49.

9. This "OP" designation itself reflected ONI's transfer from the Administration Division to the Operations Division of the Navy Department, which occurred in August 1946. See ONI OPINTEL "Lessons Learned" Symposium.

10. The Chief of Naval Intelligence was redesignated a "Director" in November 1948 in order to correspond with the analogous titles given to the heads of Army and Air Force intelligence and of the Central Intelligence Agency.

11. For an account of these various postwar changes, see Packard, *Century of U.S. Naval Intelligence,* 219–22; see also *OPINTEL Chronology,* ONI OPINTEL "Lessons Learned" Symposium.

12. Showers, videotaped interview.

13. Packard, *Century of U.S. Naval Intelligence,* 221–22; see also Naval Maritime Intelligence Center, *Naval Maritime Intelligence Center: October 1991–7 January 1993* (command history dated March 26, 1993), 1, ONI Historian's Files.

14. Packard, *Century of U.S. Naval Intelligence,* 222; see also undated notes in collection of NFOIO/NOSIC Command Histories maintained by the ONI Command. The renaming of Y1 as NFOIO was apparently just a by-product of the physical move to Fort Meade, which took the organization out from under the wing of the Navy Department and placed it under the aegis of the Severn River Naval Command—the operational "hat" of the superintendent of the U.S. Naval Academy. In this new guise, the organization could no longer bear the Navy Department designation "Y1." Information from informal conversations with Rear Adm. Donald M. Showers, USN (Ret.), the first head of NFOIO.

15. Packard, *Century of U.S. Naval Intelligence,* 222.

16. As Reddig recounts, NFOIO's establishment at Fort Meade continued the "symbiotic relationship" between Naval Intelligence and cryptology that had begun with such promise during the war (Reddig, "OSIS Culture," 2–3).

17. Ibid., 2–3.

18. Personal daily briefings for the CNO from ONI's Operational Intelligence Branch had begun in September 1949, under Adm. Forrest Sherman. *OPINTEL Chronology.*

19. This was the Shipping Intelligence Center of the Commander Naval Forces Far East (COMNAVFE) Intelligence Section organized at the end of 1950, which "collated, evaluated, and disseminated reports

of sightings received through air, surface, subsurface, and radar searches and reports from coast watchers" (Packard, *Century of U.S. Naval Intelligence,* 415).

20. Miyamoto Musashi, *The Book of Five Rings,* trans. Thomas Cleary (Boston: Shambhala, 1994), 34.

21. Rear Adm. Edward D. Sheafer, *Strategic Planning for the Office of Naval Intelligence: Vision and Direction for the Future* (July 1992), 2; see also Studeman, slide presentation, noting that "It is the *people* that can make the difference . . . [and] continuing training and education are critical."

22. Joseph Amato, presentation at ONI OPINTEL "Lessons Learned" Symposium.

23. *OPINTEL Chronology.*

24. See generally ONI, "Our Story," 12, 19.

25. See Packard, *Century of U.S. Naval Intelligence,* 374–77; see also National Maritime Intelligence Center, "History of the Intelligence Specialist Rating" (June 6, 1998), at http://www.nmicic.gov/mipm/hist.htm.

26. Reddig, "OSIS Culture," 4–5.

27. Photogrammetry is "the art or science of obtaining reliable measurements from photographic images" (Watson et al., *United States Intelligence,* 437).

28. NMIC, "History," 1; see also *Photographic Interpretation and Radar Target Intelligence Newsletter* VI, no. 2 (April 1958): 5, which describes BUPERS NOTICE 14400 of February 7, 1958, establishing PT rating.

29. Information supplied to the author by Capt. William Manthorpe, USN (Ret.), on July 9, 2000.

30. Reddig, "OSIS Culture," 4.

31. Prior to 1963, DNIs were chosen exclusively from the ranks of unrestricted line officers. Capt. William H. J. Manthorpe, USN (Ret.), interview by Lt. Comdr. M. D. Mizrahi, USNR (April 24, 1996); see also ONI, "Our Story," 20.

32. Packard, *Century of U.S. Naval Intelligence,* 241.

33. See Grant, *U-boat Intelligence,* 10 and 71, describing the use of hydrophones in antisubmarine operations, e.g., by French patrol boats off Calais in August 1918.

34. See Owen R. Cote Jr., *The Third Battle: Innovation in the U.S. Navy's Silent Cold War Struggle with Soviet Submarines* (Newport, R.I.: Naval War College Press, Newport Papers No. 16, 2003), 16–17, quoting Maurice Ewing and J. Lamar Worzel, "Long-Range Sound Transmission:" *The Geological Society of America Memoir* 27 (October 15, 1948): 1.

35. Cote, *Third Battle,* 17, citing Frank Andrews, "The Evolution of SubDevGru 12," *Submarine Review* (April 1983): 4; Massachusetts Institute of Technology, "Project Hartwell, A Report on Security of Overseas Transport," September 21, 1950.

36. See Jeffrey T. Richelson, *The U.S. Intelligence Community,* 3rd. ed. (Boulder, Colo.: Westview, 1995), 211; Lautenschläger, "Technology and the Evolution of Naval Warfare," 173, 216; see also generally Norman Polmar, "The U.S. Navy: Sonars, Part 2," U.S. Naval Institute *Proceedings* 107 (September 1981): 135–36; Joel S. Wit, "Advances in Antisubmarine Warfare," *Scientific American* (February 1981): 32; Alan Hyman, "Ocean Surveillance from Land, Air, and Space," *Naval Forces* 3, no. 2 (1982): 58–59; David Miller and Chris Miller, *Modern Naval Combat* (New York: Crescent, 1986), 65.

37. IUSS/CAESAR Alumni Association Web site, "Integrated Undersea Surveillance System (IUSS) History, 1950–1997," at http://www. iusscaa.org/history.htm (accessed June 2, 2002, and September 27, 2003).

38. *OPINTEL Chronology.*

39. Manthorpe, interview.

40. Information provided informally in discussions with retired Rear Adm. Donald M. Showers, Rear Adm. Sumner Shapiro, and Capt. John Q. Edwards by Comdr. David A. Rosenberg, USNR, in 1997–98.

41. Alternative routes—through the narrow and shallow waters of the Baltic Sea's western exits or out of the Black Sea through the Turkish-controlled Bosporus into the Mediterranean—were even more confining, and perhaps prohibitive in an environment of general war. For this reason, the Soviet Northern Fleet (based on or near the Kola Peninsula in the Barents Sea) and Pacific Fleet (based on or near the Kamchatka Peninsula and/or Vladivostok on the mainland) were the principal concerns of NATO and U.S. naval planners.

42. See generally Wit, "Advances in Antisubmarine Warfare," 31, 36–37.

43. See Dotsenko, "Soviet Art of Naval Warfare," 27.

44. Wit, "Advances in Antisubmarine Warfare," 36.

45. Ibid., 32.

46. Richelson, *U.S. Intelligence Community,* 211.

47. Packard, *Century of U.S. Naval Intelligence,* 220.

48. See Showers, presentation.

49. Manthorpe, interview. As Manthorpe recalls, as a 1630 sent straight from the Naval Academy to ONI, he used to be jibed by Rear Adm. Charles Martell—then the Deputy DNI and an unrestricted line officer with significant at-sea experience—that "you will know nothing about the Navy until you go to sea." Fortunately, five years later Martell was able to overcome the reluctance of the DNI, Rear Adm. Rufus Taylor, and take Manthorpe (by then a lieutenant commander) to sea as Martell's Acting N-2. This would not have been possible without the support of the Atlantic Fleet's shore-based ocean surveillance node. See information supplied to the author by Capt. William Manthorpe, USN (Ret.), on July 9, 2000.

50. Ibid.

51. David A. Rosenberg, "American Naval Strategy in the Era of the Third World War: An Inquiry into the Structure and Process of General War at Sea," in N. A. M. Rodger, ed., *Naval Power in the Twentieth Century* (Annapolis, Md.: Naval Institute Press, 1996), 242, 245.

Chapter 3: The 1960s

1. Rosenberg, "History of World War III," 97, 207–9.

2. Ibid., 210, quoting President Jimmy Carter, *Military Strategy and Force Posture Review Final Report,* Presidential Review Memorandum: PRM/NSC-10 (June 6, 1977), 8–9.

3. By 1967 the United States had forty-one Polaris ballistic missile submarines (SSBNs) in commission. Lautenschläger, "Submarine in Naval Warfare," 238, 275.

4. See Dotsenko, "Soviet Art of Naval Warfare," 22, 28–29.

5. Ibid.

6. Lautenschläger, "Submarine in Naval Warfare," 273.

7. Reddig, "OSIS Culture," 9.

8. See Rear Adm. Sumner Shapiro, USN (Ret.), presentation at ONI OPINTEL "Lessons Learned" Symposium.

9. According to Captain Manthorpe, for a time in the 1960s the U.S. Navy regarded Soviet naval aviation threats as being an even higher priority than that posed by Soviet submarines (Manthorpe, interview).

10. Vice Adm. David Richardson, USN (Ret.), notes for presentation at ONI OPINTEL "Lessons Learned" Symposium.

11. See, e.g., Watson et al., *United States Intelligence,* 279.

12. Studeman, interview, describing HUMINT as having traditionally been of only "marginal interest" to Naval Intelligence.

13. See generally Richelson, *U.S. Intelligence Community,* 192–93.

14. Despite the acronym, it should be noted, this was a separate organization from the *National* Photographic Interpretation Center, which was run by the Central Intelligence Agency.

15. *NAVPIC: Historical Report for 1961* (January 17, 1962), 1, ONI Historian's Files.

16. This phrasing is taken from the Navy Unit Commendation received by the center for its work during the Cuban Missile Crisis. See Naval Intelligence Support Center, Office of Naval Warfare Capabilities, *A Chronology, Command History, Legal Authorities and Organization Charts Depicting the Development of Navy Photographic Interpretation and Scientific and Technical Intelligence Activities 1941–1975* (May 1975), 4, ONI Historian's Files.

17. See U.S. Naval Research Laboratory, "Galactic Radiation and Background (GRAB) Satellite Declassified: NRL Built and Deployed First Reconnaissance Satellite System," Press Release 41–98r (June 17, 1998) and pamphlet, Naval Research Laboratory, *GRAB: Galactic RAdiation and Background, First Reconnaissance Satellite* (Washington, D.C.: Naval Research Laboratory, Code 8000, 1998).

18. Packard, *Century of U.S. Naval Intelligence,* 245.

19. Defense Intelligence Agency, *Instruction No. 60–8* (September 22, 1969), 1, ONI Historian's Files.

20. Packard, *Century of U.S. Naval Intelligence,* 245.

21. Reddig, "OSIS Culture," 10.

22. Studeman, slide presentation.

23. Naval Reconnaissance and Technical Support Center, *Historical Review—1964* (February 17, 1965), 1–2, ONI Historian's Files.

24. Naval Reconnaissance and Technical Support Center, *Historical Review—1969* (February 13, 1970), 1, ONI Historian's Files.

25. Packard, *Century of U.S. Naval Intelligence,* 244.

26. Ibid., 243.

27. Naval Reconnaissance and Technical Support Center, *Historical Review—1968* (February 18, 1969), 2, ONI Historian's Files.

28. Packard, *Century of U.S. Naval Intelligence,* 246.

29. Reddig, "OSIS Culture," 5–6.

30. Packard, *Century of U.S. Naval Intelligence,* 245.

31. See Capt. Larry Wright, USN (Ret.), interview by Lt. Comdr. M. D. Mizrahi, USNR, June 25, 1996, discussing the impact of automation upon the daily tasks of OPINTEL analysts.

32. Rear Adm. Thomas A. Brooks, USN (Ret.), videotaped interview by Comdr. Stephen W. Scalenghe, Suitland, Md., January 8, 2000.

33. Reddig, "OSIS Culture," 6.

34. Cf. Jan M. Van Tol, "Military Innovation and Carrier Aviation: Analysis," *Joint Forces Quarterly* (Autumn/Winter 1997–98): 97, 98–9, arguing that the key element to the success of the U.S. Navy during the interwar period was being conscious of the need for change even while being unsure of its ultimate direction; Thomas C. Hone and Mark D. Mandales, "Interwar Innovation in Three Navies: U.S. Navy, Royal Navy, Imperial Japanese Navy," *Naval War College Review* XL, no. 2 (Spring 1987): 63, 76–80, noting importance to warfare developments of the gradual refinement and application of existing technologies, and the key role of organizational adaptability and flexibility in making this possible.

35. Showers, presentation; Capt. George B. Pressly, USN (Ret.), presentation at ONI OPINTEL "Lessons Learned" Symposium; Shapiro, presentation.

36. See, e.g., Amato, presentation.

37. Studeman, presentation.

38. The designator "1635" was given to Naval Reserve intelligence officers whose duties corresponded to the cadre of active-duty 1630s.

39. Quoted by Reddig, "OSIS Culture," 5.

40. See ibid.; see also Manthorpe, interview.

41. See generally Vice Adm. J. M. McConnell, USN (Ret.), interview by Lt. Comdr. M. D. Mizrahi, USNR, August 13, 1996; Wright, interview.

42. See, e.g., Jeremiah, videotaped interview; Vice Adm. Thomas R. Wilson, USN, videotaped interview by Comdr. Stephen W. Scalenghe, Suitland, Md., February 4, 2000; Shapiro, videotaped interview.

43. Jeremiah, videotaped interview.

44. Rear Adm. Donald P. Harvey, USN (Ret.), presentation at ONI OPINTEL "Lessons Learned" Symposium.

45. Wright, interview. According to Captain Wright, in fact, U.S. and Soviet submarines would even occasionally "bump into each other in the middle of the night." See also Desmond Ball, "Nuclear War at Sea," in *Naval Strategy and National Security,* Steven Miller and Stephen van Evera, eds. (Princeton, N.J.: Princeton University Press, 1988), 304 ("The sea is the only area where nuclear weapons platforms of the U.S. and the Soviet Union actually come into physical contact.").

46. Herman, *Intelligence Power,* 121.

47. Shapiro, videotaped interview.

48. See Rear Adm. Thomas R. Wilson, USN, presentation at ONI OPINTEL "Lessons Learned" Symposium.

49. Rear Adm. Lowell E. Jacoby, USN, videotaped interview by Comdr. Stephen W. Scalenghe, Suitland, Md., February 5, 2000.

50. Wilson, videotaped interview.

51. Jacoby, "Operational Intelligence," 102–3.

52. Allen Dulles, *The Craft of Intelligence* (New York: Harper and Row, 1963), 175.

53. Manthorpe, interview.

54. Cf. Studeman, slide presentation, describing the "first obligations" of OPINTEL as "penetrate the threat" and "know your customer." It is important, of course, that these obligations be kept in a prudent balance. Just as too little knowledge of one's own operational environment will lead the intelligence professional to provide information that fails to meet his commander's needs, too close an identification with the "Blue" warfighter may induce him to acquire the warfighter's preconceptions (and perhaps misconceptions) about the enemy. See generally Herman, *Intelligence Power,* 110–11.

55. Rear Adm. John L. Marocchi, USN (Ret.), presentation at ONI OPINTEL "Lessons Learned" Symposium; see also Manthorpe, interview.

56. Wilson, videotaped interview.

57. Richard L. Haver, videotaped interview by Comdr. Stephen W. Scalenghe, Suitland, Md., February 6, 2000.

58. Jacoby, videotaped interview; Jeremiah, videotaped interview.

59. Shapiro, videotaped interview.

60. Haver, videotaped interview.

61. See generally T. Brooks, videotaped interview. ("The most important aspect of OPINTEL which endures is the Naval Intelligence OPINTEL culture—which identifies the Intel officer directly as a support element to the tactical commander. We are a service industry, and dedicate ourselves to understanding the tactical commander and his problems—to understanding how we can bring the assets of the [Intelligence Community] in a focused fashion to bear specifically on those problems.")

62. See generally Herman, *Intelligence Power,* 45–46 and 293–95. Adm. Edmund P. Giambastiani Jr., then-commander of U.S. submarine forces in the Atlantic, prefers a more religious metaphor, describing the good intelligence officer as an "evangelist" who preaches the gospel of intelligence and its potential to the warfighting community. Vice Adm. Edmund P. Giambastiani Jr., USN, presentation at ONI OPINTEL "Lessons Learned" Symposium.

63. Jon Tetsuro Sumida, "'The Best Laid Plans': The Development of British Battle-Fleet Tactics, 1919–1942," *International History Review* XIV, no. 4 (November 1992): 661, 693.

64. Beesly, *Very Special Intelligence,* xiii (from the introduction by W. J. R. Gardner).

65. Ibid., xiv.

66. Herman, *Intelligence Power,* 45.

67. Marocchi, presentation.

68. Sheafer, *Strategic Planning,* 2.

69. Vice Adm. David Richardson, himself a former Sixth Fleet operational commander closely involved in this dynamic, dates the development of such intimate relationships to 1966. "They *did not,*" he has emphasized, "previously exist as norms in the operational commander/intelligence relationship." Vice Adm. David Richardson, USN (Ret.), letter to Lt. Christopher Ford, USNR (August 26, 1998). Richardson also recalls that he did not himself acquire "any understanding of operational intelligence" until his *third* year as a flag officer—at which

point his Carrier Division 7 operations officer "opened my eyes" by observing that "if we run a better flight deck, we improve maybe five percent, *but* if we choose targets more wisely, we double or treble our effectiveness." Richardson, notes of presentation.

70. See Richard L. Haver, presentation at ONI OPINTEL "Lessons Learned" Symposium; Rear Adm. Edward D. Sheafer, USN (Ret.), presentation at ONI OPINTEL "Lessons Learned" Symposium.

71. Herman, *Intelligence Power,* 102.

72. Beesly, *Very Special Intelligence,* 69 and 73.

73. Studeman, slide presentation.

74. Ibid.

75. Cf. Comdr. R. L. Shreadley, USN, "The Naval War in Vietnam, 1950–1970," *Proceedings: Naval Review 1971* 97, no. 819 (May 1971): 182, 187, 188–91, and 209, discussing the Navy's involvement from 1965 and the development of new "Brown water" tactics and operations in a riverine environment.

76. Pressly, presentation. Captain Pressly gave a presentation based upon information provided by former NSA Deputy Director Rear Adm. James S. McFarland, USN (Ret.), who was unable to attend the symposium.

77. Wright, interview.

78. Rear Adm. James S. McFarland, USN (Ret.), notes for presentation at ONI OPINTEL "Lessons Learned" Symposium. Rear Admiral McFarland was unable to attend the symposium, but has generously provided the authors with notes of the presentation he prepared for the occasion.

Chapter 4: OSIS Comes of Age

1. Rosenberg, "American Naval Strategy," 242, 246.

2. Dotsenko, "Soviet Art of Naval Warfare," 22, 29–30.

3. Rosenberg, "American Naval Strategy," 248.

4. Lautenschläger, "Submarine in Naval Warfare," 238, 275.

5. Manthorpe, interview; see also Rear Adm. Lowell E. Jacoby, presentation at ONI OPINTEL "Lessons Learned" Symposium.

6. This point was made by various participants at ONI OPINTEL "Lessons Learned" Symposium, most notably among them Adm. William O. Studeman, USN (Ret.).

7. Packard, *Century of U.S. Naval Intelligence,* 245.

8. Richardson, letter to Ford.

9. Pressly, slide presentation.

10. Wright, interview.

11. Reddig, "OSIS Culture," 6.

12. Pressly, slide presentation.

13. Ibid.

14. Rear Adm. James S. McFarland, USN (Ret.), slide presentation prepared for ONI OPINTEL "Lessons Learned" Symposium. Rear Admiral McFarland was unable to attend the symposium, but Capt. George Pressly, USN (Ret.), gave his presentation in the admiral's absence.

15. Pressly, presentation, and McFarland, presentation.

16. Pressly, presentation.

17. McFarland, presentation.

18. Ibid.

19. T. Brooks, videotaped interview.

20. McFarland, presentation.

21. Similar innovations were under way at this time at FOSIC Norfolk. There, in fact, the CSG staff—technically attached to the theater command (CINCLANT)—came to be located in direct support of a component command intelligence activity. *OPINTEL Chronology.*

22. McFarland, presentation.

23. Wright, interview.

24. McFarland, presentation.

25. Pressly, presentation.

26. McFarland, presentation.

27. Memorandum from OIC, NFOIO to Commanding Officer, Naval Intelligence Support Center, *Ocean Surveillance Information Division/NOSIC Portable Building* (September 29, 1972) (attaching copy of original Contract N62477–70–0091 for building, dated March 1970), ONI Historian's Files.

28. See Packard, *Century of U.S. Naval Intelligence,* 223; see also Memorandum from OIC, NFOIO to Commanding Officer, Naval Intelligence Support Center; Naval Maritime Intelligence Center, *Naval Maritime Intelligence Center,* 1.

29. Pressly, presentation.

30. See undated notes in collection of NFOIO/NOSIC Command Histories maintained by ONI Command Historian Patricia Maynard, ONI Historian's Files.

31. Navy Field Operational Intelligence Office, *NFOIO History 1972* (February 15, 1973), 8; see also ibid., 6, describing NFOIO mission in peacetime as being to "exploit processed SIGINT in the production of finished operational intelligence . . . [including] providing for the timely dissemination of such intelligence so as to permit effective use by authorized recipients" and in wartime to continue with "the above with greater emphasis on analysis and operational intelligence production efforts in support of the operating forces afloat." ONI Historian's Files.

32. Reddig, "OSIS Culture," 8.

33. NFOIO, *NFOIO History 1972,* 2.

34. Navy Ocean Surveillance Information Center, *NOSIC Input for 1976 Command History* (February 25, 1977), 4, ONI Historian's Files. This report was originally sent only to the CNO, but in July 1976 its dissemination was expanded to include the commanders of the Atlantic and Pacific fleets (CINCLANTFLT and CINCPACFLT), as well as the commander of U.S. Naval forces in Europe (CINCUSNAVEUR).

35. Ibid.

36. Pressly, presentation.

37. Reddig, "OSIS Culture," 7.

38. See generally Memorandum from Commander, Naval Intelligence Command, to the Director of Naval History (OP–09B9) (August 1, 1973) (with attachments), ONI Historian's Files; Pressly, slide presentation; Reddig, "OSIS Culture," 7; Richelson, *U.S. Intelligence Community,* 105 and 115; Memorandum from Commander, U.S. Naval Communication Station, Yokusuka, Japan, to Officer in Charge, FOSIF, *Interservice Support Agreement (ISSA) 5H-N-70278–0205–1* (January 19, 1972), giving FOSIF WESTPAC use of portion of building at station, ONI Historian's Files.

39. J. R. Reddig, for example, describes the FOSIFs, in particular, as being "alone, unafraid and almost entirely dedicated to direct support to forward naval operations" (Reddig, "OSIS Culture," 8).

40. Memorandum from Commander, Naval Intelligence Command, to Director of Naval History (OP-09B9) (April 29, 1974) (with attachments), 76.

41. See generally Navy Ocean Surveillance Information Center, *NOSIC Input for 1976 Command History* (February 25, 1977), 1, ONI Historian's Files; McConnell, interview.

42. Wright, interview.

43. Ibid.

44. *NAVINTCOM-42 Command History Submission for 1974* (undated), 10, ONI Historian's Files.

45. Navy Ocean Surveillance Information Center, *NOSIC Command History—1974* (February 3, 1975), 3, ONI Historian's Files.

46. Naval Intelligence Support Center, *NISC-10: Historical Review—1976* (March 13, 1977), 12, ONI Historian's Files.

47. Navy Ocean Surveillance Information Center, *NOSIC Input for 1975 Command History* (February 11, 1976), 5, ONI Historian's Files.

48. Harrison, presentation.

49. See, e.g., Reddig, "OSIS Culture," 8.

50. See Navy Ocean Surveillance Information Center, *NOSIC Input for 1976 Command History* (February 25, 1977) 7, ONI Historian's Files.

51. Memorandum from Commander, Naval Intelligence Command, to the Director of Naval History (OP-09B9) (August 1, 1973) (with attachments), 63.

52. Studeman, interview.

53. Wright, interview. Wright attributes some annoyance with the term "all-source fusion" to Richard Haver and other analysts who were intimately familiar with some of the "black programs" under way during this period.

54. Pressly, presentation, and McFarland, presentation.

55. Haver, videotaped interview.

56. McFarland, presentation.

57. Navy Ocean Surveillance Information Center, *NOSIC Command History* (February 3, 1975), 1, ONI Historian's Files.

58. Harrison, presentation.

59. Commander, Naval Intelligence Command, *COMNAVINTCOM-NOTE 5450* (January 22, 1970), 1–2, ONI Historian's Files.

60. See Watson et al., *United States Intelligence,* 402.

61. See *History of the Ocean Surveillance Information System* (undated), attachment to Commander, Naval Intelligence Command,

memorandum to the Director of Naval History (OP-09B9) (April 29, 1974), 76; see also NFOIO, *NFOIO History 1972,* 3, both in ONI Historian's Files.

62. NFOIO, *NFOIO History 1972,* 1.

63. Ibid., 3.

64. *NOSIC Command History—1974* (February 3, 1975); see also NFOIO, *NFOIO History 1972,* 1; Director of Naval Intelligence, *Report to the Chief of Naval Operations by the Director of Naval Intelligence Fiscal 74* (September 11, 1974), V-6; Officer in Charge, Navy Field Operational Intelligence Office, memorandum to Director of Naval Intelligence, *Graphics Display Console Environment* (November 19, 1973), all in ONI Historian's Files.

65. Harrison, presentation.

66. Navy Ocean Surveillance Information Center, *NOSIC Input for 1975 Command History* (February 11, 1976), 7.

67. Ibid.

68. *NAVINTCOM-42 Command History Submission for 1974* (undated), 3 and 7–9; Navy Ocean Surveillance Information Center, *NOSIC Input for 1975 Command History* (February 11, 1976), 8, recounting allocation of $559,000 for development of new software package to handle inputs from new system.

69. *NAVINTCOM-42 Command History Submission for 1974* (undated), 1, ONI Historian's Files. The same document also recounts that FOSIF WESTPAC (Kamiseya) and FOSIF Rota both had enormous difficulties with their new BR-700 computers—problems that required the complete cannibalization of their backup units in order to keep the system functioning. Ibid., 2.

70. Packard, *Century of U.S. Naval Intelligence,* 246.

71. Naval Reconnaissance and Technical Support Center, *Historical Review—1971* (February 16, 1972), 14, ONI Historian's Files.

72. Commander, Naval Intelligence Command, memorandum to the Director of Naval History (August 1, 1973) (with attachments), 62.

73. Ibid.

74. Packard, *Century of U.S. Naval Intelligence,* 247.

75. NFOIO, *NFOIO History 1972,* 1.

76. Officer in Charge, Navy Field Operational Intelligence Office, memorandum to Chief of Naval Operations, *AUTOSEVOCOM Termi-*

nal, Requirement for (October 14, 1971), 1–2, discussing these deficiencies and requesting access to AUTOSEVOCOM telephone network.

77. Commander, Naval Intelligence Command, memorandum to the Director for Naval History (OP-09B9) (August 1, 1973) (with attachments), 62; *1973 History of the Ocean Surveillance Information System,* attachment to Commander, Naval Intelligence Command, memorandum to the Director for Naval History (OP-09B9) (April 29, 1974) (with attachments), 74, both in ONI Historian's Files.

78. Officer in Charge, Navy Field Operational Intelligence Office, to Commander, Naval Intelligence Command (January 16, 1973), 1, ONI Historian's Files.

79. Commander, Naval Intelligence Command, memorandum to the Director of Naval History (OP-09B9) (August 1, 1973) (with attachments), 63; see also Director of Naval Intelligence, *Report to the Chief of Naval Operations by the Director of Naval Intelligence Fiscal 74* (September 11, 1974), ix, discussing installation of additional computers and expanded databases and noting Naval Intelligence Command's objective to "complete the automation" of OSIS; *NAVINTCOM-42 Command History Submission for 1974* (undated), 1, recounting purchases of new computer systems, all in ONI Historian's Files.

80. Commander, Naval Intelligence Command, memorandum to the Director for Naval History (OP-09B9) (August 1, 1973) (with attachments), 62.

81. Navy Ocean Surveillance Information Center, *NOSIC Command History—1974* (February 3, 1975), 2; Navy Ocean Surveillance Information Center, *NOSIC Input for 1975 Command History* (February 11, 1976), 6.

82. *OPINTEL Chronology.*

83. *NAVINTCOM-42 Command History Submission for 1974* (undated), 11; see also Harrison, presentation.

84. Commander, Naval Intelligence Command, memorandum to the Director for Naval History (OP-09B9) (August 1, 1973) (with attachments), 63, discussing contents of TDP 35–15; see also Commander, Naval Intelligence Command, memorandum to the Director for Naval History (OP-09B9) (April 29, 1974) (with attachments), 74, recounting approval of TDP 35–15, both in ONI Historian's Files.

85. *NAVINTCOM-42 Command History Submission for 1974* (undated), 2. A study in April 1973 had concluded that "the relationship between

OSIS and other related command and control systems should be reexamined for duplication of effort." *1973 History of the Ocean Surveillance Information System,* attachment to Commander, Naval Intelligence Command, memorandum to Director of Naval History (OP-09B9) (April 29, 1974) (with attachments), 76.

86. See generally Studeman, interview.

87. For a discussion of network-centric warfare, see Vice Adm. Arthur K. Cebrowski, USN, and John J. Garstka, "Network-Centric Warfare: Its Origin and Future," U.S. Naval Institute *Proceedings* (January 1998), 28.

88. Commander, Naval Intelligence Command, memorandum to the Director for Naval History (OP-09B9) (August 1, 1973) (with attachments), 62.

89. See generally Wright, interview, and Studeman, interview.

90. See Pressly, presentation, discussing occasional role of FOSIF Rota in transmitting operational traffic; see also Studeman, interview, noting that Naval Intelligence has traditionally been ahead of the Navy's regular C^2 community in the speed and accuracy of information transmittal.

91. See Shapiro, presentation; Harrison, presentation.

92. See, e.g., McConnell, interview.

93. Harrison, presentation.

94. Haver, videotaped interview.

95. Ibid.

96. Shapiro, videotaped interview.

97. Watson et al., *United States Intelligence,* 400. According to one veteran of Navy OPINTEL during this period, in fact, the strong "OPINTEL culture" proved to be in one respect a long-term weakness of Naval Intelligence. According to Vice Adm. Mike McConnell, the overwhelming priority ONI placed upon operational intelligence led it to neglect long-term planning and budgeting in comparison with the efforts of other U.S. military services (e.g., the Air Force). See McConnell, interview.

98. NMIC, *History;* Naval Intelligence Command, *NAVINTCOM History for CY-1975 Basic Narrative* (undated), 15.

99. Naval Intelligence Command, *NAVINTCOM History for CY-1975 Basic Narrative* (undated), 15.

100. Naval Intelligence Command, *NAVINTCOM Historical Review— 1976* (undated), 22.

101. Pressly, presentation. Captain Pressly described these personnel as "inexperienced, but . . . willing," and regarded their employment as a success.

102. Navy Ocean Surveillance Information Center, *NOSIC Command History—1974* (February 3, 1975), 1.

103. Watson et al., *United States Intelligence,* 411; see also Rear Adm. Edward D. Sheafer, *Posture Statement* (May 3, 1993), 4, describing OSIS as a crucial ONI contribution "in modern times" to the U.S. Navy.

104. Rosenberg, "American Naval Strategy," 249.

105. Adm. William A. Owens, *High Seas: The Naval Passage to an Uncharted World* (Annapolis, Md.: U.S. Naval Institute, 1995), 134.

106. Cf. Cebrowski and Garstka, "Network-Centric Warfare," 30, recounting that fundamental enabling dynamic of network-centric warfare is an application of "Metcalfe's law," which holds that the value-added payoff of network-centric computing increases geometrically with the number of integrated computing nodes in the network; see also Rear Adm. Isaiah C. Cole, USN (Ret.), presentation at ONI OPINTEL "Lessons Learned" Symposium, noting that the cryptologic side of the OPINTEL community understood from an early date many of the principles that underlie modern concepts of "knowledge superiority in information operations."

107. Bates, presentation; see also Amato, presentation, noting OPINTEL's lack of focus until the Korean War drove home the threat from the Communist Bloc.

108. Studeman, interview.

109. NFOIO, *NFOIO History 1972,* 1–2.

110. DNI, *Report to the Chief Fiscal 74,* ix–x.

111. *1973 History of the Ocean Surveillance Information System,* attachment to Commander, Naval Intelligence Command, memorandum to the Director of Naval History (OP-09B9) (April 29, 1974) (with attachments), 76.

112. Navy Ocean Surveillance Information Center, *NOSIC Command History—1974* (February 3, 1975), 3–4; see DNI, *Report to the Chief, Fiscal 74,* V–5 and V–6.

113. See McFarland, presentation.

114. See Navy Ocean Surveillance Information Center, *NOSIC Input for 1975 Command History* (February 11, 1976), 3 and 6; Navy Ocean

Surveillance Information Center, *NOSIC Input for 1976 Command History* (February 25, 1977), 3–4, both in ONI Historian's Files.

115. DNI, *Report to the Chief, Fiscal 74*, vi–vii.

116. NFOIO, *NFOIO History 1972*, 1.

Chapter 5: "High OPINTEL" in the Era of the "Maritime Strategy"

1. Mrs. Walt Kelly and Bill Crouch Jr., eds., *The Best of Pogo* (New York: Simon and Schuster, 1982), "We have met the enemy and they are us," parodying Commo. Oliver Hazard Perry's famous letter to Gen. William Henry Harrison, September 10, 1813, onboard USS *Niagara* after the battle of Lake Erie: "We have met the enemy; and they are ours. Two ships, two Brigs, one schooner, and one Sloop."

2. John B. Hattendorf, "The Evolution of the Maritime Strategy," *Naval War College Review* XLI, no. 3 (Summer 1988): 7, 11.

3. Rosenberg, "History of World War III," 197, 216.

4. Herman, *Intelligence Power*, 85.

5. John B. Hattendorf, *The Evolution of the U.S. Navy's Maritime Strategy, 1977–1986* (Newport, R.I.: Center for Naval Warfare Studies, Naval War College, 1989), declassified text, 35; see also T. Brooks, videotaped interview, describing U.S. views of Soviet strategy prior to Maritime Strategy period as being "a lot of mirror-imaging, a lot of reliving the last war."

6. See Hattendorf, "Evolution of the Maritime Strategy," 11.

7. Director of Central Intelligence, *Soviet Naval Strategy and Programs through the 1990s, NIE 11–15–82D* (March 1983) (declassified version) [hereinafter *NIE 11–15–82D*], 14.

8. Hattendorf, "Evolution of the Maritime Strategy," 12; see also Rosenberg, "American Naval Strategy," 242, 250.

9. Robert W. Herrick, *Soviet Naval Strategy: Fifty Years of Theory and Practice* (Annapolis, Md.: Naval Institute Press, 1968).

10. Adm. William Small, USN (Ret.), letter to Lt. Christopher Ford, USNR (March 7, 2000), 1; Hattendorf, *Evolution of the U.S. Navy's Maritime Strategy*, 37.

11. Hattendorf, *Evolution of the U.S. Navy's Maritime Strategy*, 41–43.

12. See Hattendorf, "Evolution of the Maritime Strategy," 12–13. Two other major works on the defensive focus of the Soviet navy suggested Moscow's naval power might be devoted to the establishment and protection of ballistic-missile submarine "bastions." See James L. George, ed., *Problems of Sea Power as We Approach the Twenty-first Century* (Washington, D.C.: American Enterprise Institute for Public Policy Research, 1977), especially George's introduction, 1–9, and the chapter by James M. McConnell, "Strategy and Missions of the Soviet Navy in the Year 2000," 39–67; James M. McConnell, "Military-Political Tasks of the Soviet Navy in Peace and War," in U.S. Congress, House of Representatives, *Soviet Oceans Development, Prepared for the Use of the Committee on Commerce and National Ocean Policy* (Washington, D.C.: Government Printing Office, 1976), 183–209; and Bradford Dismukes and James M. McConnell, eds., *Soviet Naval Diplomacy* (New York: Pergamon Press/Center for Naval Analyses, 1977), 1–36.

13. See, e.g., Hattendorf, *Evolution of the U.S. Navy's Maritime Strategy,* 36 ("It took a rather long time for a different attitude and interpretation to prevail within the U.S. Navy.") and 37 ("This conclusion was a controversial one which has not always sat easily with the Intelligence Community.").

14. Cf. Hattendorf, *Evolution of the U.S. Navy's Maritime Strategy,* 47–49, describing debates over CNA's analyses of Soviet strategy, which were resolved to ONI's satisfaction only in early 1981.

15. Ibid., 53.

16. Loch Johnson, *Secret Agencies: U.S. Intelligence in a Hostile World* (New Haven, Conn.: Yale University Press, 1996), 178.

17. Hattendorf, *Evolution of the U.S. Navy's Maritime Strategy,* 45.

18. T. Brooks, videotaped interview.

19. Ibid.

20. Ibid.

21. See Hattendorf, *Evolution of the U.S. Navy's Maritime Strategy,* 44, 50, and 56–57.

22. Reddig, "OSIS Culture," 1.

23. Rear Adm. Thomas A. Brooks, USN (Ret.), and Capt. Bill Manthorpe, USN (Ret.), "Setting the Record Straight," *Naval Intelligence Professionals Quarterly* XII, no. 2 (April 1996): 1. Perception management, in this context, relates to the importance to strategic planning of

incorporating anticipated enemy reactions and assumptions into one's own planning. If the adversary, for example, believes that one will take certain actions and that these actions will have a certain effect, actual or apparent preparations for these actions can themselves powerfully affect enemy planning and behavior long before the initiation of actual combat operations. Such approaches can have dramatic effects in controlling or shaping the outcome of crisis situations well short of actual warfare.

24. Adm. William Small, USN (Ret.), "Some Thoughts on OPINTEL," unpublished monograph (September 9, 1998), 2.

25. Hattendorf, *Evolution of the U.S. Navy's Maritime Strategy,* 36.

26. Jeremiah, videotaped interview.

27. Johnson, *Secret Agencies,* 178.

28. Brooks and Manthorpe, "Setting the Record Straight," 1.

29. David A. Rosenberg, "Process: The Realities of Formulating Modern Naval Strategy," in *Mahan Is Not Enough,* James Goldrick and John Hattendorf, eds. (Newport, R.I.: Naval War College Press, 1993), 141, 158; see also Rosenberg, "History of World War III," 213.

30. See Brooks and Manthorpe, "Setting the Record Straight," 2.

31. Rosenberg, "History of World War III," 216 (quoting Capt. Linton Brooks, USN [Ret.]).

32. T. Brooks, videotaped interview.

33. Ibid.

34. One Soviet author saw this approach as having clear historical roots in "Lenin's thesis of reliable defense of the socialist homeland" itself. See Dotsenko, "Soviet Art of Naval Warfare," 22.

35. Adm. James D. Watkins, USN, "The Maritime Strategy," U.S. Naval Institute *Proceedings,* Special Supplement (January 1986), 4, 7.

36. *NIE 11–15–82D,* 22.

37. Ibid., 15.

38. See Watkins, "Maritime Strategy," 7, arguing that the Soviet navy's role in a conflict would be to protect the Soviet homeland and Soviet SSBNs, "which provide the Soviets with their ultimate strategic reserve," while "other roles, such as interdicting sea lines of communication or supporting the Soviet Army, while important, will probably be secondary."

39. *NIE 11–15–82D,* 14; see also ibid., 5.

40. Watkins, "Maritime Strategy," 7. "The Soviets would particularly like to be able to destroy our ballistic missile submarines, but lack the antisubmarine warfare capability to implement such a mission."

41. Ibid., 5; see also ibid., 20, discussing the importance of defense against U.S. aircraft carriers as "a critical element of several important naval tasks."

42. Brooks and Manthorpe, "Setting the Record Straight," 2.

43. Hattendorf, "Evolution of the Maritime Strategy," 7, 16; see also Small, "Some Thoughts on OPINTEL," 3; Rosenberg, "Process," 161.

44. Rosenberg, "Process," 160; see also Hattendorf, *Evolution of the U.S. Navy's Maritime Strategy,* 71–72, describing OP-603 and its role in preparing the briefing for the Directorate of Naval Warfare (OP-095) that "later became known as the Maritime Strategy."

45. Ibid. The ATP was originally a special panel of the CNO's executive board, but it later became a separate component; the ATP's OPNAV sponsor was the vice chief of Naval Operations. See Comdr. J. C. Williams, "OPNAV Decision Process Review," memorandum of May 27, 1987, unclassified administrative paper, ONI Historian's Files; see also David A. Rosenberg, "Intelligence and Maritime Strategy, 1945–1990," lecture slides from Naval War College presentation (undated). Support for the ATP came from the ATP Working Group run by Rear Adms. Bill Studeman and Roger Bacon (Brooks and Manthorpe, "Setting the Record Straight," 2).

46. OPNAV Instruction 5420.2M (May 7, 1983).

47. Rosenberg, "Process," 157–59.

48. Small, "Some Thoughts on OPINTEL," 1–2. Such a perspective was invaluable, for until the "deep penetrations" of the 1970s, U.S. military intelligence relied principally upon technical means (e.g., SIGINT and satellite imagery) for its understanding of the Soviet Union. Such methods were "relatively unilluminating about underlying Soviet motivations. These needed regular access to higher-level message-like sources and a sustained effort to interpret them" (Herman, *Intelligence Power,* 85).

49. Small, letter to Ford, (March 7, 2000), 1.

50. Brooks and Manthorpe, "Setting the Record Straight," 1.

51. Linton F. Brooks, "Naval Power and National Security," *International Security* 11, no. 2 (Fall 1986): 16, 17 (quoting James A. Barber Jr.,

"From the Executive Director," U.S. Naval Institute *Proceedings,* Special Supplement [January 1986], 1).

52. Small, "Some Thoughts on OPINTEL," 2.

53. See, e.g., John Mearsheimer, "A Strategic Misstep," *International Security* 11, no. 2 (Fall 1986): 47.

54. See Rosenberg, "Process," 162.

55. See Haver, presentation.

56. For a general discussion of the organizational, professional, and personal factors that helped make the Navy more receptive to the "new thinking" behind the Maritime Strategy, see Rosenberg, "Process," 150–67.

57. Ibid., 150–51.

58. Small, letter to Ford, (March 7, 2000), 1.

59. See Rosenberg, "Process," 168, suggesting that Rickover's retirement helped "release the brakes" upon strategic thinking; cf. Watkins, "The Maritime Strategy," 15, noting in 1986 that "the most striking and far-reaching trend within the naval profession in recent years has been [its] emphasis on strategy as the focus of naval thought, planning, resource allocation, and operational employment."

60. Small, letter to Ford, (March 7, 2000), 1.

61. Jacoby, videotaped interview.

62. T. Brooks, videotaped interview.

63. Ibid.

64. See generally Hattendorf, *Evolution of the U.S. Navy's Maritime Strategy,* 15–16 and 65–66.

65. Ibid., 19, 22–25, and 61–62.

66. See, e.g., ibid., 53–54.

67. Ibid., 51–52.

68. Ibid., 109–18.

69. Small, letter to Ford, (March 7, 2000), 2.

70. Adm. William N. Small, USN, memorandum to Director of Navy Program Planning (December 18, 1981) [declassified], provided to Comdr. David A. Rosenberg by staff members of Op-603.

71. Adm. William N. Small, USN, memorandum to OP-095 and OP-06 (March 1, 1982) [declassified], provided to Comdr. David A. Rosen-

berg by staff members of OP-603. Such new analysis, Small wrote, "may well change many of the assumptions currently explicit in our systems requirements." Ibid.

72. Adm. William N. Small, USN, handwritten notes on memorandum from Vice Adm. S. R. Foley, USN (March 15, 1982) [emphasis in original], provided to Comdr. David A. Rosenberg by staff members of OP-603. Small emphasized the need for drawing a distinction between "defeating the Soviet Navy and winning the war." "How great a distinction [there is]," he wrote, "depends upon one's view of our *concepts of maritime operations.*" Ibid. [emphasis in original].

73. Vice Adm. S. R. Foley, USN, memorandum to Adm. William Small, USN (March 15, 1982), 1.

74. See Small, letter to Ford, (March 7, 2000), 1.

75. Hattendorf, *Evolution of the U.S. Navy's Maritime Strategy,* 54–55 and 83.

76. Small, letter to Ford, (March 7, 2000), 1.

77. Hattendorf, *Evolution of the U.S. Navy's Maritime Strategy,* 55.

78. Navy Field Operational Intelligence Office [NFOIO], *History, 1977* (March 1, 1978), ONI Historian's Files, 9. See also Lt. David A. Rosenberg, USNR, "Being 'Red': The Challenge of Taking the Soviet Side at War Games at the Naval War College," *Naval War College Review* XLI (Winter 1988): 81–93.

79. NAVINTCOM Notice 5450 (June 11, 1979), ONI Historian's Files, 1.

80. Commanding Officer, NFOIO, Memorandum to Director of Naval History (OP-09BH), "Command History for CY 1981 (OPNAV Report 5750–1)" (April 15, 1982), ONI Historian's Files, 13. In 1982, in fact, SSG support was apparently the detachment's principal mission. See NFOIO, *Command History 1982* (undated), ONI Historian's Files, 8, listing SSG support first under the description of detachment mission, and introducing the war-gaming role with the phrase "in addition."

81. See NFOIO, *Command History 1982* (undated), 8; NAVOPINT-CEN, *Command History 1984* (February 28, 1985), 20; NAVOPINTCEN, *Command History 1985* (March 13, 1986), 19; NAVOPINTCEN, *Command History 1987* (May 20, 1987); NAVOPINTCEN, *Command History 1986* (March 16, 1987), 21–22, all in ONI Historian's Files.

82. NAVOPINTCEN, *Command History 1986* (March 16, 1987), 21. Not surprisingly, however—given the remarkable changes then under

way in the Soviet Union during Mikhail Gorbachev's years of *pere-stroika* and *glasnost*—the detachment's focus upon Maritime Strategy–related support waned in the late 1980s. By 1989, for example, Newport Detachment mission statements focused upon war gaming and no longer emphasized support for cutting-edge Soviet naval analysis. See NAVOPINTCEN, *Command History 1989* (June 26, 1990), 2.

83. Hattendorf, *Evolution of the U.S. Navy's Maritime Strategy*, 55.

84. Ibid.

85. T. Brooks, videotaped interview.

86. Rosenberg, "Process," 150 and 159.

87. Sun Tzu, "Art of War," in *The Seven Military Classics of Ancient China*, Ralph D. Sawyer, ed. (Boulder, Colo.: Westview, 1993), 157, 183.

88. Rosenberg, "American Naval Strategy," 243.

89. Rosenberg, "History of World War III," 212–14.

90. See ibid., 211.

91. See, e.g., Hattendorf, *Evolution of the U.S. Navy's Maritime Strategy*, 145–48, describing some changes in emphasis under follow-on convocations of the Strategic Studies Group.

92. See McConnell, interview; L. Brooks, "Naval Power and National Security," 23.

93. See Rosenberg, "Process," 161–62; see also L. Brooks, "Naval Power and National Security," 23; Gregory L. Vistica, *Fall from Glory* (New York: Touchstone, 1997), 214 and 217–18.

94. Vistica, *Fall from Glory*, 214.

95. Rosenberg, "History of World War III," 213.

96. *NIE 11–15–82D*, 5 and 15–16; see also L. Brooks, "Naval Power and National Security," 21. "To implement this strategy, the bulk of the Soviet navy must be used to protect defensive bastions near the Soviet Union, with only limited forces deployed into the broad ocean areas"; Watkins, "Maritime Strategy," 7.

97. Wit, "Advances in Antisubmarine Warfare," 31, 40.

98. Ronald Wilson Reagan, *National Security Strategy of the United States* (January 1987), 29–30, quoted in Hattendorf, *Evolution of the U.S. Navy's Maritime Strategy*, 25.

99. L. Brooks, "Naval Power and National Security," 26.

100. Hattendorf, "Evolution of the Maritime Strategy," 24.

101. L. Brooks, "Naval Power and National Security," 24 and 28.

102. Ibid., 28–29.

103. See generally, e.g., Ball, "Nuclear War at Sea," 323 and 328–29; Mearsheimer, "Strategic Misstep," 51, 79–80, and 90–92.

104. Cf. Rosenberg, lecture slides; Rosenberg, "Process," 159.

105. Hattendorf, *Evolution of the U.S. Navy's Maritime Strategy,* 88, quoting Comdr. Kenneth McGruther [emphasis in original].

106. Ibid., 91.

107. See Mearsheimer, "A Strategic Misstep," 92–98.

108. See, e.g., Alvin A. Snyder, *Warriors of Disinformation: American Propaganda, Soviet Lies, and the Winning of the Cold War—An Insider's Account* (New York: Arcade, 1995), 120–25.

109. Rosenberg, "History of World War III," 214.

110. Small, letter to Ford, (March 7, 2000), 2; see also Adm. William Small, USN (Ret.), letter to Lt. Christopher Ford, USNR (March 10, 2000), 1.

111. Small, letter to Ford, (March 7, 2000), 2.

112. Commanding Officer, NFOIO, memorandum to Director of Naval History (OP-09BH), "Command History for CY 1980" (March 11, 1981), ONI Historian's Files, 1 and 4. The special reports from the Iran-Iraq war task force were discontinued, however, after the return of U.S. hostages from Iran in January 1981. Commanding Officer, NFOIO, memorandum to Director of Naval History (OP-09BH), "Command History for CY 1981, (OPNAV Report 5750–1)" (April 15, 1982), 3.

113. Commanding Officer, NFOIO, memorandum to Director of Naval History (OP-09BH), "Command History for CY 1980" (March 11, 1981), 6.

114. Ibid., 4.

115. McConnell, interview.

116. Ibid.

117. Commanding Officer, NFOIO, memorandum to Director of Naval History (OP-09BH), "Command History for CY 1981 (OPNAV Report 5750–1)" (April 15, 1982), 13–14; see also Commanding Officer, NFOIO, memorandum to Director of Naval History (OP-09BH), "Command History for CY 1980" (March 11, 1981), 9.

118. Commanding Officer, NFOIO, memorandum to Director of Naval History (OP-09BH), "Command History for CY 1981 (OPNAV Report 5750–1)" (April 15, 1982), 20.

119. Commanding Officer, NFOIO, memorandum to Director of Naval History (OP-09BH), "Command History for CY 1980" (March 11, 1981), 3–4. Later that year, a twenty-four-hour watch was also established specifically to follow "Soviet operations bearing on readiness estimates." Ibid.

120. Commanding Officer, NFOIO, memorandum to Director of Naval History (OP-09BH), "Command History for CY 1981 (OPNAV Report 5750–1)" (April 15, 1982), 21.

121. NAVOPINTCEN, *Command History 1989* (June 26, 1990), 1; see also Watson et al., *United States Intelligence,* 400.

122. Commanding Officer, NFOIO, memorandum to Director of Naval History (OP-09BH), "Command History for CY 1981 (OPNAV Report 5750–1)" (April 15, 1982), 20. Buoyed by such commitments of personnel, technology, and money, NFOIO's operations analysis branch also doubled the number of "time-sensitive, quick-look analytical responses to the fleet" in 1981, primarily through providing better "feedback to [United States] SSBN Commanding Officers on ACINT and other items of interest from their previous patrols." Ibid., 14.

123. NAVOPINTCEN, *Command History 1985* (March 13, 1986), 21.

124. NAVOPINTCEN, *Command History 1986* (March 16, 1987), 23–24.

125. NAVOPINTCEN, *Command History 1988* (undated), 29; NAVOPINTCEN, *Command History 1987* (May 20, 1987), 29.

126. Commanding Officer, NFOIO, memorandum to Director of Naval History (OP-09BH), "Command History for CY 1981 (OPNAV Report 5750–1)" (April 15, 1982), 6 and 20.

127. NFOIO, *Command History 1982,* 2.

128. NAVOPINTCEN, *Command History 1985* (March 13, 1986); Commanding Officer, NFOIO, memorandum to Director of Naval History (OP-09BH), "Command History for CY 1981 (OPNAV Report 5750–1)" (April 15, 1982), 20.

129. Commanding Officer, NFOIO, memorandum to Director of Naval History (OP-09BH), "Command History for CY 1981 (OPNAV Report 5750–1)" (April 15, 1982), 20.

130. Ibid., 19.

131. NIPPSA, *Calendar Year 1984 History—Naval Intelligence Processing System Support Activity (NIPSSA)* (undated), ONI Historian's Files, 2.

132. See Commanding Officer, NFOIO, memorandum to Director of Naval History (OP-09BH), "Command History for CY 1979" (October 7, 1980), 2 and 4; Commanding Officer, NFOIO, memorandum to Director of Naval History (OP-09BH), "Command History for CY 1980" (March 11, 1981), 2 and 4.

133. Commanding Officer, NFOIO, memorandum to Director of Naval History (OP-09BH), "Command History for CY 1980" (March 11, 1981), 2.

134. NAVOPINTCEN, *Command History 1983* (undated), 17–18.

135. Ibid., 18; see also NAVOPINTCEN, *Command History 1984* (February 28, 1985), ONI Historian's Files, 12, recounting efforts to set up British OBU site.

136. NAVOPINTCEN, *Command History 1985* (March 13, 1986), ONI Historian's Files, 14. The prototype teleconferencing capabilities from which the link to FOSIC PAC was developed had been developed by the Defense Advanced Research Projects Agency (DARPA). NAVOPINTCEN, *Command History 1984* (February 28, 1985), 13.

137. NAVOPINTCEN, *Command History 1984* (February 28, 1985), 12. Additional automated systems being developed at this time included the Developmental Surface Analysis Testbed (DSURT), the Developmental Submarine Analysis Testbed (DSAT), and the Developmental Aircraft Reports Tracker (DART), all of which were designed to assist processing, correlation, and interpretation of multisource analysis on the specified variety of Soviet naval forces. See ibid., 13; NIPPSA, *Calendar Year 1984 History—Naval Intelligence Processing System Support Activity (NIPSSA)* (undated), ONI Historian's Files, 13–15.

138. NAVOPINTCEN, *Command History 1986* (March 16, 1987), 15.

139. NIPPSA, *Calendar Year 1984 History—Naval Intelligence Processing System Support Activity (NIPSSA)* (undated), 12.

140. Ibid., 11, discussion of acquisition of new IBM computers for SEAWATCH III, and 13 (quotation); NAVOPINTCEN, *Command History 1983* (undated), 18, recounting approval of SEAWATCH III A Level Specification; see also NAVOPINTCEN, *Command History 1984* (February 28, 1985), 12, discussing replacement of computer console and mainframe modernization for SEAWATCH II; NAVOPINTCEN,

Command History 1986 (March 16, 1987), 15, describing SEAWATCH III as major project of newly reorganized Intelligence Systems Department within NAVOPINTCEN. SEAWATCH III was designed to be compatible with the OBU technology. See NAVOPINTCEN, *Command History 1984,* 11–12.

141. Wit, "Advances in Antisubmarine Warfare," 35.

142. Throughout this period, the Undersea Warfare Technology Department at the Naval Intelligence Support Center (NISC) continued to build and analyze databases of ACINT information on Soviet submarine radiated noise levels, as well as acoustic signature information on foreign ships and submarines. See Commanding Officer, NISC, memorandum to Director of Naval History (OP-09B9), "Command History 1980" (June 18, 1982).

143. Lautenschläger, "Technology and the Evolution of Naval Warfare," 173, 217.

144. Wit, "Advances in Antisubmarine Warfare," 32.

145. Reddig, "OSIS Culture," 4.

146. In 1986, for example—in response to a surge of Soviet attack submarines into the Atlantic—the Navy turned to Harvard oceanographer Allan Robinson for help in analyzing peculiar acoustic "holes in the sea" in which Soviet submarines had learned to hide. These "holes" were created by loops of warm water that eddied off of the Gulf Stream into cooler areas of the ocean, thereby creating isolated areas out of which sound propagated less easily. See William J. Cromie, "Ocean Weather Prediction System Developed," *Harvard College Gazette* (May 2000): 7.

147. Commanding Officer, NFOIO, memorandum to Director of Naval History (OP-09BH), "Command History for CY 1981 (OPNAV Report 5750–1)" (April 15, 1982), 6.

148. Herman, *Intelligence Power,* 109, 252.

149. See generally Ball, "Nuclear War at Sea," 321–22; Rosenberg, "American Naval Strategy," 250.

150. Rosenberg, "Process," 158.

151. Jeremiah, videotaped interview. One measure of the extent to which the Soviets recognized the apparently ever-present danger of attack by U.S. submarines was their effort to develop radical approaches to ASW countermeasures. The *Shkval* (Squall) rocket-powered underwater weapon, for example, represented one such

approach. Essentially an unguided torpedo, this 200-knot weapon was a last-chance weapon that was designed on the assumption that the first warning a Soviet submarine would have of its impending doom at the hands of an attacking NATO submarine would be the sound of a NATO torpedo being fired. The *Shkval* was designed to be fired immediately back down the bearing of the attacking torpedo's transient noise, with the aim of destroying both the attacking submarine and the incoming weapon with a nuclear explosion. See John Downing, "How Shkval Ensured Soviet SSBN Survivability," *Jane's Intelligence Review* (November 1, 1999). In effect, *Shkval* was the physical embodiment of the Soviet High Command's realization that U.S. Navy OPINTEL could place SSNs in a position to threaten to sink Soviet ballistic missile submarines at will, even within "bastions" in the northern Atlantic and Pacific seas.

152. See Wit, "Advances in Antisubmarine Warfare," 31, 35–36, 39.

153. *NIE 11–15–82D,* 16.

154. Ibid., 35.

155. See, e.g., Commanding Officer, Naval Intelligence Support Center, Memorandum to Director of Naval History, "Command History 1982" (March 4, 1983); Commanding Officer, Naval Intelligence Support Center, Memorandum to Director of Naval History (OP-09B9), "Command History 1980" (June 18, 1982), iv–2, both in ONI Historian's Files.

156. See Reddig, "OSIS Culture," 12–13.

157. *NIE 11–15–82D,* 16.

158. See *NIE 11–15–82D,* 52–53.

159. Ibid., 35. Because improvements in Soviet ASW during the mid-1980s were expected to be offset by the need to cover the far larger patrol areas anticipated for U.S. *Ohio*-class submarines carrying longer-ranged Trident missiles, U.S. planners estimated that Soviet anti-SSBN capabilities would remain "modest" for some years to come. See ibid., 5–6, 53.

160. Shapiro, videotaped interview.

161. Wilson, interview.

162. Rosenberg, "Process," 248.

163. See, e.g., Shapiro, videotaped interview ("I think that this probably had a lot to do with our winning the Cold War."); Wilson, interview,

arguing that the Maritime Strategy "certainly had a lot to do with help-ing end the Cold War."

Chapter 6: Transition, Refocus, and the Future

1. Herman, *Intelligence Power,* 341, quoting Stansfield Turner, "Intelligence for a New World Order," *Foreign Affairs* 70, no. 4 (Autumn 1991): 150.

2. U.S. Joint Chiefs of Staff, *National Military Strategy of the United States* (January 1992), 1.

3. See generally Sheafer, *Posture Statement,* 8.

4. Ibid., 1–2.

5. Johnson, *Secret Agencies,* 54 (citing Robert M. Gates).

6. Sheafer, *Strategic Planning,* 6.

7. L. Edgar Prina, "A Forum of Excellence," *Sea Power* (August 1997): 41, 42 (quoting Vice Adm. J. O. Ellis Jr., USN); see also Stude-man, interview, which identified major challenges for OPINTEL in the modern era when "the CNN factor" can lead national decision makers to focus and refocus rapidly upon distant trouble spots.

8. Dulles, *Craft of Intelligence,* 50, 231.

9. See, e.g., Sheafer, *Posture Statement,* 6.

10. U.S. Department of the Navy, *Lessons of the Falklands: Summary Report* (February 1983): 47.

11. NAVMIC, *Naval Maritime Intelligence Center,* 20.

12. NAVOPINTCEN, *Command History 1990* (July 1, 1991), ONI His-torian's Files, 28.

13. Office of Naval Intelligence, *Command History 1993* (undated), ONI Historian's Files, 69.

14. NAVOPINTCEN, *Command History 1990* (July 1, 1991), ONI His-torian's Files, 29.

15. U.S. Department of the Navy, *From the Sea* (Washington, D.C.: Department of the Navy, 1992), 2.

16. U.S. Joint Chiefs of Staff, *National Military Strategy of the United States,* 1.

17. U.S. Department of the Navy, *From the Sea,* 5.

18. U.S. Department of the Navy, *Forward . . . from the Sea* (Washington, D.C.: Department of the Navy, 1994), 2.

19. See generally Reddig, "OSIS Culture," 15; Richelson, *U.S. Intelligence Community,* 102. The Joint Analysis Center in England was apparently given the acronym "JAC" out of deference to British sensibilities. In U.K. usage, "JIC" signified the Joint Intelligence Committee, a high-level interdepartmental organization that coordinates British intelligence policy. JAC engendered no such confusion. See Herman, *Intelligence Power,* 30–31, 113–14, and 260–61.

20. See, e.g., Robert W. Noonan, "Split-Based Intelligence for Central Region Operations," *American Intelligence Journal* (1997): 15.

21. McConnell, slide presentation prepared for ONI OPINTEL "Lessons Learned" Symposium.

22. Jacoby, "Operational Intelligence," 102, 103.

23. See Reddig, "OSIS Culture," 15.

24. See, e.g., Owens, *High Seas,* 134, discussing development of OSIS in response to Soviet submarine threat and noting that other U.S. military services subsequently "developed similar total-force integration in response to a broad spectrum of other military problems"; see also Showers, presentation, noting that collocation at NSA of OPINTEL staffs and cryptologists in Navy practice became a model for similar organizational changes in U.S. Army and Air Force.

25. Studeman, interview.

26. See Sheafer, remarks at ONI OPINTEL "Lessons Learned" Symposium, discussing the role of Navy OPINTEL veterans in building new joint watchfloors.

27. Shapiro, videotaped interview.

28. Manthorpe, interview.

29. Reddig, "OSIS Culture," 15; see also Harvey, remarks at ONI OPINTEL "Lessons Learned" Symposium, noting that OSIS nodes were powerful models and that other U.S. military services learned many lessons from the organization of Navy OPINTEL; Sheafer, remarks at ONI OPINTEL "Lessons Learned" Symposium, noting the degree to which OSIS "graduates" have thrived in the world of joint-service OPINTEL.

30. Jacoby, videotaped interview.

31. Ibid.

32. McConnell, interview.

33. Studeman, interview.

34. See, e.g., Reddig, "OSIS Culture," 15–18; see also Wright, interview.

35. McConnell, presentation; see also Shapiro, remarks at ONI OPIN-TEL "Lessons Learned" Symposium, describing OSIS as prototype for new watchfloors; Shapiro, videotaped interview, "In [the] Joint Intelligence Centers that you have today, it's OSIS by another name in the Joint arena."

36. See, e.g., Johnson, *Secret Agencies,* 40–41.

37. See, e.g., Federal Bureau of Investigation, "FBI Announces a Major Restructuring of FBI Headquarters" (November 11, 1999).

38. Haver, videotaped interview.

39. Jacoby, remarks at ONI OPINTEL "Lessons Learned" Symposium; Jacoby, videotaped interview.

40. See Sheafer, *Strategic Planning,* 1–6.

41. Ibid., 5.

42. Naval Maritime Intelligence Center, *Command History 1991* (January 28, 1992), 1; Naval Intelligence Command, *Basic Historical Narrative for Commander, Naval Intelligence Command, for CY 91* (August 1, 1992), 1, both in ONI Historian's Files; Richelson, *U.S. Intelligence Community,* 76.

43. NAVMIC Navy Maritime Operations Department, input to *Command History,* 1 (appearing within Naval Maritime Intelligence Center, *Command History 1991* [January 28, 1992], ONI Historian's Files).

44. Rear Admiral Brooks, however, notes that this consolidation—which took place on his watch and that of Rear Adm. Ted Sheafer—may not have been due to any broader conception of organizational rectitude. As Brooks puts it, "This was really imposed upon us and not something that we undertook voluntarily." It was, he said, a compromise with the Defense Department leadership and Congress: "a lesser of two evils choice in the face of a determined drive by DIA [the Defense Intelligence Agency] to effectively take over Service Intelligence." Rear Adm. Thomas A. Brooks, USN (Ret.), e-mail message to Lt. Christopher Ford, USNR (February 24, 2000).

45. Office of Naval Intelligence, *Command History 1993* (undated), ONI Historian's Files, 1; Richelson, *U.S. Intelligence Community,* 76.

46. Ibid., 2. Groundbreaking for the new purpose-built facility had taken place four years earlier, in October 1989. See Naval Intelligence Activity, *Ground Breaking Ceremony* (October 23, 1989) (event pamphlet/program), ONI Historian's Files.

47. See, e.g., Office of Naval Intelligence, *Command History 1993*, discussing Newport Detachment.

48. NAVOPINTCEN, *Command History 1989* (June 26, 1990), ONI Historian's Files, 29.

49. NAVOPINTCEN, *Command History 1990* (July 1, 1991), ONI Historian's Files, 29–30.

50. See ONI, "Our Story," 12.

51. Office of Naval Intelligence, *Command History 1994* (June 29, 1995), ONI Historian's Files, 8.

52. Office of Naval Intelligence, *Command History 1995* (May 30, 1996), ONI Historian's Files, 10.

53. See John Donnelly, "The Quest for Bandwidth," *Military Information Technology* (June/July 1998), 8.

54. NAVOPINTCEN, *Command History 1988* [sic, Command History for 1978 was mislabeled 1988] (May 20, 1987), ONI Historian's Files, 19–20. SEAWATCH III was "expected to provide the long-term storage of positional data from all incoming data sources." NAVOPINTCEN, *Command History 1989* (June 26, 1990), ONI Historian's Files, 19.

55. NAVMARINTCEN, *Naval Maritime Intelligence Center,* 20. Because of various developmental problems, SEAWATCH III had also been given to an entirely new contractor in 1988. NAVOPINTCEN, *Command History 1988* (undated), 17.

56. See Naval Intelligence Activity, *Calendar Year 1990 History— Naval Intelligence Activity (NIA)* (March 25, 1991), 3, noting database conversion; NAVMARINTCEN, *Naval Maritime Intelligence Center,* noting transition complete; see also NAVOPINTCEN, *Command History 1990* (July 1, 1991), 16, noting continuing teething problems with SEAWATCH III and postponement of initial operational capability (IOC), all histories in ONI Historian's Files.

57. See T. Brooks, e-mail message to Ford, (February 24, 2000), "To my recollection, Seawatch III was not really fully operational until some time after my watch, which ended in summer 1991."

58. NAVOPINTCEN, *Command History 1988* [sic] (May 20, 1987), ONI Historian's Files, 19–20.

59. See generally, e.g., Naval Intelligence Activity, *Calendar Year 1990 History—Naval Intelligence Activity (NIA)* (March 25, 1991), ONI Historian's Files, 9.

60. NAVMARINTCEN, *Naval Maritime Intelligence Center,* 9.

61. Office of Naval Intelligence, *ONI Command History 1993,* 74.

62. Office of Naval Intelligence, *Command History 1994,* 113.

63. NAVOPINTCEN, *Command History 1988* (undated), 17.

64. NAVOPINTCEN, *Command History 1989* (June 26, 1990), 19.

65. Office of Naval Intelligence, *Command History 1997* (undated), ONI Historian's Files, 22.

66. Office of Naval Intelligence, *Command History 1994,* 129.

67. "Purple" is military slang for joint-service work; it represents the hypothetical uniform color one would get by blending Army and Marine varieties of "green" with Air Force, Coast Guard, and Navy varieties of "blue."

68. Office of Naval Intelligence, *ONI Command History 1993,* 130–31.

69. See Office of Naval Intelligence, *ONI Command History 1993,* 131, describing installation of 120 JDISS units; Office of Naval Intelligence, *Command History 1995* (May 30, 1996), ONI Historian's Files, 144–45, describing installation of 1,330 JDISS in 1994, and 1,434 of JDISS version 1.01 and 1,110 of JDISS version 2.0 in 1995.

70. Office of Naval Intelligence, *Command History 1995,* 147; see also Office of Naval Intelligence, *ONI Command History 1993,* 131, discussing interest expressed by various foreign governments in JDISS at that point.

71. See Sheafer, *Strategic Planning,* 18. "Interactive analysis can be performed remotely through database sharing, on-line inter-analyst graphical and data processing and teleconferencing"; see also Reddig, "OSIS Culture," 18.

72. Office of Naval Intelligence, *Command History 1995,* 145; see also Office of Naval Intelligence, *ONI Command History 1993,* 129–30, discussing JDISS developments and efforts to integrate systems.

73. Office of Naval Intelligence, *Command History 1997,* 107; see also Office of Naval Intelligence, *ONI Command History 1993,* 129, describing JDISS "direct support to, and . . . significant impact on, real-world JTF military operations in Southwest Asia, Somalia, Haiti, Korea, and Bosnia Herzegovina." To the list of operations supported by JDISS

should also be added Noncombatant Evacuation Operations (NEOs) in Albania and Central Africa, see Office of Naval Intelligence, *Command History 1997,* 107, as well as the NATO air campaign against Yugoslavia during the Kosovo conflict of 1999.

74. Reddig, "OSIS Culture," 18; see also Jacoby, videotaped interview, where he notes, "We put the same basic capabilities on ships in the mid-90s [that existed only on OSIS watchfloors ashore in previous years]"; Studeman, remarks, describing development of the "telephone company model" of organization, involving "pushing fusion to the front."

75. Cebrowski and Garstka, "Network-Centric Warfare," 28, 33.

76. Reddig, "OSIS Culture," 19.

77. Donnelly, "Quest for Bandwidth," 8.

78. See Layton, *"And I Was There,"* 361–62.

79. See, e.g., Jacoby, remarks; Richardson, letter to Ford, 1.

80. Noonan, "Split-Based Intelligence for Central Region Operations," 18–19.

81. See Reddig, "OSIS Culture," 18.

82. Particularly since forward-based or "afloat" intelligence staffs were increasingly tempted to deploy without expensive and space-consuming traditional libraries of paper (or even CD-ROM) reference materials, the loss of satellite communications would instantly cripple late-1990s OPINTEL staffs. Training regimes were also slow to recognize the need to train intelligence professionals in "low-tech work-arounds" designed to permit meaningful intelligence support activity with only low-bandwidth connectivity.

83. Noonan, "Split-Based Intelligence for Central Region Operations," 18–19, discussing CENTCOM plans for "split-based" JIC and noting that with the latest high-bandwidth communications tools, forward-based JIC elements should easily be able to interact with CENT-JIC cadres back in the Continental United States (CONUS).

84. McConnell, slide presentation.

85. See, e.g., Wright, interview.

86. See Showers, Pressly, and Shapiro, remarks at ONI OPINTEL "Lessons Learned" Symposium.

87. T. Brooks, e-mail message to Ford, (January 12, 2000).

88. Jacoby, USN, "Operational Intelligence," 103.

89. Studeman, remarks; see also Rear Adm. H. Winsor Whiton, USN, remarks at ONI OPINTEL "Lessons Learned" Symposium, noting that the sensitivity of new intelligence sources is likely to increase.

90. See Capt. George B. Pressly, USN (Ret.), remarks given on behalf of Rear Adm. James S. McFarland, USN (Ret.), at ONI OPINTEL "Lessons Learned" Symposium. Dialogue about sources may be more important outside the time-sensitive OPINTEL arena.

91. Haver, videotaped interview; see also Shapiro, videotaped interview, noting continuing importance of "taking all of that information and working it together . . . checking one source against the other in order to derive maximum benefit from the information that's available to you."

92. Jacoby, "Operational Intelligence," 103.

93. See Wilson and Harvey, remarks at ONI OPINTEL "Lessons Learned" Symposium, discussing the importance of inhabiting the same weapons platform in creating a uniquely integrated intelligence/operational community.

94. See Capt. George B. Pressly, USN (Ret.), Amb. Linton F. Brooks, and Rear Adm. Edmund P. Sheafer, USN (Ret.), remarks at ONI OPINTEL "Lessons Learned" Symposium, emphasizing the need to understand "Blue" as well as "Red"; see also Studeman and Marocchi, remarks at ONI OPINTEL "Lessons Learned" Symposium, noting that intelligence is a *service* business, in which professionals need to understand their "customer."

95. Jacoby, "Operational Intelligence," 103; see also Harvey, remarks at ONI OPINTEL "Lessons Learned" Symposium.

96. Haver, videotaped interview. He stated, "To some degree, what the adversary is doing is reacting to us. If we don't know what we're doing, then we misinterpret what the reaction is. We think the reaction may be initiative [on the enemy's part], when it's the opposite—it's response." Another reason to cultivate a familiarity with both "Red" and "Blue" activity through the lens of operational intelligence, it should be noted, is that such a perspective sometimes allows the chance to uncover enemy intelligence successes. The Germans could have done so during World War II, if only they had they been more willing to admit the possibility that their codes had been compromised. See, e.g., Winton, *ULTRA at Sea,* 4, 38–39, 89–90, 104, and 181–95; Beesly, *Very Special Intelligence,* 90, 196, 281–84. This is

what the British Admiralty's Rodger Winn also came to suspect about Royal Navy ciphers during the war, based upon his careful observation of the interaction of Allied and German fleets in the Atlantic. See Beesly, *Very Special Intelligence,* 162–63. As it turns out, Winn was right: the Germans could, in fact, read many Royal Navy signals. See Winton, *ULTRA at Sea,* 83, 103, 105, and 124. During the Cold War in the late 1970s, U.S. Navy OPINTEL analysts such as Richard Haver also came to suspect that the Soviets had somehow penetrated U.S. Navy codes—a fact confirmed, altogether fortuitously, some years later with the arrest of the John Walker spy ring. See Haver, videotaped interview.

97. Sun Tzu, *The Art of War,* Ralph Sawyer, trans. (New York: Barnes and Noble, 1994), 179.

98. Jacoby, "Operational Intelligence," 103; see also Giambastiani, remarks at ONI OPINTEL "Lessons Learned" Symposium.

99. Wilson, interview.

100. See, e.g., Haver, videotaped interview. He stated, "More than anything else, we have to be good salesmen. We are *selling* information. We are *selling* that to someone. They aren't paying for it in dollars. They're paying for it in attention; they're paying for it when they turn around and use it"; Shapiro, videotaped interview. He also noted that it "frequently takes a selling job."

101. Haver, videotaped interview; see also T. Brooks, videotaped interview, making the same argument, and identifying Bobby Inman as the exemplar of a great intelligence officer in this respect when serving as an intelligence officer for CINCPACFLT: "He so well understood his commander's thought processes, requirements, needs, [and] intentions, that he could foresee what was going to be asked, that he could forearm himself by getting that data . . ."; cf. Shapiro, videotaped interview, stating, "You can't wait for them [the operators] to come in and tell them what to do. You have to tell them what they need to know. . . . Not necessarily what they *want* to know."

102. Jeremiah, videotaped interview.

103. See generally Rear Adm. Thomas A. Brooks, USN (Ret.), Richard L. Haver, and Comdr. David A. Rosenberg, USNR, remarks at ONI OPINTEL "Lessons Learned" Symposium.

104. Jacoby, videotaped interview; see also Shapiro, videotaped interview, noting, "You have to establish your credibility with the operator,

most important of all. Not only your ability, but your integrity—that he can believe what you tell him. . . . The Intelligence officer has to be prepared to do that, and by doing that he will establish his credentials, his *bona fides,* [and the] confidence that the operator has to have in him."

105. Haver, videotaped interview.

106. See Harvey, remarks.

107. Jacoby, "Operational Intelligence," 104.

108. See Sheafer and Haver, remarks at ONI OPINTEL "Lessons Learned" Symposium. Also crucial to this success was that the SIGINT community—or at least the Cryptologic Support Group staffs who worked so closely with Navy OPINTEL analysts—developed a powerful "haze grey and underway" ethic of fleet support. See Cole, remarks at ONI OPINTEL "Lessons Learned" Symposium.

109. See Shapiro, and Pressly, remarks.

110. Jacoby, "Operational Intelligence," 104.

111. Harrison, remarks at ONI OPINTEL "Lessons Learned" Symposium.

112. Richardson, letter to Ford, 1.

113. Harrison, remarks.

114. Jacoby, "Operational Intelligence," 104. This point has been made forcefully by Frederick Harrison, an architect of some of the most important ADP innovations of the 1980s and 1990s and the "father" of INTELINK. See Harrison, remarks.

115. Jacoby, ibid., 104.

116. See Pressly, remarks, noting the contributions of TAD personnel and reservists to building OPINTEL.

117. Jacoby, "Operational Intelligence," 104. See also Amato, remarks at ONI OPINTEL "Lessons Learned" Symposium, noting the importance of quality personnel to permitting OPINTEL to balance the need for coherent long-term planning with the operational imperative of always remaining flexible enough to reorient one's focus as circumstances demand.

118. Herman, *Intelligence Power,* 328.

119. Jacoby, "Operational Intelligence," 104.

120. See Whiton, remarks at ONI OPINTEL "Lessons Learned" Symposium.

121. Wilson, remarks at ONI OPINTEL "Lessons Learned" Symposium.

122. Jacoby, "Operational Intelligence," 104.

123. See, e.g., T. Brooks, videotaped interview, noting, "What is it you will improve your knowledge of? Who's the enemy today? Improve knowledge of Kosovo? [Osama] Bin Laden? Iranians? There isn't an easily identifiable single, monolithic enemy that I can spend my time better understanding. It was easier in my time: you could understand one well-defined enemy. That element is not so easy today as it was in days past."

124. Jacoby, "Operational Intelligence," 104.

125. Jacoby, videotaped interview.

126. Another question about the Navy's ability to adapt to the amorphous contemporary environment is suggested by the importance of the ATP/SSG processes of operator/intelligence interaction that were so important to the intelligence and doctrinal revolution of the Maritime Strategy. How, in the twenty-first century, is the Navy to replicate the intense focus of that period upon studying *actual* adversary decision-making and war-gaming coherent approaches to attacking the strategy of a constellation of very different potential enemies?

127. Wilson, interview.

128. If it is true, for example, that "communications will expand to utilize all available bandwidth" (see T. Brooks, e-mail message to Ford, [February 24, 2000]), so might it perhaps also be said that intelligence sensor information will expand to consume all available processing capabilities.

129. Studeman, slide presentation.

130. Ibid., emphasizing the need to balance collection and analysis; see also Dulles, *Craft of Intelligence,* 51, noting, "In addition to getting the information, there is also the question of how it should be processed and analyzed."

131. Jacoby, "Operational Intelligence," 103.

132. See Rear Adm. Thomas A. Brooks, USN (Ret.), remarks given on behalf of Dr. Alfred L. Andreassen, at ONI OPINTEL "Lessons Learned" Symposium; Ambassador Linton F. Brooks, remarks at ONI OPINTEL "Lessons Learned" Symposium.

133. Haver, videotaped interview.

134. Shapiro, videotaped interview.

135. Jacoby, videotaped interview.

136. Herman, *Intelligence Power,* 296, quoting J. McCausland, *The Gulf Conflict: A Military Analysis,* Adelphi Paper 282 (London: International Institute for Strategic Studies/Brassey's, 1993), 57.

137. McFarland, slide presentation. "Chaff" is the term for a type of self-protection device used by aircraft and naval vessels to create false and distracting radar echoes by firing "narrow metallic strips of various lengths and frequency responses" into the air around a potential target of enemy guns or missiles. See Watson et al., *United States Intelligence,* 82.

138. Herman, *Intelligence Power,* 42.

139. Studeman, remarks.

140. See Herman, *Intelligence Power,* 124.

141. See Barbara Starr, "USA's rapid targeting reaches new heights," *Jane's Defence Weekly* (March 4, 1998): 22.

142. Shapiro, remarks.

143. Herman, *Intelligence Power,* 124; see also Adm. William M. Small, USN (Ret.), remarks at ONI OPINTEL "Lessons Learned" Symposium.

144. Jacoby, "Operational Intelligence," 103; see also McConnell, slide presentation, stressing the need to "extract meaning from sensor-to-shooter chaff"; Wilson, remarks, noting importance of providing *the right information* without extraneous data. It is not enough, for example, to provide information to the operational decision-maker without explaining it "in the context of what we knew yesterday and the day before." Richardson, letter to Ford, 1.

145. McConnell, remarks. Reddig also attributes such a saying to a watchstander at FOSIC PAC in 1982. See Reddig, "OSIS Culture," 6. To whomever belongs credit for this phrasing, however, it is clear that the *quickest* intelligence is not always the best intelligence. See Giambastiani, remarks; see also Shapiro, videotaped interview, noting dangers of "sending it all to the operators directly and making them serve as their own Intelligence officers."

146. See Bryan Bender, "Buying Into Networked Warfare," *Jane's Defence Weekly* (May 13, 1998): 27, describing Vice Admiral Cebrowski.

147. Vice Adm. Arthur K. Cebrowski, "Sea Change," *Surface Warfare* (November/December 1997): 5.

148. Sheafer, *Posture Statement,* 11.

149. Jacoby, "Operational Intelligence," 103. According to Michael Herman, "Even in the Cold War the all-source [analysis] effort was under-funded compared with collection. It is now all the more necessary to ensure that it can exploit the increased volume of information at its disposal" (Herman, *Intelligence Power,* 353).

150. Studeman, remarks.

151. Jacoby, videotaped interview, noting, "There is a time and place for direct informational feed to operational systems, and what we need to do is be very precise in our thinking about where direct 'push' makes sense, and where assessment and analysis is important, and where 'pulling' information makes sense"; Wilson, interview, "When you are in a tactical fight, sometimes you are advantaged by having raw data flow straight to the decisionmaker. . . . There's a place for everything. The challenge is getting [to] mix and match . . . raw data and value-added information and intelligence in the right does—[and with the requisite] timeliness to suit the mission."

152. Cf. Small, remarks at ONI OPINTEL "Lessons Learned" Symposium, noting need to preserve role for *thought* in OPINTEL process.

153. Rear Adm. Lowell E. Jacoby, USN (Ret.), and Rear Adm. Perry M. Ratliff, USN, remarks at ONI OPINTEL "Lessons Learned" Symposium; see also Haver, remarks at ONI OPINTEL "Lessons Learned" Symposium, noting the importance to the intelligence process of value added from "arguments among analysts."

154. Reddig, "OSIS Culture," 19.

155. See Harrison and Giambastiani remarks, noting the great challenges of making sense of a blizzard of collected information.

156. Adm. Jay Johnson, USN, address to U.S. Naval Institute Annapolis Seminar and 123rd Annual Meeting, Annapolis, Md. (April 23, 1997), quoted in Cebrowski and Garstka, "Network-Centric Warfare," 29.

157. JO3 Kip Wright, USN, "Ring of Fire," *Surface Warfare* (November/December 1997): 61.

158. Cebrowski, "Sea Change," 5.

159. Adm. William A. Owens, USN (Ret.), "Intelligence in the 21st Century," *American Intelligence Journal* (Spring 1999): 15, 18–20.

160. Wright, "Ring of Fire," 62.

161. See also generally David Foxwell and Mark Hewish, "Sealing the Sea Link: A Leap in Naval Communications," *Jane's International Defence Review* (May 1998): 41, discussing "Information Technology for the 21st Century" [or "IT21"] plans to develop a single integrated, high-bandwidth information network consisting of a wide-area network [WAN] of interlinked local area networks [LANs].

162. Cebrowski, "Sea Change," 2.

163. Owens, "Intelligence in the 21st Century," 15, 19.

164. Studeman and Ratliff, remarks at ONI OPINTEL "Lessons Learned" Symposium, noting the parallels between modern concepts of warfighting based around integrated C⁴ISR (command, control, communications, computers, intelligence, surveillance, and reconnaissance) networks and "information operations" and U.S. Navy OPINTEL organization.

165. Studeman, remarks.

166. Owens, *High Seas,* 134.

167. Studeman, slide presentation.

168. Cf. George Santayana, "Those who cannot remember the past are condemned to repeat it."

169. Jacoby, "Operational Intelligence," 104.

170. See Studeman, remarks.

171. George Noel Gordon, Lord Byron, *Journal* (entry of January 28, 1821).

Bibliography

Official Sources

Selected official Command Histories of components, offices, and intelligence centers of the Naval Intelligence command and the Office of Naval Intelligence, 1961–93, in the files of the Historian, Office of Naval Intelligence, National Maritime Intelligence Center, Suitland, Md.

Selected official documentation collected for the Director of Naval Intelligence Operational Intelligence "Lessons Learned" Project, 1994–2004, in the files of the Historian, Office of Naval Intelligence, National Maritime Intelligence Center, Suitland, Md.

Official Oral History Interviews and Presentations

The following interviews and presentations were collected for the Director of Naval Intelligence Operational Intelligence "Lessons Learned" Project, 1994–2004. These records are under the control of the Historian, Office of Naval Intelligence, National Maritime Intelligence Center, Suitland, Md., and as of 2004 are not open to the public.

Amato, Joseph. Presentation and remarks at Office of Naval Intelligence Symposium. "U.S. Navy OPINTEL: Lessons Learned from the Cold War." September 12, 1998.

Bates, Capt. Richard W., USN (Ret.). Presentation and remarks to Office of Naval Intelligence Symposium. "U.S. Navy OPINTEL: Lessons Learned from the Cold War." September 12, 1998.

Brooks, Ambassador Linton F. Presentation and remarks at Office of Naval Intelligence Symposium. "U.S. Navy OPINTEL: Lessons Learned from the Cold War." September 12–13, 1998.

Brooks, Rear Adm. Thomas A., USN (Ret.). Presentation and remarks at Office of Naval Intelligence Symposium. "U.S. Navy OPINTEL: Lessons Learned from the Cold War." September 12–13, 1998.

———. Remarks given on behalf of Dr. Alfred L. Andreassen, at Office of Naval Intelligence Symposium. "U.S. Navy OPINTEL: Lessons Learned from the Cold War." September 12–13, 1998.

———. Videotaped interview by Comdr. Stephen W. Scalenghe. Office of Naval Intelligence, Suitland, Md. January 8, 2000.

Cole, Rear Adm. Isaiah C., USN (Ret.). Presentation and remarks at Office of Naval Intelligence Symposium. "U.S. Navy OPINTEL: Lessons Learned from the Cold War." September 13, 1998.

Edwards, Capt. John Q., USN (Ret.). Presentation and remarks to Office of Naval Intelligence Symposium. "U.S. Navy OPINTEL: Lessons Learned from the Cold War." September 13, 1998.

Giambastiani, Vice Adm. Edmund P., Jr., USN. Presentation and remarks at Office of Naval Intelligence Symposium. "U.S. Navy OPINTEL: Lessons Learned from the Cold War." September 13, 1998.

Harrison, Frederick. Presentation and remarks at Office of Naval Intelligence Symposium. "U.S. Navy OPINTEL: Lessons Learned from the Cold War." September 12, 1998.

Harvey, Rear Adm. Donald P., USN (Ret.). Presentation and remarks at Office of Naval Intelligence Symposium. "U.S. Navy OPINTEL: Lessons Learned from the Cold War." September 12, 1998.

Haver, Richard L. Presentation and remarks at Office of Naval Intelligence Symposium. "U.S. Navy OPINTEL: Lessons Learned from the Cold War." September 13, 1998.

———. Videotaped interview by Comdr. Stephen W. Scalenghe. Office of Naval Intelligence, Suitland, Md. February 6, 2000.

Jacoby, Rear Adm. Lowell E. Presentation and remarks at Office of Naval Intelligence Symposium. "U.S. Navy OPINTEL: Lessons Learned from the Cold War." September 13, 1998.

———. Videotaped interview by Comdr. Stephen W. Scalenghe. Office of Naval Intelligence, Suitland, Md. February 5, 2000.

Jeremiah, Adm. David. Videotaped interview by Comdr. Stephen W. Scalenghe. Office of Naval Intelligence, Suitland, Md. February 4, 2000.

Manthorpe, Capt. William H. J., USN (Ret.). Interview by Lt. Comdr. M. D. Mizrahi, USNR. April 24, 1996.

Marocchi, Rear Adm. John L., USN (Ret.). Presentation at Office of Naval Intelligence Symposium. "U.S. Navy OPINTEL: Lessons Learned from the Cold War." September 12, 1998.

McConnell, Vice Adm. John M., USN (Ret.). Interview by Lt. Comdr. M. D. Mizrahi, USNR. August 13, 1996.

————. Presentation and remarks at Office of Naval Intelligence Symposium. "U.S. Navy OPINTEL: Lessons Learned from the Cold War." September 13, 1998.

McFarland, Rear Adm. James S., USN (Ret.). Notes for presentation prepared for Office of Naval Intelligence Symposium. "U.S. Navy OPINTEL: Lessons Learned from the Cold War." September 12–13, 1998.

Pressly, Capt. George B., USN (Ret.). Presentation and remarks at Office of Naval Intelligence Symposium. "U.S. Navy OPINTEL: Lessons Learned from the Cold War." September 12, 1998.

————. Remarks given on behalf of Rear Adm. James S. McFarland, USN (Ret.), at Office of Naval Intelligence Symposium. "U.S. Navy OPINTEL: Lessons Learned from the Cold War." September 12–13, 1998.

Ratliff, Rear Adm. Perry M., USN. Presentation and remarks at Office of Naval Intelligence Symposium. "U.S. Navy OPINTEL: Lessons Learned from the Cold War." September 12–13, 1998.

Richardson, Vice Adm. David, USN (Ret.). Presentation and notes for presentation at Office of Naval Intelligence Symposium. "U.S. Navy OPINTEL: Lessons Learned from the Cold War." September 13, 1998.

Rindskopf, Rear Adm. Maurice H., USN (Ret.). Presentation and remarks at Office of Naval Intelligence Symposium. "U.S. Navy OPINTEL: Lessons Learned from the Cold War." September 12, 1998.

Shapiro, Rear Adm. Sumner, USN (Ret.). Presentation and remarks at Office of Naval Intelligence Symposium. "U.S. Navy OPINTEL: Lessons Learned from the Cold War." September 12, 1998.

————. Videotaped interview by Comdr. Stephen W. Scalenghe. Office of Naval Intelligence, Suitland, Md. January 8, 2000.

Sheafer, Rear Adm. Edward D., USN (Ret.). Presentation and remarks at Office of Naval Intelligence Symposium. "U.S. Navy OPINTEL: Lessons Learned from the Cold War." September 12–13, 1998.

Showers, Rear Adm. Donald M., USN (Ret.). Presentation and remarks at Office of Naval Intelligence Symposium. "U.S. Navy OPINTEL: Lessons Learned from the Cold War." September 12–13, 1998.

————. Videotaped interview by Comdr. Stephen W. Scalenghe. Office of Naval Intelligence, Suitland, Md. January 8, 2000.

Small, Adm. William M. Small, USN (Ret.). Presentation and remarks at Office of Naval Intelligence Symposium. "U.S. Navy OPINTEL: Lessons Learned from the Cold War." September 12–13, 1998.

Studeman, Adm. William O., USN (Ret.). Presentation and remarks to Office of Naval Intelligence Symposium. "U.S. Navy OPINTEL: Lessons Learned from the Cold War." September 13, 1998.

————. Interview by Lt. Comdr. David A. Rosenberg, USNR, and Lt. William R. Hunt, USNR. August 17, 1996.

Whiton, Rear Adm. H. Winsor, USN. Presentation and remarks at Office of Naval Intelligence Symposium. "U.S. Navy OPINTEL: Lessons Learned from the Cold War." September 12–13, 1998.

Wilson, Rear Adm. Thomas R., USN. Presentation and remarks at Office of Naval Intelligence Symposium. "U.S. Navy OPINTEL: Lessons Learned from the Cold War." September 13, 1998.

————. Videotaped interview by Comdr. Stephen W. Scalenghe. Office of Naval Intelligence, Suitland, Md. February 4, 2000.

Wright, Capt. Larry, USN (Ret.). Interview by Lt. Comdr. M. D. Mizrahi, USNR. June 25, 1996.

Books and Periodicals

Andrews, Frank. "The Evolution of SubDevGru 12." *Submarine Review* (April 1983).

Baer, George W. "U.S. Naval Strategy 1890–1945." *Naval War College Review,* no. XLIV (Winter 1991).

Ball, Desmond. "Nuclear War at Sea." In *Naval Strategy and National*

Security. Steven Miller and Stephen van Evera, eds. Princeton, N.J.: Princeton University Press, 1988.

Bamford, James. *The Puzzle Palace.* New York: Penguin, 1983.

Bath, Alan Harris. *Tracking the Axis Enemy.* Lawrence: University Press of Kansas, 1998.

Beesly, Patrick. *Very Special Intelligence: The Story of the Admiralty's Operational Intelligence Centre, 1939–1945.* London: Greenhill, 2000.

Bender, Bryan. "Buying Into Networked Warfare." *Jane's Defence Weekly* (May 13, 1998).

Benson, Robert Louis. *A History of U.S. Communications Intelligence during World War II: Policy and Administration.* U.S. Cryptologic History, Series IV, World War II, vol. 8. Ft. Meade, Md.: National Security Agency, 1997.

Beyerchen, Alan D. "Clausewitz, Nonlinearity, and the Unpredictability of War." In *Coping with the Bounds: Speculations on Nonlinearity in Military Affairs.* Tom Czerwinski, ed. Washington, D.C.: Institute for National Strategic Studies, 1998.

Brooks, Linton F. "Naval Power and National Security." *International Security* 11, no. 2. (Fall 1986).

Brooks, Thomas A., and Bill Manthorpe. "Setting the Record Straight." *Naval Intelligence Professional Quarterly* 12, no. 2 (April 1996).

Cebrowski, Arthur K. "Sea Change." *Surface Warfare* (November/December 1997).

Cebrowski, Arthur K., and John J. Garstka. "Network-Centric Warfare: Its Origin and Future." U.S. Naval Institute *Proceedings* (January 1998).

Colomb, J. C. R. "Naval Intelligence and Protection of Commerce of War." *Royal United Services Institute Journal* 24, no. 112 (1881).

Cote, Owen R., Jr. *The Third Battle: Innovation in the U.S. Navy's Silent Cold War Struggle with Soviet Submarines.* Newport, R.I.: Naval War College Press, 2003.

Cromie, William J. "Ocean Weather Prediction System Developed." *Harvard College Gazette* (May 2000).

Dismukes, Bradford, and James M. McConnell, eds. *Soviet Naval Diplomacy.* New York: Pergamon Press/Center for Naval Analyses, 1977.

Donnelly, John. "The Quest for Bandwidth." *Military Information Technology* (June/July 1998).

Dotsenko, V. "Soviet Art of Naval Warfare in the Postwar Period." *Morskoy Sbornik,* no. 7 (1989).

Downing, John. "How Shkval Ensured Soviet SSBN Survivability." *Jane's Intelligence Review* (November 1, 1999).

Dulles, Allen. *The Craft of Intelligence.* New York: Harper and Row, 1963.

———. *Great True Spy Stories.* Secaucus, N.J.: Castle, 1968.

Dunnigan, James F., and Albert A. Nofi. *Dirty Little Secrets.* New York: William Morrow, 1990.

Dvornik, Francis. *Origins of Intelligence Services.* New Brunswick, N.J.: Rutgers University Press, 1974.

Ewing, Maurice, and J. Lamar Worzel. "Long-Range Sound Transmission." *The Geological Society of America Memoir* 27 (October 15, 1948).

Federal Bureau of Investigation. "FBI Announces a Major Restructuring of FBI Headquarters." Press release, November 11, 1999.

Fishel, Edwin C. *The Secret War for the Union.* Boston: Houghton Mifflin, 1996.

Ford, Christopher A. "Dinosaur's Dilemma." U.S. Naval Institute *Proceedings* (September 1996).

Foxwell, David, and Mark Hewish. "Sealing the Sea Link: A Leap in Naval Communications." *Jane's International Defence Review* (May 1998).

George, James L., ed. *Problems of Sea Power as We Approach the Twenty-first Century.* Washington, D.C.: American Enterprise Institute for Public Policy Research, 1977.

Grant, Robert M. *U-boat Intelligence, 1914–18.* Hamden, Conn.: Archon Books, 1969.

Grey, A. M. *Warfighting: The U.S. Marine Corps Book of Strategy.* New York: Doubleday, 1995.

Hattendorf, John B. "The Evolution of the Maritime Strategy," *Naval War College Review,* XLI, no. 3 (Summer 1988).

———. *The Evolution of the U.S. Navy's Maritime Strategy, 1977–1986.* Newport, R.I.: Center for Naval Warfare Studies, Naval War College, 1989.

Herman, Michael. *Intelligence Power in Peace and War.* Cambridge: Royal Institute of International Affairs, 1996.

Herrick, Robert W. *Soviet Naval Strategy: Fifty Years of Theory and Practice.* Annapolis, Md.: Naval Institute Press, 1968.

Herwig, Holger H. "The Failure of German Sea Power, 1914–1945: Mahan, Tirpitz, and Roeder Reconsidered." *International History Review* X, no. 1 (February 1988).

Hone, Thomas C., and Mark D. Mandales. "Interwar Innovation in Three Navies: U.S. Navy, Royal Navy, Imperial Japanese Navy." *Naval War College Review* XL, no. 2 (Spring 1987).

Hyman, Alan. "Ocean Surveillance from Land, Air, and Space." *Naval Forces* 3, no. 2 (1982).

IUSS/CAESAR Alumni Association Web site. "Integrated Undersea Surveillance System (IUSS) History, 1950–1997." *http://www.iusscaa.org/history.htm.*

Jacoby, Rear Adm. Lowell E. "Operational Intelligence: Lessons from the Cold War." U.S. Naval Institute *Proceedings* (September 1999).

Jervis, Robert. "Complex Systems: The Role of Interactions." In *Complexity, Global Politics, and National Security.* David S. Alberts and Thomas J. Czerwinski, eds. Washington, D.C.: Institute for National Strategic Studies, 1999.

Johnson, Loch. *Secret Agencies: U.S. Intelligence in a Hostile World.* New Haven, Conn.: Yale University Press, 1996.

Jones, R. V. *The Wizard War.* New York: Coward, McCann, and Geoghegan, 1978.

Keegan, John. *The Price of Admiralty.* New York: Penguin, 1988.

Kelly, Mrs. Walt, and Bill Crouch Jr., eds. *The Best of Pogo.* New York: Simon and Schuster, 1982.

Kohnen, David. "F-21 and F-211: A Fresh Look into the 'Secret Room.'" In *New Interpretations in Naval History: Selected Papers from the Fourteenth Naval History Symposium.* Randy Carol Balano and Craig L. Symonds, eds. Annapolis, Md.: Naval Institute Press, 2001.

Lautenschläger, Karl. "The Submarine in Naval Warfare, 1901–2001," *International Security,* 2, no. 3 (Winter 1986–87).

———. "Technology and the Evolution of Naval Warfare." *International Security,* 8, no. 2 (Fall 1983).

Layton, Rear Adm. Edwin T., with Roger Pineau and John Costello. *"And I Was There": Pearl Harbor and Midway—Breaking the Secrets.* New York: William Morrow, 1985.

Maffeo, Steven E. *Most Secret and Confidential: Intelligence in the Age of Nelson.* Annapolis, Md.: Naval Institute Press, 2000.

McCausland, J. *The Gulf Conflict: A Military Analysis.* Adelphi Paper 282. London: International Institute for Strategic Studies/Brassey's, 1993.

McConnell, James M. "Military-Political Tasks of the Soviet Navy in Peace and War." In U.S. Congress, House of Representatives, *Soviet Oceans Development, Prepared for the Use of the Committee on Commerce and National Ocean Policy.* Washington, D.C.: Government Printing Office, 1976.

Mearsheimer, John. "A Strategic Misstep." *International Security* 11, no. 2 (Fall 1986).

Miller, David, and Chris Miller. *Modern Naval Combat.* New York: Crescent, 1986.

Milner, Marc. "The Battle of the Atlantic." *Journal of Strategic Studies* 13, no. 1 (March 1990).

———. "The Dawn of Modern Anti-Submarine Warfare: Allied Responses to the U-Boats, 1944–45." *Royal United Services Institute Journal* 134, no. 1 (Spring 1989).

Musashi, Miyamoto. *The Book of Five Rings.* Trans. Thomas Cleary. Boston: Shambhala, 1994.

Noonan, Robert W. "Split-Based Intelligence for Central Region Operations." *American Intelligence Journal* (1997).

Owens, William A. *High Seas: The Naval Passage to an Uncharted World.* Annapolis, Md.: U.S. Naval Institute, 1995.

———. "Intelligence in the 21st Century." *American Intelligence Journal* (Spring 1999).

Packard, Capt. Wyman H. *Century of U.S. Naval Intelligence.* Washington, D.C.: Department of the Navy, 1996.

Parker, Frederick D. *Pearl Harbor Revisited: United States Navy Communications Intelligence, 1924–1941.* United States Cryptologic History, Series IV, World War II, vol. 6. Ft. Meade, Md.: National Security Agency, 1994.

———. *A Priceless Advantage: U.S. Navy Communications Intelli-*

gence and the Battles of Coral Sea, Midway, and the Aleutians. United States Cryptologic History, Series IV, World War II, vol. 5. Ft. Meade, Md.: National Security Agency, 1993.

Photographic Interpretation and Radar Target Intelligence Newsletter VI, no. 2 (April 1958).

Polmar, Norman. "The U.S. Navy: Sonars, Part 2." U.S. Naval Institute *Proceedings* 107 (September 1981).

Polmar, Norman, and Thomas Allen. *Spy Book.* New York: Random House, 1997.

Polmar, Norman, and K. J. Moore. *Cold War Submarines: The Design and Construction of U.S. and Soviet Submarines.* Washington, D.C.: Brassey's, 2004.

Porch, Douglas. *The French Secret Services.* New York: Farrar, Strauss, and Giroux, 1995.

Prados, John. *Combined Fleet Decoded.* New York: Random House, 1995.

Prina, L. Edgar. "A Forum of Excellence." *Sea Power* (August 1997).

Richelson, Jeffrey T. *A Century of Spies.* New York: Oxford University Press, 1995.

———. *The U.S. Intelligence Community.* 3rd. ed. Boulder, Colo.: Westview, 1995.

Rosenberg, David A. "American Naval Strategy in the Era of the Third World War: An Inquiry into the Structure and Process of General War at Sea." In N. A. M. Rodger, ed. *Naval Power in the Twentieth Century.* Annapolis, Md.: Naval Institute Press, 1996.

———. "Being 'Red': The Challenge of Taking the Soviet Side at War Games at the Naval War College." *Naval War College Review* XLI (Winter 1988).

———. "The History of World War III, 1945–1990: A Conceptual Framework." In Robert David Johnson, ed. *On Cultural Ground: Essays in International History.* Imprint Studies in International Relations, 1. Chicago: Imprint, 1994.

———. "Process: The Realities of Formulating Modern Naval Strategy." In James Goldrick and John Hattendorf, eds., *Mahan Is Not Enough.* Newport, R.I.: Naval War College Press, 1993.

Shreadley, R. L. "The Naval War in Vietnam, 1950–1970." *Proceedings: Naval Review 1971* 97, no. 819 (May 1971).

Snyder, Alvin A. *Warriors of Disinformation: American Propaganda, Soviet Lies, and the Winning of the Cold War—An Insider's Account.* New York: Arcade, 1995.

Starr, Barbara. "USA's Rapid Targeting Reaches New Heights." *Jane's Defence Weekly* (March 4, 1998).

Sumida, Jon Tetsuro. "'The Best Laid Plans': The Development of British Battle-Fleet Tactics, 1919–1942." *International History Review* XIV, no. 4 (November 1992).

Sun Tzu. "Art of War." In *The Seven Military Classics of Ancient China.* Ralph D. Sawyer, ed. Boulder, Colo.: Westview, 1993.

———. *The Art of War.* Trans. Ralph Sawyer. New York: Barnes and Noble, 1994.

Troy, Thomas F. *Donovan and the CIA: A History of the Establishment of the CIA.* Frederick, Md.: Aletheia Books/CIA Center for the Study of Intelligence, 1981.

U.S. Department of the Navy. *From the Sea.* Washington, D.C.: Department of the Navy, 1992.

Van Tol, Jan M. "Military Innovation and Carrier Aviation: Analysis." *Joint Forces Quarterly* (Autumn/Winter 1997–98).

Vistica, Gregory L. *Fall from Glory.* New York: Touchstone, 1997.

Watkins, James D. "The Maritime Strategy." U.S. Naval Institute *Proceedings.* Special Supplement (January 1986).

Watson, Bruce, Susan Watson, and Gerald Hopple, eds. *United States Intelligence: An Encyclopedia.* New York: Garland, 1990.

Winks, Robin W. *Cloak and Gown.* New York: William Morrow, 1987.

Winterbotham, F. W. *The Ultra Secret.* New York: Harper and Row, 1974.

Winton, John. *ULTRA at Sea.* New York: William Morrow, 1988.

Wit, Joel S. "Advances in Antisubmarine Warfare." *Scientific American* (February 1981).

Wright, Kip. "Ring of Fire." *Surface Warfare* (November/December 1997).

Wright, Marshall N. "Battlespace 2000: Intelligence Communications or Deployed Naval Forces." *American Intelligence Journal* (1997).

Index

1350s (air intelligence officers), 34, 38–39, 48–49
1630s (special duty officers, intelligence), 34–35, 38–39, 48–49, 51
1635s (Naval Reserve special duty officers, intelligence), 163
600-ship Navy, 88, 89

ACINT (acoustic intelligence), 37, 61, 62, 103–4, 130, 184n142
Adams, John, 17
Aden, Gulf of, 98
ADP. *See* automated data processing
Advanced Technology Panel (ATP), 87, 96–97: war gaming and, 91–93
Air Force, U.S., 49, 50, 115, 115–16, 187n24
air intelligence officer (AI), 34
AirLand Battle theory, 94
Air Tasking Order (ATO), 119
Allies, 14
All-Source Analysis System (ASAS), 122
all-source fusion, 42–44, 105, 139: adaptation of model in the intelligence community, 116–17; analysts of, 39, 53–54; background of, 3–6; British Admiralty and, 6; importance of, 126–27, 135; influence of interconnectivity on, 71; OSIS system and, 64; World War II and, 14–15. *See*

also intelligence inputs
analysts, 20, 53–54, 70–71, 134–35, 135–38, 144n23, 145n34, 195n130
Anderson, Walter, 9
Andreassen, Alfred, 86
antisubmarine warfare (ASW), 16, 41, 99, 103, 105–6, 184–85n151
Antisubmarine Warfare Centers Command and Control System (ASW CCCS), 70
applied automated data processing (ADP), 19
Arabian Sea, 98
area of responsibility (AOR), 66
Army, U.S., 49, 50, 94, 115, 115–16, 187n24
Atlantic, Battle of, 14
Atlantic Intelligence Command (AIC), 114
Atlantic Theater, 8–12, 14
Auckland, 13
Australia, 117
AUTODIN (Department of Defense Automatic Digital Network), 104
automated data processing (ADP), 35–36, 45–48, 56, 63, 65–67, 75, 120
Automated Message Handling System (AMHS), 102
automation, 45–48, 161, 183n137. *See also* automated data processing (ADP)

About the Authors

Christopher Ford currently serves as Principal Deputy Assistant Secretary in the U.S. State Department's Bureau of Verification and Compliance. Prior to this, he served as Minority Counsel and then General Counsel to the U.S. Senate Select Committee on Intelligence. Dr. Ford's previous positions include that of Staff Director and Chief Counsel for the Permanent Subcommittee on Investigations of the Senate Governmental Affairs Committee, Chief Investigative Counsel for the Governmental Affairs Committee, and National Security Advisor to U.S. Senator Susan Collins (R-ME). Dr. Ford has also worked in private practice with the law firm of Shea & Gardner in Washington, D.C., and as Assistant Counsel to the President's Intelligence Oversight Board at the White House. Dr. Ford graduated summa cum laude from Harvard, received his doctorate from Oxford University as a Rhodes Scholar, and graduated from the Yale Law School. He is an intelligence officer in the U.S. Naval Reserve, currently with the rank of lieutenant commander, and has been joyously married to Jennifer L. Davis-Ford since 1992.

David Alan Rosenberg is a senior professor at the U.S. Naval War College. He directed Task Force History for the Vice Chief of Naval Operations in 2003–4, compiling Navy operational history in Operation IRAQI FREEDOM and the Global War on Terror. From 1996 to 2003 he served as Admiral Harry W. Hill Professor of Maritime Strategy at the National War College, and from 1990–2000 he was a tenured professor of military and naval history at Temple University. The first military historian awarded a five-year John D. and Catherine T. MacArthur Fellowship for his studies of Cold War nuclear strategy, he holds a Ph.D. in history (with honors) from the University of Chicago. A captain, special duty, intelligence, in the U.S. Naval Reserve, he originated and ran the Director of Naval Intelligence Operational Intelligence Lessons Learned Project from 1994–2004 that produced a 1998 symposium, two articles, a training video, and this book. He currently commands the Naval Reserve's largest intelligence unit, Office of Naval Intelligence 0566, recognized in 2004 as the top large unit in the Naval Reserve Intelligence Command.

The Naval Institute Press is the book-publishing arm of the U.S. Naval Institute, a private, nonprofit, membership society for sea service professionals and others who share an interest in naval and maritime affairs. Established in 1873 at the U.S. Naval Academy in Annapolis, Maryland, where its offices remain today, the Naval Institute has members worldwide.

Members of the Naval Institute support the education programs of the society and receive the influential monthly magazine *Proceedings* and discounts on fine nautical prints and on ship and aircraft photos. They also have access to the transcripts of the Institute's Oral History Program and get discounted admission to any of the Institute-sponsored seminars offered around the country. Discounts are also available to the colorful bimonthly magazine *Naval History.*

The Naval Institute's book-publishing program, begun in 1898 with basic guides to naval practices, has broadened its scope to include books of more general interest. Now the Naval Institute Press publishes about one hundred titles each year, ranging from how-to books on boating and navigation to battle histories, biographies, ship and aircraft guides, and novels. Institute members receive significant discounts on the Press's more than eight hundred books in print.

Full-time students are eligible for special half-price membership rates. Life memberships are also available.

For a free catalog describing Naval Institute Press books currently available, and for further information about joining the U.S. Naval Institute, please write to:

Membership Department
U.S. Naval Institute
291 Wood Road
Annapolis, MD 21402-5034
Telephone: (800) 233-8764
Fax: (410) 269-7940
Web address: www.navalinstitute.org